Contemporary Travel Writing of Latin America

Routledge Research in Travel Writing
EDITED BY PETER HULME, UNIVERSITY OF ESSEX,
AND TIM YOUNGS, NOTTINGHAM TRENT UNIVERSITY

1. Travel Writing, Form, and Empire
The Poetics and Politics of Mobility
Edited by Julia Kuehn and
Paul Smethurst

2. Visualizing Africa in Nineteenth-Century British Travel Accounts
Leila Koivunen

3. Contemporary Travel Writing of Latin America
Claire Lindsay

Contemporary Travel Writing of Latin America

Claire Lindsay

Taylor & Francis Group
New York   London

First published 2010
by Routledge
711 Third Avenue, New York, NY 10017

Simultaneously published in the UK
by Routledge
2 Park Square, Milton Park, Abingdon, Oxfordshire OX14 4RN

First issued in paperback 2014

Routledge is an imprint of the Taylor & Francis Group, an informa business

© 2010 Taylor & Francis

Typeset in Sabon by IBT Global.

All rights reserved. No part of this book may be reprinted or reproduced or utilised in any form or by any electronic, mechanical, or other means, now known or hereafter invented, including photocopying and recording, or in any information storage or retrieval system, without permission in writing from the publishers.

Trademark Notice: Product or corporate names may be trademarks or registered trademarks, and are used only for identification and explanation without intent to infringe.

Library of Congress Cataloging-in-Publication Data
Lindsay, Claire
 Contemporary travel writing of Latin America / by Claire Lindsay.
   p. cm.—(Routledge research in travel writing ; 3)
 Includes bibliographical references and index.
 1. Travelers' writings, Spanish American—History and criticism. 2. Spanish American prose literature—20th century—History and criticism. 3. Latin America—In literature. 4. Latin America—Description and travel. 5. Travel in literature. I. Title.
 PQ7082.T73L56 2009
 868—dc22
                        2009032893

ISBN 13: 978-0-415-99121-6 (hbk)
ISBN 13: 978-1-138-81757-9 (pbk)

Contents

List of Figures vii
Acknowledgements ix

1 Introduction: Contemporary Travel Writing of Latin America 1

2 In (Postmodern) Patagonia 18

3 Spectacular Andean Adventures 47

4 Unhomely Mexico 66

5 "Real" Ethnographies 92

Afterword 115
Notes 121
Bibliography 157
Index 169

Figures

2.1 Front cover of Luis Sepúlveda, *Full Circle: A South American Journey*, trans. by Chris Andrews (Melbourne: Lonely Planet, 1996). 30

3.1 Che Guevara dead. Rex Features Ltd. 51

A.1 A deserted Mexico City metro after the 2009 flu outbreak. Rex Features Ltd. 117

Acknowledgements

I am indebted to a number of people who have assisted in the development of this book over the last few years. I am especially grateful to Tim Youngs, Peter Hulme, and Charles Forsdick for all encouraging this volume at various stages of its development. Other colleagues and friends to whom I also owe sincere thanks for offering support, asking pertinent questions, recommending sources, reading or listening to parts of this book in earlier and other formats include: Ana Arendar, María del Pilar Blanco, Miguel Cabañas, Nick Caistor, Robert Clarke, Catherine Davies, Juan Daneri, Jacqueline Dutton, Nuala Finnegan, Eva-Lynn Jagoe, John King, Maureen Moynagh, Andrea Noble, Fernanda Peñaloza, Thea Pitman, Jean Xavier Ridon, Paul Smethurst, Juan Pablo Spicer Escalante, Philip Swanson, Mónica Szurmuk, Carl Thompson, Jennifer Valko, Claire Williams, and Jason Wilson. I thank my colleagues in the Department of Spanish and Latin American Studies at University College London, especially Jo Evans for discussions about migration, globalisation, and Lacan, and Stephen Hart, who, as head of department, has enabled an essential period of study leave to complete this book. I would also like to acknowledge my appreciation of the assistance and support of colleagues in the Department of English and Comparative Literature at Goldsmiths', University of London, where I began this research. I am grateful to my former undergraduate students there for their indulgence and enthusiasm in testing ideas about travel writing in my course "On the Road: Writing the Americas through Travel" (2004–5) and my MA and research students at UCL—especially Pam Peers, Joey Seager, Amana Khan, and Sian Ferry, who took "SPANG012 Border Narratives of Latin America" in 2007–8, and, more recently, Guadalupe Araúz and Marcelo Somarriva—with all of whom I have enjoyed fruitful discussions about travel.

The assistance of staff at the University of London Research Library, Senate House, UCL library, and the British Library in London, the Daniel Cosías Villegas library at the Colegio de Mexico, Mexico City, and at the Benson Collection at the University of Texas at Austin, especially Margo Gutiérrez, has been indispensable. Thanks are due too to Jonathan Brown and Paola Bueche at the Lozano Long Institute of Latin American Studies for facilitating my stay there as a visiting scholar. I am grateful to Erica Wetter and Elizabeth Levine at Routledge, who have been efficient and patient throughout the production process.

Needless to say, any errors or misinterpretations in what follows are entirely my own.

This project has inevitably entailed a certain amount of travel. The British Academy has funded essential research trips to Mexico City and Austin, Texas, to source primary and secondary material. They have also supported travel to overseas conferences at which papers related to parts of this book were presented: at Las Vegas, United States (LASA2004), and Montreal, Canada (LASA2007). I have presented associated material at conferences and seminars in Birmingham (2004), University of Liverpool (2006), Universidad Complutense, Madrid (2006), University of Oxford (2007), and University of Sheffield (2009): my thanks to the organisers and participants at all of those events for comments and suggestions.

I am grateful to the Arts and Humanities Research Council for a grant awarded under their Research Leave scheme, which enabled me to bring this book to completion.

Penn State University Press has granted its permission to publish excerpts from my article 'Luis Sepúlveda, Bruce Chatwin and the global travel circuit', from *Comparative Literature Studies*, 43, nos. 1–2 (2006), 55–76, material from which appears in revised form in Chapter 2. Lonely Planet has also allowed reproduction of the front cover image of their edition of Luis Sepúlveda's *Full Circle: A South American Journey*, trans. Chris Andrews (Melbourne, 1996) in the same chapter.

On a personal level, my warm thanks go to Phil Hutchinson, the assistants, and fellow students at the Mei Quan Academy in Holborn for weekly tai chi classes which have been immensely enjoyable, relaxing, and instructive in recent times. To friends and family—in particular, David Barr, Sue Harris, Mags Lewis, George Lewis, Lourdes Orozco, Pia Pichler, and, as ever, Angela Lindsay and Roger Lindsay—I am grateful for their unstinting encouragement along the way.

Above all, however, I thank Mark, who has lived with the project so closely, enthusiastically, and patiently. To him, whose love and good humour has made its writing possible, I dedicate this book.

1 Introduction
Contemporary Travel Writing of Latin America

"Many lives are now inextricably linked with representations, and thus we need to incorporate the complexities of expressive representation (film, novels, travel accounts) into our ethnographies, not only as technical adjuncts but as primary material with which to construct and interrogate our own representations."[1]

At a staff training seminar at my former institution, I took part in what turned out to be a memorable and culturally revealing ice-breaking activity. The exercise was a familiar one: participants had to describe their departmental affiliations and research expertise to the person sitting next to them, after which they were to introduce their neighbour with the information gleaned to the rest of the group. After the required exchange of information had taken place and I had presented my partner (an Italian psychology specialist researching Alzheimer's and responses to trauma), she then introduced me, to my surprise, as a researcher of human rights and tourism in Latin America. Something had definitely been lost in translation, for I had told my colleague that I worked on Latin American women writers (the project I was completing at the time) and on narratives of travel in the region (the project I was starting). How had I acquired this new—and, I admit to thinking at the time, slightly more radical—professional identity? I concede that my colleague might have misheard me: this was not the first time that my "women writers" had been mistaken for "human rights", for I am quite softly spoken. I admit also that some element of transference might have occurred in the light of the gap between our particular disciplines. I am not exactly sure, however, how travel narratives became tourism (although, of course, they are not unrelated) and, least of all, how such combined interests corresponded to my then location as a lecturer in an English and comparative literature department. Nevertheless, what did happen in that exchange was that Latin America emerged as a tourist destination with human rights issues. A minor misunderstanding, to be sure, but nevertheless one that has stayed with me in subsequent years as I have researched this, my second book.

On one level, then, what happened at that seminar is no more than an amusing anecdote, the result of poor auditory conditions, disciplinary entrenchment, and possibly ice-breaking exercise fatigue to boot. On another level, however, the episode also brings into focus compelling questions about cultural stereotypes, modalities of travel, and, ultimately, the place of Latin America in the Euro-American imaginary. It is precisely such issues that underpin this study of contemporary travel writing of Latin America. My former colleague might not have gleaned her impression of Latin America from reading any travel books, of course, although, as Dennis Porter points out, written accounts of places and their peoples "have traditionally been the vehicle by which our knowledge of things foreign has been mediated."[2] Nevertheless, her specific associations with the region and conception of travel there correspond to a number of commonplace ideas that have been, if not engendered, certainly perpetuated by journey narratives, and which have become crystallized in the Western geographical imagination. According to that well-rehearsed but paradoxical script, the region is an exotic destination for the (adventurous) leisure traveller seeking escapism and enjoyment, the conventional motivations of the paradigmatic tourist who, in Dean MacCannell's words, is a "sightseer, mainly middle-class . . . deployed throughout the entire world in search of experience."[3] However, the "Latin America" of that formulation is also a (largely homogeneous) continent with a notorious history of social and political injustice, conditions which offer a significant "edge" to any adventure undertaken there. This study does not seek to expose those ideas as untruths, for it would be foolish to deny that some, though not all, countries in the continent have undergone recent or ancient periods of violence and improbity (for, as Mabel Moraña et al. point out, "The Latin American modern subject is the product of a traumatic origin")[4], just as it would be misguided to fail to recognise the increasing importance of tourism to many Latin American economies. Rather, this book will explore and evaluate the ways in which contemporary Latin American travellers have engaged with these and other "myths" in accounts of their own journeys in the region.

In essence, this book is about how contemporary travellers from Latin America write their journeys at and about home. In its consideration of modern narrative forms and experiences of travel, the book is about the practice as well as the representation of journeys there in the late twentieth century. In contrast to other analyses of travel writing in Latin America which focus on Euro-American journeys to the continent, this study enquires into how "regional" travellers have negotiated this hybrid but volatile form, which has been fashioned in large part by their foreign predecessors. Some of the travellers discussed in this study—who include Luis Sepúlveda, Mempo Giardinelli, Andrés Ruggeri, Ana García Bergua, Silvia Molina, María Luisa Puga, Rubén Martínez and Luis Alberto Urrea—will be familiar to readers with a knowledge of Latin America, whereas others may be less recognizable. Insofar as they are all writers of literary fiction as well as travel narratives, and some even trained or amateur ethnographers, they are not unlike many contemporary practitioners of the form in other parts of the world. Nevertheless, these "middlebrow adventurers" are not professional travel writers of the ilk of Bill Bryson or Paul Theroux in the anglophone tradition: there are few if any of those in Latin America, Mexico's Jorge Ibargüengoitia being perhaps the closest example of a contemporary serial travel writer of sorts. The proponents of the form in this study, then, following Maureen Moynagh's pithy but effective formulation, are very much "writer-travellers rather than travel writers".[5] Moreover, the motivations for their journeys vary and include the more conventional "literary" commission as well as projects of political or social commitment. This study is not only concerned with how contemporary Latin American travellers of this kind "write back" to and within a fundamentally metropolitan discourse, therefore. It also explores what kinds of epistemologies of travel are at stake in their journey experiences. If expansion and exploration have been the dominant models of transit to and within this region, *Contemporary Travel Writing of Latin America* asks which paradigms of mobility inform modern Latin American travellers' accounts of journeys in the "periphery". Taking my cue, as have others, from James Clifford, I approach travel here in full recognition of what he calls its "historical taintedness", that is, "its associations with gendered, racial bodies, class privilege, specific means of conveyance".[6] Indeed, the term's very taint throws into relief the modalities of travel considered here, the narratives of which attest to changing and more nuanced conceptions of the idea of "travel" itself. In contrast to (and at times in concert with) those time-honoured Euro-American journeys to the region of conquest, expansion, or leisure, "domestic" journeys in Latin America adhere to a diverse range of models of transit including economic migration and political exile, as well as philosophical speculation regarding the continent's very "ontology" of travel. In its focus on contemporary Spanish- and English-language travel accounts of Latin America, then, this book seeks in part to respond to Clifford's injunction that we "listen to a wide range of 'travel stories'", for, as he suggests, "travel needs to be rethought in different traditions and historical predicaments."[7] In order to elucidate more fully both the exact scope of my enquiry as well as its methodological underpinnings, it seems appropriate at this point to outline in a more detailed fashion the parameters of my engagement first with the subject of travel writing in Latin America.

TRAVEL WRITING IN LATIN AMERICA

Travel accounts of Latin America have been written extensively from the perspective of foreign, often European, travellers, through what Mary Louise Pratt, in her landmark study, evocatively calls "imperial eyes", in narratives which have sought to convey a sense of far-flung lands visited to an audience back home. Indeed, Jason Wilson claims that "in complex ways, Latin America is *the creation* of foreigners writing about the New World" (my emphasis), the aim of whose work was "to dissipate ignorance and awaken envy . . . to offer a vision of a different place in terms of a rhetoric of cultural shock."[8] Nevertheless, travel books written by Europeans about non-European parts of the world, which have attracted most attention from scholars and critics of travel writing to date, are not only about that apparently benign process of bringing the faraway near. They "created the imperial order for Europeans 'at home'", Pratt observes, and in giving their readers a sense of familiarity with and concomitant ownership of distant parts of the world, such works became "a key instrument . . . in creating the 'domestic subject' of empire."[9] Indeed, following the large influx of military, scientific, and leisure travellers in Latin America from the colonial period onwards, journeys of expansion and exploration became the paradigmatic experiences of the foreign traveller there and continue to persist in myriad forms. As Porter notes, these include: "diplomacy, emigration, forced exile, and trade . . . religious or political pilgrimage, aesthetic education, anthropological enquiry, and the pursuit of a bronzer body or a bigger wave."[10] Moreover, such journeys and their accounts have had tremendous impact in and beyond the region itself, both of a positive and negative kind. Alexander von Humboldt, for example, for the portrayal of the equinoctial regions of the continent in his journey accounts, was considered by Simón Bolívar to have "[done] more for the Americas than all the conquistadores",[11] while in other cases the exploration and research carried out by travellers there had a direct or indirect military application. As Roberto González Echeverría points out, the efforts of travellers such as Captain Richard Burton, who were also military men, "had in some instances a revolutionary impact on Latin American societies."[12] Whether revered or reviled, since the early modern period such travel books have established and perpetuated a range of enduring myths about the continent, especially in relation to its natural resources, for, as Echeverría notes, "Latin American nature had been a source of wonder to Europeans since the discovery".[13] These myths invoked its vast and variegated land and riverscapes, an enigmatic and elusive indigenous people (who might be threatening, if not cannibalistic), as well as the lure of unearthing lost cities of gold or other natural wonders. As Neil Whitehead sums up, for foreign travellers Latin America offered "the discovery of the fantastic, the survival of the anachronistic, and the promise of marvellous monstrosity."[14] These are tropes which have survived centuries in travel mythology, the tourist site with human rights problems conjured up by my colleague mentioned earlier—a destination (still) for Europeans to "discover" through leisure travel but one with primitive and potentially corrupt systems of social justice—being just one contemporary iteration of those ideas.

If much travel writing about Latin America has been written from an outsider's perspective, it is also true that much existing scholarship in this area to date has focused on its production in the colonial era or on the output of the long nineteenth century. While this is not the occasion to provide a detailed overview of all of that work, it is fair to say that much of it has been (necessarily) concerned with unravelling the genre's imperialist underpinnings, as well as tracing, or problematizing, the surviving vestiges of such ideologies in periods of particular dynamism and transit.[15] Thus, Michael Kowalewski's observation that "Criticism of modern (by which I mean twentieth-century) travel writing has been scanty" remains valid.[16] This book aims to redress that imbalance by examining contemporary journey narratives that have been written by travellers from and about the region in the late twentieth century. *Contemporary Travel Writing of Latin America* seeks to explore how Latin American travellers have constructed journey narratives at home, largely, although not exclusively, in Spanish, the "of" in my title pointing as much to the travellers' regional affiliations as to what their books are about (although the question of identity itself may be articulated in fraught or volatile terms). In doing so, this book seeks to contest the notion that, as Steve Clark puts it, "travel writing is inevitably one-way traffic" as well as to complicate the idea that the travel encounter is always about "simple relations of domination and subordination".[17] Travel writing of the kind considered here has tended to receive little if any critical attention to date, however, not only because of a particular fetishization of its earlier, "imperial" forms but also due to questions of translation (or, what Loredana Polezzi describes elsewhere as the "eminently Anglo-centric" character of much existing critical work on travel writing and a tendency to "marginalise texts written in languages other than English").[18] To be sure, the question of the coverage and consideration of travel books in a variety of languages is already being addressed in what is a burgeoning area of study, for, as Peter Hulme and Tim Youngs point out, "travel writing has played an important role in recent years in the creation of an international literary field."[19] The increasing number of book-length studies on travel writing by scholars in the field of modern languages of late, such as those of Charles Forsdick, Angela Pérez Mejía, Thea Pitman, David Scott, and Polezzi herself, attests to the welcome early expansion of this particular field of enquiry's attention to source material and questions of travel in non-anglophone cultures and languages. My own study owes a considerable debt to this body of work: in its focus on travel writing of Latin America it seeks as much to draw on, dialogue with, and amplify this increasingly international corpus of scholarship as to engage with critical work on travel and its writing in the anglophone tradition. In equal measure it aims to speak to and enhance an emerging body of critical texts on travel writing in and from Latin America which, often in article-length studies, unpublished doctoral theses and in a small but growing number of monographic studies to date, has tended to take an author- or more narrow nationally based approach to the form in the continent.[20]

It is not only for reasons of linguistic bias or accessibility, however, that "domestic" travel writing of the sort under consideration in this book might occupy a discrete realm in the critical imagination. It is due also to some residual indifference towards, if not devaluation of, the very type of journey on which it rests. The journeys undertaken in such accounts have perhaps suffered from another kind of "taint", this time of the terms commonly used to describe them, such as "domestic", which have local, small-scale, and often feminised connotations (in another context, for example, compare the sound of the "Home" to the "Grand" Tour). Until recent times and with specific exceptions, these kinds of journey have been underestimated as somehow more banal and inferior than the apparently more dramatic intercultural or transatlantic encounter. For Tzvetan Todorov, for example, travelogues require spatial movement to a physically located elsewhere and, as such, they "entrench a Western and European point of view".[21] In consequence, Todorov claims that "A journey in France would not result in a 'travel narrative'" because it would "clearly lack the feeling of alterity in relation to the people and lands described."[22] Nevertheless, Todorov's disavowal of the possibilities of the journey in and through home territory is overstated, in my view. In this respect, I concur with North American traveller Paul Theroux, who is right (if not, otherwise, a terribly sympathetic travel writer himself on Latin America) when he says that the journey near home is in fact "the most difficult of all travel subjects".[23] It is a difficult subject because of an enduring preference for the consumption and examination of English-language journey accounts of places "elsewhere" and also because to travel at "home", notwithstanding its perceived ordinariness, can be a fundamentally (and sometimes unexpectedly) complex enterprise. On one level, the freedom of movement or escape from conventions typically associated with travel "abroad" is not necessarily as immediately apparent on the journey in "home" territory, an aspect which can function to circumscribe and/or galvanize the traveller in equal measure. Indeed, the circumscriptions of the home journey can in fact be productive rather than limiting, as examples as diverse as Iain Sinclair's psychogeographical tours of London in the anglophone tradition, Héctor Perea's literary-philosophical explorations of Mexico City, and Jorge Macchi's multimedia *Buenos Aires Tour* in the context of Latin America all illustrate in different ways.[24] Latin America is an especially fascinating site of travel in this regard, where vast distances, variegated geographies within and across nation-states as well as a strong tradition of regional and ethnic identities mean that home territories are not always necessarily very well known, familiar or even considered home at all to the regional traveller. In this context, Clifford's assertion that "home [can be] a site of unrestful differences" is especially resonant.[25] Writing about such journeys thus also corresponds to some degree to Kowalewski's characterisation of the domestic travel narrative as "celebrating the local or unfamiliar . . . [or] exposing or investigating conditions at home that most would prefer to ignore",[26] except that in the case of travel writing of Latin America the destinations can often be local *and* unfamiliar. That is, as with other regions of the world with comparable levels of topographical, cultural, and ethnic diversity, Latin America can offer the home traveller just as much of the "cultural shock" Wilson referred to earlier in respect of foreign travel and its accounts.

Nevertheless, the journey "at home" in Latin America is further complicated by the fact that, thanks to the long tradition of imperialist travel writing mentioned earlier, it might also appear to be always-already written. The home journey, then, is a difficult subject in this respect also because it presents a particular kind of discursive dilemma for the regional traveller, relating precisely to the rhetorical tools and strategies employed in the construction of the journey narrative. In effect, this is the paradox of what Pratt calls the neo-colonial cultural dilemma, in which "one is forced to be a second-class member of a club in which membership is not optional."[27] As can be inferred by my use of scare quotation marks in preceding paragraphs, then, the term "domestic" (as much as its corresponding antonym "foreign") transpires to be an unsatisfactory and at times inappropriate one to describe some of the primary material under discussion in what follows. For that reason I avoid the sustained use of the word "domestic" here, preferring the unmodified term "travel writing", in part due to its less asymmetrical tenor. Indeed, if, as Paul Fussell reminds us, there is disagreement over the very terms by which "travel writing" is classified ("Criticism has never quite known what to call books like these", he writes),[28] the stakes are even higher when such definitions and related expressions, originally elaborated in and with reference to largely anglophone cultures, are deployed in the so-called neocolony. This is another reason why this book's endeavour to interrogate and, where appropriate, recalibrate some of the vocabulary commonly used to talk about the form is so necessary in these particular geographies. Differences of nationality aside, the denominations of "foreign" and "domestic" also run the risk of setting up a specious separation of the journey accounts of Euro-American and Latin American travellers. In its focus on travel narratives of Latin America, therefore, this book seeks to illuminate the hitherto un- or understudied Spanish- and English-language output of Latin American travellers, but not in order to set up an antithesis between such work and that of other visitors to the region. To insist upon any essential difference in thematic or generic terms is not only to set up a dichotomy which could ultimately prove difficult to sustain, but also to contradict the intrinsically transcultural nature of travel and travel writing: for, as Forsdick puts it, in his study of travel in francophone cultures, "any attempt to maintain divisions along national or even linguistic lines is likely to strain credibility."[29] In more specific terms, such an endeavour would also belie particular configurations of cultures, literatures, and nationalisms in Latin America which appear in many respects to be fundamentally (and ever increasingly) transnational in character. As Gareth Williams observes in relation to the last three decades in Latin America, "Something is happening to the underlying telos of nationhood and of national identity formations" as they are "being opened up and transformed with an intensity and depth that have probably never been seen or experienced before."[30] Recognising that the divisions between "foreign" and "domestic" travel accounts can be slippery is not, however, to advocate instead a woolly, universalist conception of travel writing: that, in turn, could lead to another, no less insidious neo-imperialist manoeuvre. Pitman, in an excellent article on the conception and development of "Mexican travel writing", provides a germane example of just such an exercise. She points out that in many English-language collections of "Mexican travel writing", authors of Mexican nationality are frequently and sometimes entirely excluded from the selections, the travellers of the volumes' titles presumed to be simply travellers *in* Mexico, and, as such, largely if not exclusively "citizens of (ex-)colonial powers of the Western World". This, she concludes quite rightly, ultimately reveals "a rather colonialist mentality at work".[31] In its consideration of the contemporary journey accounts of Latin American travellers, therefore, this study will consider the accommodations and negotiations at stake in their engagement with other material of this kind about the region, where applicable in different languages and from different historical periods. In sum, *Contemporary Travel Writing of Latin America* seeks to engage critically with the composite character of a corpus of recent travel accounts about the continent which merit but have yet to receive sustained consideration in their own right. In doing so it responds to Pratt's exhortation in *Imperial Eyes* to explore the heterogeneity of travel writing and its interactions with other kinds of expression in the wake of her own groundbreaking study. In particular, in its focus on contemporary travel writing *of* Latin America, and mindful of the intercultural and intertextual character of the very form, this book takes seriously her assertion that "If one studies only what the Europeans saw and said, one [risks] reproduc[ing] the monopoly on knowledge and interpretation that the imperial enterprise sought."[32]

THE TERMS OF TRAVEL WRITING

Pratt's pioneering work has without doubt been "suggestive for people thinking about similar materials from other times and places",[33] myself included. Indeed, *Imperial Eyes* has been truly far-reaching in its influence, both in the context of the study of travel writing and in Latin American and postcolonial studies more generally, with terms such as "contact zone" and the "monarch-of-all-I-survey" position now common currency in the critical vocabulary and often deployed in contexts far removed from those which gave rise to their original coinage. Notwithstanding, I do have difficulty with one particular aspect of her approach in that book, an aspect which is by no means unique to Pratt, but which also accounts in part for this study's particular focus. It is that problem which I would now like to outline in brief here, before I go on to address the scope of my own project any further.

It is in respect of Pratt's engagement with contemporary forms of mobility in the recently revised second edition of *Imperial Eyes* that her work evinces what for me is a significant shortcoming. This emerges specifically in her preference for the discussion of contemporary forms of mobility in works of literary fiction from Latin America rather than in the so-called nonfictional travel book. In an additional chapter whose themes are modernity, mobility, and globality in the neocolony, Pratt cites Horacio Quiroga's collection of short stories, *Los desterrados* ["The Exiles"], as a pertinent example of a text written from the perspective of the "travellee". Pratt sees this fictional work as even more significant because it posits Misiones, a frontier region on the Argentine-Brazilian border in which the stories are set, "not as a location, but as a destination, a terminus ... a place with the power to disrupt the circular paradigm of departure and return that produces travel literature."[34] Quiroga's Misiones thus evinces the predicament of the neocolonial position mentioned earlier: for Pratt it is "a tragicomic version of ... peripheral modernity." Pratt then goes on to draw on a range of other literary examples—from writers as diverse as Ricardo Piglia, José María Arguedas, Gabriela Mistral, and Mário de Andrade—in the course of her discussion of the "unfreedom" of the neocolony, before concluding her consideration of contemporary modes of mobility with a number of material examples, which include border crossings from Mexico to the United States and the transnational journeys of the Virgin of Zapopan. While she acknowledges the reconfiguration of enduring narratives and tropes of travel in those brief case studies, there is no mention or examination of any "nonfictional" or empirical journey narratives of the kind ordinarily associated with the category of "travel writing". This is disappointing, for, as this study will illustrate, such works are not only in print and in circulation in Latin America (and elsewhere) but, significantly, they also attest to those "new forms of citizenship and belonging ... [and] often permanent 'awayness'" mentioned by Pratt which are indicative of the region's more recent experience of globalisation.[35]

Jason Wilson performs a similar manoeuvre to Pratt's when he privileges works of creative writing over what he acknowledges is in any case a hybrid, protean form. In his overview of "Travel Literature" in Latin America (the title of the piece already some indication of his preference), Wilson claims that "There is not a strong tradition of Latin American empirical observation or of Latin American travel writing, and even less of travelling within the Latin American continent."[36] That assertion has been subsequently invalidated, of course, by Pitman's groundbreaking work on Mexican travel writing as well as that of Shannon Marie Butler on nineteenth-century travel narratives in Peru.[37] Notwithstanding, Wilson proposes that much Latin American literary fiction, especially that of the realist or regionalist type, can be seen as an attempt to "write back" to the travel narratives of foreign visitors mentioned earlier. Ultimately, he avows that for "a native tradition of verifiable observations" the reader's only recourse is in fact to poetry, such as that of Pablo Neruda, or to literary fiction by authors such as Gabriel García Márquez and, once again, Quiroga. To be sure, there is a great deal of truth in Wilson's assertions about the engagement of Latin American literary fiction and poetry with the region's varied topographies. Nevertheless, in respect of the contemporary period, his and Pratt's comments resound with an epistemology which regards "travel writing" as being of only documentary value, its stylistic or aesthetic qualities somehow secondary, and decidedly second best, to its counterpart of "travel literature". To talk about contemporary travel writing in Latin America in relation only to literary texts, moreover, as do both critics, without taking into account "nonfictional" travel books of the kind considered here, seems to me to be a tantalizingly truncated endeavour. As Butler remarks, in comments which are equally applicable to Wilson, Pratt's insistence in her study not only on travel literature but in large part on European travel texts results in a "missed opportunity to explore what the genre of travel writing itself offers [as well as the] direct contestation of European representations of Latin American culture in the travel texts written by Latin Americans themselves."[38] Indeed, Porter's reminder that "One of the positive results of the poststructuralist critique ... has been that we no longer fetishize so-called creative writing as something essentially separate from and superior to writing of other kinds"[39] is thus especially timely in this respect. In that light, this book seeks to engage with a corpus of Latin American travellers' largely "nonfictional" travel accounts, while recognising that that term must in any case be held under erasure, especially in the context of a form with such a troubled relationship with factual and fictional discourses.[40] Nevertheless, the material under consideration here is largely "nonfictional" in the sense that, although the journey narratives may well deploy figurative strategies, rest on, and create fictions of their own, they are not works of literary fiction of the kind favoured by Pratt and Wilson; instead, they are based on empirical journeys undertaken (in large part) by their authors. My focus on these travel texts, then, aims to bring to light the issues at stake in their engagement with existing discourses and mythologies of travel, rather than to make value judgments as to their aesthetic qualities.

The evident tensions that emerge from Pratt's and Wilson's positions inevitably raise the question of terminology and it is to that topic that I now turn briefly in order to clarify my own use of terms in this study, rather than to arrive at a conclusive definition of this category of writing.[41] Fussell succinctly characterises the problem of having to use two words to describe the form at all: "Perhaps it is when we cannot satisfactorily designate a kind of work with a single word [such as epic, novel, romance]," he writes, "but must invoke two [like war memoir or travel book] that we sense we're entering complicated territory, where description, let alone definition, is hazardous, an act closer to exploration than to travel."[42] Travel books are hard to define precisely because of their complex associations with other forms, including the essay, the pastoral, the picaresque, and the quest romance. As Patrick Holland and Graham Huggan put it, travel writing is "a hybrid genre that straddles categories and disciplines . . . running from picaresque adventure to philosophical treatise, political commentary, ecological parable, and spiritual quest"[43] and the material considered here is no exception. Jan Borm, in an essay on the related range of terms available, proposes that travel writing is not a genre at all, however, "but a collective term for a variety of texts both predominantly fictional and non-fictional whose main theme is travel."[44] Given that the literary is at work in the form, he suggests that the phrases "literature of travel" or "travel literature" should in fact be regarded as synonyms of "travel writing", in which light works by Jonathan Raban and Redmond O'Hanlon could be considered alongside the *Odyssey* and *Robinson Crusoe*. Meanwhile, Borm characterises the travel book as: *"any narrative characterised by a non-fiction dominant that relates (almost always) in the first person a journey or journeys that the reader supposes to have taken place in reality while assuming or presupposing that author, narrator and principal character are but one or identical"* (original emphasis).[45] In terms of my own selection of texts, they fall largely under the auspices of Borm's categorisation of the "travel book", in which the nonfiction dominant is prevalent.[46] Nevertheless, the phrase "travel writing" will also appear in these pages as a synonym of the "travel book" and "travelogue", any one of those expressions operating as a means of distinguishing a selection of works which are predicated on empirical journeys undertaken in large part by their "writer-travellers". I refrain from using the term "travel literature" here with any consistency, however, despite the correlation of its equivalent, *literatura de viaje*, in the criticism in Spanish (or any rendition of the more awkward term to translate, *crónica de viaje*).[47] This is in large part because it retains an association with the literary fiction foregrounded by Pratt and Wilson and possibly even with the category of "travel novel" examined more recently by Stephen Levin in his study of anglophone travel texts.[48] The corpus of travel books examined in what follows, then, is representative of what Wilson referred to (but effectively sidestepped) as empirically observed travel writing.

CONTEMPORARY TRAVEL WRITING OF LATIN AMERICA

This book aims to illuminate and conceptualise contemporary journey accounts from Latin America through a series of case studies concerning four key sites of travel there, each of which engenders particular configurations of travel and travel narrative: Patagonia, the Andes, Mexico, and the Mexico-U.S. border.[49] While the volume is organised around those different but much mythologised sites, and while I am interested in the ways in which the selected accounts engage with existing place myths relating to those destinations, my concerns are not only, or always, spatial in every chapter. Indeed, in terms of the "Andean" focus of Chapter 3, that description is admittedly something of a misnomer, as the journey at hand in fact covers vast reaches of the continent beyond that mountainous expanse, including Amazonia and parts of Central America. Notwithstanding, the "Andean" epithet provides a convenient and resonant designation in terms of the character of the arduous quest narrative analysed in that discussion. Thus, I am also interested in how these travellers intervene in and reconfigure orthodox discourses such as adventure and ethnography in their work. Each chapter, then, considers two or more travel texts which thematize different and often contrasting journey experiences of a particular site, country or route. This approach has a number of advantages over the broad historical survey: it provides a closer proximity to and understanding of the range of voices articulated in the region's contemporary travel writing; it offers the possibility of comparative analysis of the travel texts and travellers at hand; and it also brings into focus the complex discursive construction of those journeys and their different destinations. It is only through this kind of thorough regionally and historically contextualised close reading that a full sense of the formal and epistemological complexity of these travel books can be appreciated. The selection of sites or zones of study in this book is not intended to be exhaustive, however, and some highly fabled destinations—such as Cuba or other parts of the Caribbean, for example—are not covered here. This is in part due to the fact that there is already fine interdisciplinary work on such places as travel destinations in the public domain.[50] Resting in part too on a selection of the region's contemporary travel writing available in print, this book seeks through its case studies not to arrive at a definitive interpretation or decryption of the form in Latin America, but instead to formulate a more subtle and proportionate vocabulary with which to conceptualise this material than is currently available in travel writing or Latin American studies and to advance some suggestive theoretical approaches for the further study of its expressions in other parts of the region and beyond.

Nevertheless, the travel texts chosen for consideration here are significant as a corpus in various different ways: either because of their circulation in, or engagement with, international travel writing "circuits" (as in the cases of the material considered in Chapters 2, 3 and 5), or for their appearance in specific, commissioned series of travel books in the region (as in the case of the texts analysed in Chapter 4). Moreover, this heterogeneous material speaks in different ways to the transformations of contemporary neoliberalism—a period marked by an acceleration in mobility due to processes of re-democratisation, globalisation, and radical economic reorganisation—which have fostered so much debate amongst scholars in Latin American studies in recent years. It is thus worth noting here some of the prevailing characteristics of what Thomas Perreault and Patricia Martin describe as "a mobile project in Latin America",[51] as it provides an essential underpinning to the textual and contextual analyses to follow.

In the 1990s, after years of military dictatorship in parts of the continent, many Latin American countries began to recover from the previous, so-called "lost decade" by adopting sweeping neoliberal reforms. Those transformations varied from country to country, the specificities of which are explored at greater length with regard to each of the individual case studies.[52] In more general terms, of course, neoliberalism stems from an economic theory developed in the United States in the 1960s and 1970s, and closely associated with the University of Chicago, which later emerged as a set of political and economic policies under Reagan and Thatcher in the 1980s. Neoliberalism is perhaps most commonly thought of as an endeavour to liberalise (particularly international) trade, to privatise national industries and state-controlled services, to reduce certain state functions, especially in the area of social services, and to introduce market-oriented practices in a reduced state sector, as well as to deregulate business practices. In Latin America, it is often seen as a successor to the political-economic policies of import substitution industrialisation (ISI), which promoted inward economic growth and industrialisation by limiting foreign trade and investment through measures such as quotas and subsidies for domestic industry. The language of social justice which often accompanied ISI, together with periods of substantial economic growth throughout the region, meant that some of its economic instabilities remained hidden until the debt crisis of the 1980s. Then, governments in almost every country of the continent turned to the IMF (International Monetary Fund) and World Bank to keep their economies afloat. Loans were awarded which were predicated on the condition of structural readjustment programmes, which in turn ushered in processes of neoliberal reform for most Latin American countries, the objectives of which became known as the "Washington Consensus". Neoliberalism brought in its wake a resurgence of neopopulism in the political systems of several countries and although, as Perreault and Martin point out, it has produced new subjectivities and "reconfigured social relations in ways that are not strictly destructive", it has also "exacerbated, rather than reduced, the [region's] uneven geographies of development."[53] As Kurt Weyland has argued, the implementation of neoliberalism has been a complex process, therefore, "affect[ing] Latin American democracy in opposite, even contradictory ways."[54] On one level it has strengthened democratic rule, in the sense that the involvement of Latin American countries in the world economy has led external powers and regional partners to seek to promote and protect democracy there. On another level, neoliberalism has considerably weakened internal political challenges to the survival of civilian rule (such as communism and socialism), a shift in the domestic balance of power which, as Weyland observes, "precludes any bold equity-enhancing reforms designed to combat Latin America's pronounced social inequality."[55]

The region's continued and often turbulent insertion into this period of late capitalism has interested scholars in a range of disciplines in Latin American studies, who in different ways and with diverse methodologies have sought to engage with the emergence of the neoliberal social order. While my aim here is not to offer a comprehensive survey of such work, I do want to highlight a couple of instances from cultural studies in order to frame this book further. Gareth Williams, for example, in *The Other Side of the Popular*, notes how the formation of the nation-state in the region (since the early decades of the twentieth century through to the debt crisis of the 1980s) rested on the institutionalisation of the concept of the people and the popular. The economic and political transformations of the last three decades, however, have fundamentally altered that relationship so that the insertion of Latin American nations into global networks has "ungrounded the nation-state and, alongside it, the transformational potential of the national-popular."[56] As such, Williams contends that foundational critical paradigms anchored in the consolidation of the nation-state are no longer valid; subalternity provides "an alternative fundamental but non-foundational critical perspective" from which to "grapple with the complexities of the current cultural and political configurations in Latin America."[57] Interested, like Williams, in subalternity, Francine Masiello, in *The Art of Transition*, considers how cultural experimentation in Argentina and Chile cultivates tensions in a neoliberal era, how it "interrupt[s] the comfortable 'flow' of postdictatorship regimes, so easily given to the sale of 'difference' yet so often indifferent to the depths of experience."[58] Masiello identifies aesthetic strategies of concealment and revelation to name and represent the "real", among which she sees the re-emergence of a subaltern marked particularly by gender.[59] While I do not identify this study with Williams' or Masiello's particular strain of Latin Americanism nor with their insistence on subalternity (although my interest in a form which might be seen as "minor" could be seen to be analogous), there is an obvious convergence of interests in the ways in which cultural production is bound up in the social and political transformations of the period.[60] This study's analysis of empirical accounts of journeys through neoliberal geographies, in which there is arguably a closer proximity to the materiality of structural readjustment as well as to flesh-and-blood subalterns at stake, is intended to be seen as complementary to the efforts of Williams, Masiello and others in seeking "an evaluation of the ways in which to think about [the period] in cultural and political terms."[61] Although it is focused on a more discrete but intrinsically "transnational" range of written production than either of those or other studies of culture under neoliberalism to date, this book nevertheless shares similar ambitions.[62] I invoke these studies of contemporary Latin American culture, therefore, in order to situate this book within debates in the field of the travel-writing studies, as indicated previously, as well as within an emerging corpus of critical work concerned with the cultural implications of the region's entry into neoliberal globalisation. As Arjun Appadurai suggests in the chapter's epigraph, travel accounts (should) now number among the key cultural texts that provide a means of exploring subjectivity in an increasingly globalised world.

In its endeavour to formulate a more expressive and compatible vocabulary for the study of journey accounts of Latin American travellers during this period, *Contemporary Travel Writing of Latin America*, like other recent studies of the form, draws inspiration for its conceptual framework from a wide variety of disciplines, including anthropology, sociology, literary and cultural studies, and continental philosophy. The approach is deliberately eclectic, its intention being to resist any overarching "explanation" or "theory" of this corpus, which might circumscribe rather than enable the exegeses of the diverse material. As such, in the course of each case study, space is devoted to the discussion and implications of the particular theoretical paradigms invoked. While much scholarly literature on travel writing is broadly informed by postcolonial criticism and theory, and notwithstanding some degree of relevance to the work carried out here (in the light of a certain correspondence of globalisation and neocolonialism), I share the reservations of other scholars about fully appropriating and endorsing such theories in a context which is neither fully "postcolonial" nor closely affiliated to the specific geographical or historical sources of those ideas.[63] Given the thematic and temporal focus of this book on notions of transit and identity in contemporary Latin America, and mindful of issues pertaining to cultural specificity, I draw on and sometimes modulate several key theoretical concepts such as nomadism (Deleuze and Guattari, Braidotti), the foreigner/stranger (Derrida, Ahmed), mourning and melancholy (Derrida, Butler, Bartra), all of which find a resonance in the discussion of indigenised notions at work in the travel writing under discussion. Recourse to such ideas, however, especially those from a continental philosophical tradition, is a matter not of replacing one borrowed set of concepts with another. Rather, it is a question of establishing a suggestive engagement with an adopted range of theoretical tools which are commensurate with, and which open up a transatlantic conversation appropriate to, the complexities and characteristics of my chosen corpus. For, as Moraña et al. put it, "a fruitful dialogue can be established [between First World paradigms and the analysis of peripheral societies], particularly due to the fact that cultural frontiers are today more permeable than ever."[64] In tandem with a consideration of the spatial and discursive issues at stake in journey narratives of Latin America in relation to their imperial(ist) heritage, therefore, this book also aims to introduce a relatively little-known body of work to nonspecialist readers with an interest in the form by exploring a number of issues of broader currency and debate in the field of travel-writing studies. These include questions of the exotic, the sublime, belatedness, as well as of the interplay of gender and ethics with the articulation of different forms of mobility.

The first of my case studies considers the encoding of what Paul Theroux famously called the "ultimate nowhere place"[65] in two contemporary travel books by Luis Sepúlveda, *Patagonia Express (Full Circle: A South American Journey*, 1995/6), and Mempo Giardinelli, *Final de novela en Patagonia (Novel's End in Patagonia*, 2000). It enquires into how these travel texts can be situated within the context of prevailing images and conceptions of Patagonia in travel mythology, such as the symbolic function of its perennially empty landscape. The chapter examines Sepúlveda's and Giardinelli's positions in relation not only to the broad European legacy of travel narrative but also, more specifically, to the persistent influence of English writer Bruce Chatwin, whose 1977 *In Patagonia* looms large over contemporary travel writing of this site. In doing so, it explores Sepúlveda's and Giardinelli's respective variations on "nomadism" and "literary tourism" as well as the ways in which their travel accounts engage ideas of the exotic and the global in the context of the southern cone's experience of late modernity. Drawing on theories of globalisation and translation, this chapter ultimately conceptualises the Patagonia of Sepúlveda's and Giardinelli's travelogues as a heterotopic space in Michel Foucault's terms: not as a romanticised "other" space on the margins, however, but as a heterotopia of crisis, whereby the word "crisis" takes on a particular complexion in individual and collective terms.

Chapter 3 theorises the nexus of adventure and politics in *América en bicicleta* (*America by Bicycle*, 2001), the account of a 15,000-km bicycle journey by Argentine activist and anthropologist Andrés Ruggeri from Buenos Aires to Havana in protest against the U.S. economic blockade of Cuba. In seeking to conceptualise Ruggeri's experience as part of a new breed of traveller, the contemporary "politico-cyclist", the chapter illuminates a fundamental tension at the heart of his travel book, which is haunted by the spectre of Ernesto Che Guevara's *Diarios de Motocicleta: Notas de viaje* [*The Motorcycle Diaries*]. That is, the journey account hinges on an apparent paradox between, on the one hand, this traveller's affiliation with the iconic Guevara and certain "elite" discourses of mobility, and, as his elemental but epic journey is transformed into a media spectacle, Ruggeri's own ambivalent process of celebrification. In this chapter, therefore, I consider the implications of Ruggeri's disavowal of his political precursor, the symbolic function of his means of transport, as well as his ambivalent engagement with the textual imprimatur of adventure. Taking my cue from ideas from Georg Simmel and Jacques Derrida, I suggest that Ruggeri might be seen as a "spectral adventurer" whose journey operates as much as a reaction to as an expression of spectacularised postmodernity.

The following chapter addresses the contributions of three women writers, María Luisa Puga (*Crónicas de una oriunda del kilómetro X en Michoacán* [*Chronicles of a Native of Km X in Michoacán*], 1995), Silvia Molina (*Campeche, imagen de eternidad* [*Campeche, Image of Eternity*], 1996) and Ana García Bergua (*Postales del puerto* [*Postcards from the Port*],

1997), to a series of regional travel books commissioned by the Mexican Council for Culture and the Arts (CONACULTA) during the mid 1990s. It assesses the production of these journey narratives within a context which takes into account considerations of gender, in part in order to conceptualise the enduring discursive unease evident in their travel books, in part also to address a particular oversight in the scholarship on travel writing in this context to date. Situating its objectives alongside feminist interventions in travel-writing studies, therefore, such as those of Mary Louise Pratt, Shirley Foster, and Sara Mills, the chapter considers the enduring significance of literary conceptions of femininity in formal and critical contexts. Furthermore, the chapter also traces the recurrence of symptoms of a broader *fin de siècle* malaise in Mexico in these writers' travelogues, notably in emerging positions of schizophrenia and strangerhood.

The final chapter considers travel texts about the Mexico-U.S. border by Rubén Martínez (*Crossing Over: A Mexican Family on the Migrant Trail*, 2002) and Luis Alberto Urrea (*The Devil's Highway*, 2004) which follow the "ghost steps" of undocumented migrants' failed attempts to cross from south to north. It situates these "thana-travel texts" within a significant counter-discourse to celebratory postmodern theorizing both of this site and of the figure of the migrant during the 1990s, as well as within recent material transformations in migratory behaviour. The chapter also reconsiders debates about the travel narrative's longstanding engagement with and ambivalence in respect of the fictive which, I contend, is the source of these morbid travelogues' affective and political power. For, while certain affiliations with ethnography can be identified in both cases, these travel texts speak in different ways to the centrality and particularity of the fictive in the contemporary experience and articulation of border crossings at this site. In effect, then, this chapter addresses the operation and implications of these works' narratological and thematic properties which, in light of Judith Butler's recent work on vulnerability and mourning, open them up to suggestive readings in a broader philosophical context. In doing so, it aims to provide a fuller understanding of these particular travel accounts and, as in other parts of the book, to engage in broader critical questions relating to the limitations, or the expediency of the reformulation, of certain interpretative tools in the study of contemporary travel writing of Latin America.

2 In (Postmodern) Patagonia

> "The Pampa and the Desert (which is what Patagonia used to be called) are our literary lands *par excellence*."[1]

Like other areas of the world implicated in processes of Western imperialism, and despite—or perhaps because of—its inaccessible and inhospitable nature, Patagonia has galvanised the imagination of travellers throughout history. As a result, it has accrued dense layers of textuality as myriad travellers have followed in the footsteps of early, largely European voyagers of discovery or scientific exploration there, such as Ferdinand Magellan, Antonio Pigafetta, Charles Darwin, Robert Fitzroy, and others. The significance of those travellers' accounts of the region is such that not only have they been read and consumed widely (and even republished in new editions of late)[2] but some of them are now considered intrinsic to a national literature and culture in Argentina and Chile.[3] Moreover, many of those travellers' experiences have had an impact far beyond the culture of travel: Darwin's journey on the *Beagle* eventually had the singular effect of transforming the history of scientific thought, for example, while Fitzroy's logbooks and instruments of the same trip contributed more broadly to the science of meteorology.[4] Furthermore, the legacy of European travellers such as these—notwithstanding the political or scientific ramifications of their works back home—is written into the region's cartography. As Fernanda Peñaloza writes, "a brief sampling of the toponymy of Patagonia demonstrates these [travel] texts' appropriative power over naming and representing the region: there is an Andean mountain range called Darwin ... a lake called Musters and a volcano called Hudson",[5] names which Argentine journalist Roberto Payró sardonically noted were "all of them difficult to pronounce for those who speak a Latin tongue."[6] Patagonia is thus a space which is "inevitably overdetermined", one that, if it were included in their study, Patrick Holland and Graham Huggan would describe as a zone of repetition, around which various apparently "unshakable" mythologies have been generated.[7] Among these myths feature the idea that "Patagonia en el imaginario occidental es metáfora de últimas fronteras y aventuras" [Patagonia in the Western imaginary is a metaphor of the ultimate frontier and adventure][8] as well as the notion that, to quote North American travel writer Paul Theroux's now famous aphorism, "it is the ultimate nowhere place."[9]

Patagonia is more than a construction of and in European travel discourse, of course, as Payró illustrated in his work; it has had its own enduring power in the Argentine and Chilean imaginaries. Indeed, Chris Moss claims that for metropolitan inhabitants of the countries of the Southern Cone, the broad notion of *el sur* [the South] "is nothing like the myths Europeans spin about Patagonia."[10] While the very concept of the South is geographically diffuse, incorporating Patagonia, the pampa and other south- and westerly-lying regions (as Eva-Lynn Jagoe notes, "it holds little cartographic allegiance"),[11] nevertheless it has featured prominently in Spanish-language travel and fictional writing, particularly in the formulation and consolidation of ideas about nationhood during the nineteenth century. To write about Patagonia, about the South, has always presented a particular discursive dilemma for the "domestic" literary tourist, therefore, whereby to write about the region has meant "also to position oneself within a European discourse about its land and its inhabitants."[12] That is, to engage with the South has always involved for Argentine and Chilean writers a necessary process of (dis)engagement with or from existing mythologies engendered and sustained by European travellers. As Jens Andermann writes in the case of Argentina in his influential study *Mapas de poder*:

> [El 'viaje nacional'] reivindica la tradición de tomar posesión, mediante la letra, de tierras que hasta el momento habían estado fuera de su alcance, en nombre de los valores que esta letra representa: la cultura, la civilisación, la productividad. Pero al mismo tiempo, la escritura tiene que marcar su propia distancia respecto del modelo imperial que hace suyo: nacionaliza entonces el espacio por el que viaja, mostrándolo como algo intrínsecamente propio antes aun de haber sido enfocado por el observador. El espacio pasa a ser lo consagrado, el depósito de argentinidad con la que se ensancha la visión del viajero.[13]

> [(The 'national journey') restores the tradition of taking possession, through writing, of lands that until then had been out of reach, in the name of the very values that writing represents: culture, civilisation, productivity. But at the same time, writing has to mark its own distance in respect of the imperial model that it makes its own: it therefore nationalises the space travelled, showing it as something intrinsically its own before it had even been seen by the observer. Space then becomes consecrated, a repository of 'Argentine-ness' with which the traveller's vision is broadened.]

Scholars such as Andermann, Jagoe, Ernesto Livon-Grosman, and Gabriela Nouzeilles have all done important and illuminating work on Patagonian travel texts of the nineteenth and early twentieth centuries, by writers including W. H. Hudson, Lucio Mansilla, Francisco P. Moreno, and Roberto Arlt, all of whom "read and responded to European, and especially British, narratives about the region."[14] This chapter seeks to amplify this work on "Spanish-language" travellers to Patagonia, who to some degree have also left their mark on its geography: there is both a national park and glacier named after Moreno, for instance, while that traveller bestowed "celebratory, almost chauvinistic names"[15] such as Lago Argentino [Argentine Lake] and Lago San Martín [San Martin lake] on other features of the landscape. My analysis departs from prevailing critical tendencies, however, both in respect of its singular historical and transnational focus and in terms of its conceptual framework. Although, as for Nouzeilles, it is the heterotopic quality of the region which informs my readings of the travel books at hand, in what follows I return to Michel Foucault's notion of heterotopia—that is, among other things, a space which simultaneously incorporates several, "incompatible" sites—in order to conceptualise their particular delineation of Patagonia.

This chapter will consider two contemporary travel books about Patagonia by authors from Chile and Argentina, Luis Sepúlveda's *Patagonia Express* [*Full Circle: A South American Journey*] and Mempo Giardinelli's *Final de novela en Patagonia* [*Novel's End in Patagonia*], which, despite their international distribution and recognition, have yet to receive any sustained critical analysis to date. It will explore how these travellers negotiate Patagonia's patently ambivalent discursive heritage at a time when, as Jagoe observes, "twentieth century writers appeal to the South in moments of national crisis when the idea of [nationhood] is challenged."[16] The decade of the 1990s is indeed a period in which questions of regional identity are at issue, although for quite different reasons than in the era of nation formation. As well as engaging with the region's particular place myths, this chapter also seeks to contest, or demythologise, another kind of fiction which is emerging about the area, which propounds a vacuum in its production of contemporary travel narratives. In his recent book on Patagonia, for example, Chris Moss claims that "[Aimé] Tschiffely aside, Argentine and Chilean writers have yet to produce a modern travelogue about Patagonia" and "there is no real tradition of travel writing in the contemporary [southern cone] literary culture."[17] By disregarding Sepúlveda's and Giardinelli's travel books, however (which receive no mention at all in what is an otherwise comprehensive and highly accessible survey of Patagonia's cultural history), and by dismissing the emerging body of travel texts from the region, Moss begins to resemble his own rather uncharitable characterisation of the contemporary travel writer as a "literary bulldozer".[18] While he is quite right that travelogues "open up certain routes and close others down", nevertheless, in this case Moss could well be accused of cutting off a compelling—and revealing—route into the subject of his own book.[19] In taking up this line of enquiry, therefore, I shall illustrate how contemporary Spanish-language travellers, in acknowledgment of their literary heritage, have marshalled the journey to Patagonia less, as their European forebears did, as a means of experiencing the utopian possibilities of the region, although that impulse is still in evidence to some degree. Rather, Giardinelli's and Sepúlveda's travel texts speak in different and sometimes complex ways to the region's experience of postmodernity and to burgeoning processes of globalisation. How, then, can Sepúlveda's and Giardinelli's travel books be situated within the context of prevailing myths about Patagonia, such as that of its perennially empty landscape? What positions do these contemporary Spanish-language travel writers take up in relation to the exoticist legacy of European travellers, specifically, that of the British author Bruce Chatwin, who is the pole star of their particular constellation and whose 1977 travel text is invoked in this chapter's title? And how do these "regional" travel texts thematize the idea and experience of the "global"? Before considering these issues, I turn first to further consideration of Patagonia's place in travel mythology and to some pertinent historical contextualisation.

MYTHOLOGIES AND HISTORIES

The myths generated by travellers about Patagonia are complex and often antithetical. On one level, as Nouzeilles points out in her excellent survey of these representations in Patagonian journey narratives, travel to this apparently limitless, empty land meant to vanish to end of the world, to step outside of history. In this respect, Patagonia is conceived as a last frontier, an unconquerable hostile desert, an impression due no doubt in part to the territory's "eerie experience of infinity",[20] and in part to what Sylvia Iparraguirre calls "el choque étnico: el espectáculo del otro distinto que no se puede asimilar" [ethnic shock: the spectacle of the other that cannot be assimilated].[21] Patagonia's encoding as the ultimate limit place has also had to do with its time-honoured status as an independent territory, for centuries (and even after colonisation) apparently beyond the jurisdiction of any particular nation-state.[22] On another level, however, the area played significant roles in the definition of imperial modernity as well as in the production of knowledge about history and nature. As such, as Hernán Santiváñez Vieyra notes, since the nineteenth century Patagonia has signified "el paraíso perdido y la tierra prometida a la vez" [simultaneously a lost paradise and promised land],[23] a point articulated in slightly different terms by Livon-Grosman, who conceives of the region as founded on a double layer of myth, "el de la región como un territorio primigenio y tierra de nadie, y el de ese territorio como parte integral de la nación" [that of the region as an *ur* territory and no man's land and that of the land as integral to the nation]. Indeed, Livon-Grosman also draws attention to the specific structure of power in which Patagonia functions as "una zona maleable para el imaginario europeo *primero* y criollo *después*" [a malleable zone for the European imaginary first and the national imaginary second] (my emphasis).[24] Notwithstanding, Patagonia's more fecund possibilities were recognised and promoted in the interior by the Argentine state in the nineteenth century: first, as a promised land (rich in resources and at threat from foreign invasion) and second, as a landscape embodying the very idea of the national state.[25] This was evinced perhaps most famously in the work of anthropologist and naturalist Francisco P. Moreno, who in his *Viaje a la Patagonia austral* [*Travels to Austral Patagonia*] mapped and classified the region and brought to national attention the economic potential of its "virgin" territory.[26] In more recent times, in the wake of the various effects of globalisation (such as rapid urbanization, industrial pollution, and global warming), Patagonia's myths have not waned. Rather, as Iparraguirre notes, ideas such as that of "[el] paisaje real con su indudable halo de exotismo, lejanía y misterio" [a real landscape with its aura of exoticism, distance, and mystery] persist.[27] The difference in the contemporary period is that they act as a magnet for a particular kind of traveller, so that, as Nouzeilles observes, "Patagonia has become the concern of environmental organisations and a powerful fetish for adventure tourism."[28]

Bruce Chatwin's *In Patagonia*, perhaps now "the most widely read work about South America's bright-skied south",[29] has played a significant role in the more recent mythologisation of this region in the anglophone tradition, as has his travelling persona in that and other works such as *The Songlines*. For Nicholas Shakespeare, this is because the English writer stood for the "promotable ideal of the literate adventurer": "inquisitive, spiritual and global", Chatwin became "an archetype for the urbane traveller and a voice for Generation X."[30] For David Taylor, however, the Englishman was more of a "connoisseur of exile",[31] the construction of a particular travelling self made possible "only through being in certain material ways a late beneficiary of empire (educated at Marlborough, one of the youngest ever directors at Sotheby's, internationally sponsored protégé of Cape)."[32] As a corollary, it is arguable whether Chatwin's 1977 account is "about" Patagonia at all; it is renowned more for its portrayal of a particular kind of self-imposed exile and its pervasive citation of other works of travel literature than, say, for its depiction of landscape. Thus, for Manfred Pfister, the unusual density of intertextual reference in Chatwin's Patagonian "travelogue" (a term the English writer would have abhorred) is symptomatic of the "postmodernization" of that text, where the intertexts are part of the object perceived. As such, Pfister claims, "*In Patagonia* is at least as much about the fantasies about Patagonia as it is about Patagonia itself."[33] In formal terms too, Chatwin's "unflappable, detached, discreet" stance (he is, according to Pfister, "a pose rather than a subject")[34] is reinforced by the "bleak, chiselled style" of *In Patagonia* where "the narratives are in constant flight from prolonged involvement", inferring a calculated distance from what is portrayed.[35] The Englishman might well have appreciated the now canonical status of that book, although, as Paul McGee argues, "anyone who searches for a fundamentally believable image of Tierra del Fuego will find this collection of ninety-seven travel fragments decidedly lacking in guidance... the only meaning articulated in [the book] is the pointlessness of meaning itself."[36]

Chatwin's iconic "nomadic" persona and his inimitable style have weighed heavily on subsequent travel writers to/in the region, and in what follows I shall consider the formal and symbolic articulations of that legacy by Sepúlveda and Giardinelli. First, however, a brief word about contemporary historical developments in Chile and Argentina, characterised by processes of redemocratisation in both countries since the mid-1980s, as it is against this context that my readings of their more recent kinds of adventure and journey accounts are cast.

Following brutal military dictatorships during the 1970s, and in compliance with emerging trends elsewhere in the continent, the return to democracy in the southern cone was characterised by the widespread adoption and implementation of neoliberal ideologies in government. Nevertheless, the transitions to democratic rule were by no means identical in each country.[37] Like his counterparts in Mexico and Peru, Carlos Menem, who had campaigned for election on a traditional Peronist rhetoric, adopted policies of privatisation and economic liberalisation in order to counter the effect of a period of rampant hyperinflation in Argentina. During the ten years of his presidency (1989–1999) he introduced a range of austerity measures and a programme of capitalist restructuring in order to stabilise the country's economy.[38] This was Argentina's so-called great transformation, orchestrated and implemented in large part by Menem's Finance Minister Domingo Cavallo, which depended on the sale of national industries and state-owned companies as well as the increasing transnationalisation of the economy.[39] The achievement of economic stability, however, had severe social costs. One of these, as Luis Alberto Romero points out, was unemployment, which became "a structural characteristic of the new economy",[40] while the Convertibility Law, which had established a fixed exchange rate and pegged the new *peso* to the U.S. dollar, in effect became "a corset that support[ed] at the same time as it asphyxiate[d]".[41] A corollary of this was the widespread impoverishment of the middle classes, which led to strikes and civil unrest as more people slipped into the lower class and many beneath the poverty line. Endemic political corruption was another feature of Menem's decade-long administration (with many of his ministers accused of personally benefitting from the privatisations, for example). In Chile, meanwhile, the transition to democracy began somewhat later, General Augusto Pinochet's dictatorship lasting seventeen years from the date of his overthrow of Salvador Allende's fledgling, democratically elected Popular Unity government in 1973. Nevertheless, while other neighbouring but essentially fragile democracies in the region postponed structural adjustment for fear of triggering social unrest, as Kurt Weyland notes, "radical market reforms were pushed through in Chile [by Pinochet] with the force of arms."[42] Since 1990, however, a succession of centre-left Concertación governments (under, respectively, Patricio Aylwin [1990–1994],

Eduardo Frei [1994–2000], Ricardo Lagos [2000–2006], and Michelle Bachelet [2006–]) have attempted to forge and consolidate a democratic future for the country, which, like its immediate neighbour, continues to be "cloaked in the shadow of its authoritarian past". As Michael Lazarra observes, the transition governments have been interested primarily in representing Chile as an "economic tiger" and a model for other nations to envy, so that their new consensus-based politics has effectively became synonymous with amnesia:

> [Redemocratisation] meant . . . the annulment of politics as it was practiced in Chile before 1973, that is, politics as a struggle among competing visions of society, and its replacement by a neoliberal regime put into place by Pinochet, a regime that preserved in its very makeup many characteristics of the authoritarian government that preceded it.[43]

Chilean sociologist José Joaquín Brunner has compared this more recent climate of democratic recovery to the period of "ideological inflation" in Latin America in the 1960s, which favoured "revolution as the means of national liberation, social integration, and economic development". Since the mid-1980s, he claims that "the opposite tendency finds itself reinforced, namely, the reappraisal of secularism in culture." Norbert Lechner concurs that in the political sphere there has been what he calls an emotional "enfriamiento" [cooling], which has been accompanied by the "disseminat[ion] [of] values of civil tolerance and . . . a certain spirit of negotiation".[44] What both Brunner and Lechner draw attention to is a shift towards a "disenchanted" notion of politics in Latin America, which "restricts it to specific areas, taking away its omnipotence and freeing it from its anchorage in absolute principles in order to make it more flexible and adjustable to immediate challenges".[45] Such transformations in the region's political spheres are consonant with broader developments which sociologists such as Ulrich Beck, Mike Featherstone, and Anthony Giddens variously call reflexive modernization or globalisation, a period of late modernity in which its very structures have become destabilised. In contrast to the metanarrative of modernity and its rhetoric of progress and achievement, a reflexive modernity indicates a "radicalisation" of modernization, in which context reflexivity is less a question of individual agency than a matter of the destabilisation of institutions, whether political or financial. As a result, and partly due also to other phenomena (such as global warming) which have encouraged reflection on the very modernizing processes which have brought them about, individuals are likely to search for other possible modes of belonging and of positioning themselves in relation to the world. Beck suggests, for example, that in a period of reflexive modernity (or what he calls a "risk society") individuals turn to a number of different forms of "sub politics", rather than the institutional politics, for identity and agency.[46] As we shall see in the following section, in speaking to those very processes, Sepúlveda's Patagonian travelogue might well be read as a "reflexive (auto)biography" of sorts.

GLOBAL EXILES

Published in Spanish in 1995, and translated the following year into English as *Full Circle: A South American Journey* for inclusion in the Lonely Planet Journeys series of travel books, Luis Sepúlveda's *Patagonia Express* relates in part the author's return to a Chile from which he had been exiled for many years. In Chile, Sepúlveda had worked as a theatre director, writer and was also active for many years in Allende's Popular Unity government. When it fell in the military coup of 1973, he was imprisoned for twenty-eight years, a sentence which was quashed in 1976 thanks to a successful campaign for his release on an expatriation clause by the German section of Amnesty International. Initially reluctant to go to Europe (and follow in the footsteps of many other political exiles from the Southern Cone in this period), Sepúlveda subsequently spent some years "travelling" around Latin America. After becoming involved in and imprisoned for further left-wing activism in Nicaragua, he finally left for Germany in 1980.[47] It was not until 1988, however, after some twelve years in exile, that he returned to his native Chile. *Patagonia Express* loosely details some of these journeys and, as such, is perhaps the most autobiographical work by this writer to date, despite his disclaimer in the book's prologue ("no está en mis planes escribir un libro de memorias" [I am not planning to write my memoirs] 189).[48] Indeed, the four parts of the volume each deal with an "expedition" of the kind described in that biographical synopsis, ranging from his youthful conversion to communism, the years of imprisonment, expatriation from Chile and journeys to other Latin American countries, the return to Patagonia from Europe some years later, as well as the final trip to Martos, in southern Spain, a journey which represents the fulfilment of a promise to return to his grandfather's birthplace made in the opening chapters of the book.

In the course of *Patagonia Express*, Sepúlveda repeatedly invokes the memory of Chatwin, whose *In Patagonia* he characterises as "uno de los mejores libros de viajes de todos los tiempos" (90) [one of the best travel books ever written, 89]. Indeed, the Chilean writer's appeals to the English traveller range from explicit citations, as in the opening of the third part of *Patagonia Express* which reconstructs what may be an apocryphal meeting between the two authors in Barcelona, to other allusions, such as to Chatwin's preferred apparatus of the moleskin notebook and to the notion of a form of nomadism. Moreover, the demography of Sepúlveda's Patagonian landscape—made up of pilots, rebels and European fugitives of Nazism—while on one level a testament to the hybrid makeup of the region's dispersed population, is in other ways reminiscent of Chatwin's own cast of characters from *In Patagonia*, although Chilean migrants tend to be foregrounded in *Patagonia Express* at the expense of the expected sheep farmers and Welsh settlers. Furthermore, as in the work of his English precursor, such a "heterogeneous collection of people [and] stories"[49] in Sepúlveda's travelogue takes precedence over any detailed description of the landscape or means of conveyance between destinations. Indeed, the lack of continuity between chapters in *Patagonia Express* renders it in some ways as elliptical and laconic as Chatwin's original volume.

The theme of exile is perhaps the most obvious issue on which these two authors' journey narratives converge, although, as Casey Blanton observes, in any case most contemporary travel writers now share a sense of themselves as exiles. Indeed, Blanton maintains that "part of the darkness of their books comes from their tendency to portray a world full of exiles, even a world exiled from itself."[50] The bleak Patagonian landscape provides an ideal backdrop for such ontological explorations ("It's perfect," writes Theroux)[51] and has in turn passed into travel mythology as a blank canvas onto which the writer might project and explore selfhood, especially the "unknown" of the self.[52] For Chatwin, the interest in exile, according to Taylor, was largely intellectual, providing material for the formulation of his "highly idiosyncratic personal mythology" of nomadism.[53] If Chatwin's interest in exile was academic, for the Chilean author it is clearly individual, however, a particularity that is evinced in two ways: first, in Sepúlveda's performance as intimate friend to those travellees he encounters along the way (many of them political exiles from Pinochet's regime), a strategy which is about proximity, rather than distance; and second, in his volume's formal and thematic endorsement of a particular ideology of mobility.

Structurally, *Patagonia Express* marks a full circle (underscored in the title of the English translation) with its denouement comprising the completion of a quest, the fulfilment of a promise made in the book's opening section to Sepúlveda's grandfather (a Republican refugee from Franco's Spain) to go back to his hometown of Martos. This is confirmed on Sepúlveda's arrival in Spain at the end of the book: "yo supe por fin se había cerrado el círculo, pues me encontraba en el punto de partida del viaje empezado por mi abuelo" [I knew that at last I had come full circle: I was at the starting point of the journey my grandfather began] (178). Crucially, however, closure at the end of *Patagonia Express* constitutes not a return to Chile but rather relocation in Europe. In this regard, it consolidates a movement by the traveller-narrator towards a position of reconciliation precisely with his location in exile. Significantly, however, Sepúlveda diffuses the importance of specific location, appearing rather to settle on and in the very condition of displacement. A particular formula crystallising this idea is reiterated in a number of exchanges and encounters in the later stages of the travel book, which suggests that ultimately, "uno es de donde mejor se siente" (177) [the place you feel best is where you belong", 182]. Indeed, the denouement confirms the possibility of making a home in exile, wherever that might be—Chile instead of Spain (for his grandfather) or Europe instead of Chile (for Sepúlveda)—and in this sense it reveals an impulse common to many other works of travel writing, "not so much to leave home as to find home".[54] In effect, the ending also proposes a fluid, contingent configuration of national identity (through that formula's grammatical construction "es de" in Spanish, which denotes nationality) which is reinforced elsewhere by Sepúlveda, who claims, for example, that "No soy un escritor chileno" [I'm not a Chilean writer].[55] Tim Youngs observes that in their Patagonian travel narratives neither Chatwin nor Theroux "seems to know where or to what he belongs".[56] In *Patagonia Express*, however, Sepúlveda does at least assert a sense of *not* belonging: while the general concept of home might well be presented with some fluidity, the conclusion for the author himself is an unequivocal disavowal of Chile and Chilean national identity. Significantly, there is also an apparent absence of any anxiety at this conclusion (or the "darkness" noted by Blanton), which is otherwise manifest elsewhere in many other travellers' experiences of exile. This is an epistemology we might call "harmonious deterritorialisation", the awkwardness of the very phrase capturing something of the concept's own unorthodox character. Thus, for Sepúlveda a journey to nowhere—to recite Theroux's famous conception of Patagonia—brings into focus a sense of somewhere (home), which effectively might be anywhere, "donde mejor se siente" [where you feel best] (177).

Underpinning Sepúlveda's particular epistemology of displacement in *Patagonia Express* is an ideological journey also charted in the course of the travelogue. The first two parts of the account, which is as much a memoir as it is a travel book, deal with the writer's young adulthood in Chile, his imprisonment and torture in Temuco, and the subsequent difficulties he encounters moving around Latin America as a political exile. In effect, these sections recount a period marked by the defeat of Allende's government in the 1973 coup, the installation of military dictatorship, and the propagation of an official campaign of terror there and elsewhere in the Southern Cone, a period denominated by Sepúlveda as "un viaje a ninguna parte" [a journey to nowhere].[57] In the third section of *Patagonia Express*, however, Sepúlveda returns to the region at the end of the 1980s, during which time Chile was on the verge of its transition to democracy. In this part of the travelogue, Sepúlveda encounters many political exiles of the recent Pinochet era, all of whom we are led to assume were involved in leftist politics but who, during this period, are otherwise engaged in diverse projects of "resistance" which have little to do with affiliation to a political party whose aims have been so publicly and painfully defeated. One example of what we might see as a kind of *enfriamiento* evident in *Patagonia Express*, on the one hand an ideological repositioning with regard to a radical left, on the other a move towards a form of "sub politics" in a redemocratised Chile, comes towards the end of the book's third section.[58] Sepúlveda recounts the story of Klaus Kucimavic, a former Nazi collaborator who sought refuge in Patagonia from Tito's partisans and who is known in the area as Carlos Carpintero, the local inventor. It turns out that Kucimavic is also a professor of physics who, whilst in exile, is awarded an alternative Nobel prize for his measurements of the hole in the ozone layer. We learn that Sepúlveda had been sent to interview him at the time of the conferment of the prize, some years before. Despite collecting enough raw material for a long article, however, Sepúlveda refrains from publishing it, claiming that "de haberlo publicado, hubiera roto la armonía de los habitantes de Río Mayo" [if I had published it I would have upset the harmony of Río Mayo], adding, "Kucimavic pasó a ser, también para mí, Carlitos Carpintero" (150) [for me too, Kucimavic became Carlos Carpintero, 153]. Sepúlveda's reconciliation with this character's Patagonian alias appears not only to echo a mood of political renegotiation, therefore, but also to synthesize an ideological repositioning on his part that has taken place over the course of the book. In other words, it appears to reflect a cooling ("enfriamiento") of his earlier leftist activism, which had led to "nowhere", in favour of an increasing concern for and engagement in environmental issues, in which area he is able to find common ground with someone who in days past would have been his political adversary. Such a shift to a form of "sub politics" is born out in the last chapter of this section of *Patagonia Express* in Sepúlveda's acquaintance and subsequent friendship with the pilot Captain Palacios. We learn that after a first chance and thoroughly unpromising encounter Sepúlveda and Palacios become friends thanks to their shared interest in protecting the environment and endangered species. They team up to make a documentary on the extermination of Amazonian crocodiles whose skin, as Sepúlveda describes, ends up on show in European fashion parades.[59] It is through such episodes, then, that *Patagonia Express* becomes a "reflexive [auto]biography" in a literal sense, detailing a process of ideological repositioning by Sepúlveda and other exiles he meets in the light of their "disenchantment" not only with the consequences of late modernity, of course, but also with a radical left in Latin America.[60]

TRANSLATING TRAVEL

And yet there is another sense of the "global" that needs to be considered in respect of Sepúlveda, although one which is perhaps not as benign as that of the discussion so far. This is a formulation of the global that is not associated with actual transit but rather with transnational networks of translation and consumption. It is a journey undertaken this time by the text itself across languages, from Spanish to English, and which has to do as much with the mechanics of translation as it has with the translatability of Sepúlveda's work.

One of the reasons that the Chilean has achieved such international recognition is not only because of his more recent location in Europe and access to publishing opportunities there but also because of the availability of much of his work in translation. He is, according to one of his reviewers, next to Gabriel García Márquez and Isabel Allende, "el escritor [latinoamericano] más leído en Europa" [the most read Latin American writer in Europe],[61] a position that the reviewer attributes precisely to the author's greater success in his literary career since his settlement in Germany. As I mentioned earlier, *Patagonia Express* was translated into English a year after its initial publication, for inclusion in the Lonely Planet Journeys series of travel literature (a series which includes a range of writers, including Zoë Brân, William Dalrymple, and Eric Newby). The book was translated as *Full Circle: A South American Journey*, with a significant change in title that effectively erases any indication of specific location for the English-language reader, substituting the generic and rather nebulous "South America" for Patagonia.[62] This amendment was suggested by the commissioning editor at the time due to the proximity of the "Spanish" title (which has in any case little Spanish in it) to that of Paul Theroux's 1979 travel book *Old Patagonia Express*.[63] There was a further modification made to the English version, however, which is worthy of note here. The prologue, "Apuntes sobre estos apuntes" [Notes on these Notes], was moved to the back of the English-language volume because the Lonely Planet editor "felt that the original placement was confusing and that the narrative was more forceful if the reader was led straight into the actual story, and the Notes formed an epilogue."[64] It is in the prologue, however, that Sepúlveda also offers an explanation for the choice of *Patagonia Express* as a title. He explains that the epithet is borrowed from a train that no longer runs in the region but which "continúa viajando en la memoria de los hombres y mujeres de la Patagonia" (11) [goes on travelling in the memories of the men and women of Patagonia]. The more specific association of the train to a station which was the site of the 1921 anarchist revolt led by Antonio Soto is unravelled (sympathetically, it might be noted, in comparison with Chatwin's account of it) in a later chapter of *Patagonia Express*.[65] This anecdote in the prologue forms one of the first of many other references (apart from the title itself) to political revolt or resistance in the Spanish original. The displacement of the prologue, however, together with the erasure of place (and the train's name) in the English title effectively decontextualize, dehistoricize and depoliticize this travelogue for the "monolingual" reader. While *Patagonia Express* is clearly not a radical political or historical text of the order of, say, Eduardo Galeano's *Venas abiertas de América Latina* [*Open Veins of Latin America*], nevertheless the English translation has clearly undergone some mollification in this way. A further implication of the publisher's decision to move the prologue to the back of the translated volume is that English-speaking readers would not immediately understand Sepúlveda's pseudo-Borgesian disavowal of the text as autobiography, accustomed as they are to consuming such life narratives from the "Third World", including Latin America.⁶⁶ As Nicholas Murray points out, however, with regard to concerns over the "philosophical" content of Chatwin's *The Songlines*, which in fact became a financial, critical, and popular success for the author (as well as the apogee of his intellectual life), readers can sometimes be more perceptive and adventurous than anticipated.⁶⁷ Nevertheless, in the form suggested by Lonely Planet, the publisher *par excellence* of guidebooks for the independent traveller, Sepúlveda's travelogue has been mitigated in order to be made "suitable for all markets".⁶⁸

The paratextual apparatus surrounding the English translation reinforces the process of its adaptation for an international audience already

Figure 2.1 Front cover of Luis Sepúlveda, *Full Circle: A South American Journey*, trans. Chris Andrews (Melbourne: Lonely Planet, 1996).

familiar with a certain kind of literature from Latin America. The back cover blurb draws attention to Sepúlveda's "vivid, sometimes surreal pictures of a continent where the distinction between reality and fiction is often blurred" and describes how the author "conjures up extravagant characters in extraordinary situations" in the course of the travelogue. There is an endorsement from the Spanish daily *El País* commending (rather oddly) the author's "detachment" as well as his "humour and vibrant prose". The book's cover (Figure 2.1) completes this metamorphosis, albeit in an apparently paradoxical manner, foregrounding an image of incarceration and freedom. The picture comprises a view of a prison cell with the proverbial three-barred window, cast for the most part in dark shadow, with a packed rucksack at the ready in one corner, a map of "South America" etched into the wall in another. The bright blue view from the cell's window on the right-hand side corner of the cover image, of the snow-capped mountains and lakes (complete with a boat on the water, wind in its sails), puts the finishing touches to this time-honoured representation of the region for the independent traveller/backpacker, the target audience of this translation. Ultimately, "South America" is confirmed as a place with a dark and troubled history, but one which promises adventure, a little danger even, as well as outstanding natural beauty. Through the cover image and back-cover blurb, therefore, Sepúlveda's text is locked into a literary ghetto of "difference", in which "South America" signifies alternatively the exotic and/or the political: a potent combination of the two characterised by Timothy Brennan as the "politico-exotic".[69] In the form suggested by Lonely Planet, therefore, Sepúlveda's travelogue is ensured its passage into what Graham Huggan calls the "global mode of mass market consumption".[70]

Another reason why Sepúlveda's work has been met with appreciation amongst an international audience, however, and why it has proved attractive to publishers such as Lonely Planet, is undoubtedly because of its inherent translatability. As Michael Cronin points out in his book *Translation and Globalisation*, in a context in which bookshops across the globe are now subject to the same pressures as other retail outlets, the emphasis in publishing is on "accessible, readable books which favour a translation strategy of least resistance and maximum naturalisation".[71] Sepúlveda's translatability has to do precisely with accessibility and readability, not only in terms of his narrative style, but also in terms of his more general depiction of "South America" and, I would suggest, the very ideology of travel endorsed in *Patagonia Express*. In interviews, for example, the Chilean author frequently stakes a claim for the qualities of simplicity and accessibility, repeatedly claiming to be part of a "new" generation of Latin American writers, distinct from those of the "Boom", such as Gabriel García Márquez, whom he takes to task for their "large impenetrable tomes plagued by obstacles".[72] He maintains that his own "younger" generation rejects the baroque style of their "Boom" precursors in favour of a return to storytelling and an economy of language and form. In this respect, Sepúlveda is typical of what Brennan calls a third wave of "shrewd, good-hearted and politically-responsible" Third World writers on the international literary scene whose "well-crafted public personae in many ways depend on rejecting aestheticism".[73] In its stylistic and structural simplicity, *Patagonia Express* would certainly seem to bear out this particular ideology. Yet, I would suggest that, contrary to his own claims, Sepúlveda's particular aesthetic effectively reinforces many of the still pervasive exoticist images of Latin America currently in circulation in the global literary market. Ultimately, *Patagonia Express* presents an image of a region where strange (almost magic) events occur with frequency but which are for the most part inoffensive and benign. Sepúlveda's Patagonia is a place where idiosyncratic lying competitions are held ("¿Existirá en el mundo otro torneo como éste, un torneo de mentiras?", 110 [Where else in the world would you find a tournament like this, a tournament of lies?, 108]) and which is home to a cast of characters such as don Nicanor Estrada, who is buried upright on his embalmed steed in full gaucho regalia. The following anecdote (related in order to bolster another reported secondhand from Bruce Chatwin regarding the peculiarity of the Patagonian people) is exemplary in this respect:

> Un profesor argentino me contó una historia insuperable. Uno de sus alumnos escribió sobre un reloj: 'El reloj sirve para pesar los atrasos. El reloj también se descompone y así como los autos pierden aceite, el reloj pierde tiempo'. ¿Alguien habló de la muerte del surrealismo? (91)
>
> [An Argentinian teacher told me a priceless story. One of his students wrote the following about clocks: 'We use clocks to weigh delays. Clocks break down too, and just as cars lose oil, clocks lose time.' Did somebody mention the death of surrealism? 89–90]

As in this instance, the tone of the rest of the travelogue is largely congenial and lighthearted so that even the sections dealing with Sepúlveda's imprisonment and torture in Temuco are "spiced up" to form sympathetic episodes, often of a comic character. There is one, for example, in which a warder, nicknamed Margarito, asks Sepúlveda's opinion of his own literary endeavours, which turn out to have been plagiarised from a Mexican poet. For his refusal to pander to the warder's literary pretensions, Sepúlveda ends up in solitary confinement: "en el cubo juré y rejuré que nunca me dedicaría a la crítica literaria" (35) [in the cube I swore over and over again never to become a literary critic, 32]. *Patagonia Express* therefore depends upon a number of fixed images and a cast of regular characters which are not only familiar to metropolitan readers but which effectively satisfy their desire for exotic appeal. Furthermore, the liberal travel and identity politics of *Patagonia Express*, that possibility posited by Sepúlveda of a kind of harmonious deterritorialisation, are also likely to appeal to and resound with an audience of independent travellers and backpackers. If, as Holland

and Huggan claim, Chatwin's special appeal is bound up with the allure of the nomad-individualist, Sepúlveda's is surely reliant on this particular combination of the exotic and the anodyne.

In aesthetic terms as well as in respect of the widespread acclaim he enjoys outside of his native Chile, Sepúlveda might be productively compared to another ex-patriot, Ariel Dorfman. Catherine Boyle has recently reconsidered the international success of Dorfman's 1991 play *Death and the Maiden* (a success not repeated in his native country), which was translated into English and also made into a feature-length film by Roman Polanski, released in 1994.[74] Boyle argues that the source culture of Dorfman's play is not Chile at all but rather Western, North American, European. She writes:

> What makes the play so readily transferable are the core codes and meanings, the sympathies and sense of awareness that adapt easily to these countries and, above all, to countries in comparable periods of transition . . . Dorfman's work is not difficult to translate because he speaks a univocal international language . . . The end result is seductive but, finally, empty.[75]

Although not entirely vacuous, Sepúlveda's work is equally seductive on a number of levels. Like Dorfman's play, however, *Patagonia Express* appears to encapsulate even in its title the "light rhythm of . . . diversion" that characterises the aesthetics of redemocratisation, as described by Chilean critic Nelly Richard, in which reference to the past must not present any rough edges or communicative harshness. Richard writes that "La memoria de la dictadura que circula por las vías del mercado entra en ese juego de signos velozmente reciclados que no se toman el tiempo de hacer de la historia algo más que una breve mención al pasar" [The memory of the dictatorship that is disseminated by the market enters into that play of signs that are rapidly recycled and do no more than mention history in passing].[76] As I have argued, the seemingly congenial *Patagonia Express* is made to appear even blander in its English translation, for it is precisely such an aesthetic that is embraced by and consumed eagerly in the global travel writing market. If "translation is the outcome of the carrying over the text which is sufficiently portable to be able to survive the journey", then Sepúlveda's travelogue would appear to present a test case of just such a text, for, to quote Cronin once again, "one factor which makes the journey easier is if the load is lighter."[77]

LITERARY TOURISTS

Mempo Giardinelli's journey to Patagonia some years later than the Chilean writer is also bound up in what starts to look like an almost endogamous circuit of travel writing relations in respect of this particular site. This is made explicit in an acknowledgment in the course of his travelogue, *Final de novela en Patagonia* [*Novel's End in Patagonia*] ("De pronto pienso en Luis Sepúlveda ... uno de mis hermanos literarios" [Suddenly I think of Luis Sepúlveda ... one of my literary brothers]) and by means of the Premio Grandes Viajeros [Great Travellers' Prize] conferred on the author by a committee on which Sepúlveda sat.[78] There is, then, something of what Holland and Huggan call "the mutual puffery of a handful of card-carrying club members" at work here.[79] Bruce Chatwin also features as part of this concatenation: while Giardinelli's invocation of the English author is considerably less favourable than that of his "Chilean" contemporary, nevertheless there are a number of convergences with the English writer's work. That is, on one level, Giardinelli's experience in Patagonia transpires to be as much a journey of "literary tourism" as that of Chatwin's in *In Patagonia*. I shall return to the more and less explicit citations of Chatwin in *Final de novela* shortly, but for the moment observe that the title of the Argentine author's volume neatly prefigures a journey that is literary in inspiration (the first chapters of his travelogue in fact lament the enormous scope of the existing travel literature about the region) and in motivation, with the author claiming that he needs to "despegarme de lo cotidiano para concentrarme en la novela que venía trabajando y que tenía completamente atascada, como un hueso en la garganta" [disconnect from everyday life to concentrate on the novel I had been working on and that was completely stalled, like a bone stuck in my throat] (16). The premise of Giardinelli's travel account therefore resounds in large part with a highly conventional desire for escapism and solitude, motivations which have long impelled the modern journey, as Eric Leed points out: "The ancients valued travel as an explication of human fate and necessity, for moderns, it is an expression of freedom and an escape from necessity and purpose."[80] Like Sepúlveda, the Argentine writer spent a period in exile from his native country during its military dictatorship, in his case in Mexico, where between 1976 and 1984 he taught at the Universidad Iberoamericana de México.[81] *Final de novela* is based on a journey undertaken in early 2000 with his friend Fernando Operé, departing from his native Chaco region in the northeast of Argentina south to Patagonia, a route that extends from one "periphery" of Argentina to another. While Cristina Sánchez-Blanco reads a history of travel writing and its construction of space retrospectively from the publication of Giardinelli's travelogue, rightly noting that "se vuelven a repetir 'enunciados' descriptivos de conceptos que han sido fundacionales en la literatura de viajes y exploraciones que redescubrieron el Nuevo Mundo" [tropes which have been foundational in travel writing and of journeys of rediscovery of the New World are repeated], my concern here is with the issues at stake in the book's more recent literary and political allusions.[82]

Indeed, it is in respect of the region's vast archive of travel literature that Giardinelli's travel book evokes some of the most common tropes and discourses associated with the long history of imperialist journeys there.

For example, a persistent masculinist nostalgia emerges in this account from the Argentine author's attempt to carve out a niche for his literary creativity on this trip. In this respect, he is very much a belated traveller in the terms outlined by Ali Behdad, that is, "lagging behind what [he] hopes to transform and write beyond".[83] Although Giardinelli acknowledges the layers of textuality at stake in both his journey and its account ("Nuestro viaje será nomás, inevitablemente, un viaje literario" [Our journey will inevitably be a literary journey], 41), he is adamant that he will not reread any of the vast body of travel literature on Patagonia before he embarks, even his friend Sepúlveda's travelogue: given that he wants to see everything "virginalmente" [in a virgin state], "todo experiencia ajena será ... negativa" [other people's experiences will be negative] (42). Like other travellers considered in the course of this study, Giardinelli asserts his intention to create *"mi viaje*, quiero construirlo paso a paso y para ello es preciso no leer otros viajes" [*my journey*, I want to build it step by step and for that reason it's imperative not to read other journeys] (41, original emphasis). The place myth of Patagonia as empty thus functions on at least two levels within the framework of this metafictional travel book. On one level, Giardinelli hankers after a void in the region's literary heritage, ultimately to fill it with his own work. Like many of his travelling precursors, however, he also depends precisely on the region's topographical and demographic vacuity, in this case, to provide an empty screen onto which the workings of his imagination can be projected, so that he can finish a novel-in-progress. This is a further implication of the book's title, *Final de novela en Patagonia*, which suggests a felicitous convergence of the completion of his novel with a journey to a region which, as mentioned earlier, is broadly conceived as the last frontier. Furthermore, if this man of letters cannot physically conquer new terrain, his journey narrative becomes instead a chronicle of his endeavours at epistemological and literary originality. Giardinelli is reflective enough, however, to acknowledge the potential pitfalls of such an endeavour:

Quería entregarme como lo hacía en este momento; con mi capacidad de asombro intacta y abierto como un lirio. No quería estar 'preparado' en ningún sentido. Era una postura que podía sonar soberbia, sin dudas, y ahora mismo, cuando lo escribo, soy consciente de que puede parecerlo. Pero no podía evitarlo, y debo decir que ni siquiera fue una decisión consciente, simplemente sucedió.

[I wanted to submit myself as I did in that moment; with my capacity for surprise open and intact like a lily. I did not want to be 'prepared' in any way. It was a position that could sound pompous, to be sure, and now as I write this I'm conscious that it could seem that way. But I could not help it, and I should say that it was not even a conscious decision, it just happened.] (53)

Here the contemporary traveller's dilemma is articulated in terms which underscore the erotics of the tourist experience. The use of a flower simile—above all, of the lily, a ubiquitous symbol of simplicity, virtue and innocence—crystallises Giardinelli's nostalgia for a pure and unbiased subjectivity and corresponds closely to the desire articulated earlier to experience Patagonia *virginalmente*. That this impulse to submit, "entregar", is described as unconscious ("simplemente sucedió") further reinforces this ultimately dubious metaphorical construction of his predicament.

Nevertheless, an extrapolation of this epistemology in relation to specific travelling precursors—and in particular a firm disavowal of the figure who has haunted contemporary travel writing about Patagonia more recently—proves to be illuminating. Unlike Sepúlveda, Giardinelli is sceptical of Chatwin, whose *In Patagonia* he singles out in an early overview of his literary antecedents:

> El [libro] del inglés ... de todos modos me dejó para siempre la sensación de haber sido yo testigo de algo ligeramente inauténtico. O quizá sentí que tenía una mirada demasiado europea para mi gusto, entendido ello como una mirada que, antes que comprender, juzga; es una mirada ... que finalmente *siempre nos juzga*.
>
> [The Englishman's book ... left me feeling that I had witnessed something slightly inauthentic. Or perhaps I felt that it had too much of a European gaze for my taste, the kind of gaze that, before understanding, judges: it's a gaze ... that ultimately *always judges us*.] (52, original emphasis)

Compared to Sepúlveda's portrayal of the Englishman as his travel buddy, Giardinelli's is a provocative depiction of Chatwin in more than one sense, notwithstanding the deference with which it is presented ("slightly inauthentic", "I felt ... for my taste"). First, in terms of Patagonian mythology, the Argentine writer is one of an increasing number to take issue with one of the principal contemporary proponents and protagonists of such myths.[84] Second, Giardinelli politicizes this critique of Chatwin in terms of hegemonic relations between Europe and Latin America. Although in doing so he sets up an antagonistic and potentially artificial dichotomy of his very own, which results in homogenising both *"us"* and "them", to some degree this anti-imperialist manoeuvre attenuates that earlier repudiation of the region's existing travel literature. Giardinelli's wilful dissociation from the literary travel-writing circuit here thus invokes another time-honoured trope of the genre he engages in *Final de novela*, which depends precisely on the assertion of the traveller's "unique" subjectivity in order to shore up difference and otherness. A corollary of this gesture, however, in this context, and specifically in respect of the accusation of inexactitude of the British author, is that Giardinelli's own subject position as an "authentic", original travel writer in Patagonia is consolidated, the legitimacy of his "postcolonial" subjectivity affirmed.

A literary feature of this journey which is manifest in more formal terms is the metafictional narrative at play throughout the account. Interwoven into almost every chapter of the book, and often indicated by a line separator and different typeface, is a separate section from the novel which Giardinelli is completing. It charts the progress of a fugitive couple, Victorio and Clelia (former protagonists of the author's 1995 work *Imposible equilibrio* [*Impossible Equilibrium*]) who are on the run in a stolen red Ford Fiesta, the same make of car that conveys Giardinelli and his travelling companion along their route south. Betrayed at every turn, these fictional characters also follow the same trajectory as their creator to Patagonia. Like Julio Cortázar and Carol Dunlop's ludic travelogue of the Paris-Marseille motorway *Los autonautas de la cosmopista* [*The Autonauts of the Cosmopiste*],[85] *Final de novela* playfully blurs the boundaries between the author's material and his characters' fictional journeys, throwing into relief that long troubled relationship between fictional and travel discourses. In addition to those excerpts from this work-in-progress, however, *Final de novela* also incorporates poems and diverse pieces of short fiction by the author (including "The time that Charles Darwin contemplated suicide") and quotations from other works such as the *Libro de Doctrina y Comportamiento* [*The Book of Doctrine and Behaviour*] by Fray Gómez de Oro y Saavedra, which comprise the travellers' mobile library. While, as Loredana Polezzi observes, "as a marginal genre, one which is often distressed and hybridised, travel writing generally grants the writer greater 'freedom of movement' than many other literary forms",[86] in this case there is considerable mobility demanded of the reader too. As such, the book is not only a highly literary travelogue in both theme and form, but also one which, ironically enough like Chatwin's *In Patagonia*, constantly impels movement in and through its composite structure.

The literary and the itinerant ultimately converge, however, in Giardinelli's philosophy of "transterración" [trans-territorialisation], which he elaborates towards the end of the travelogue. To some degree like his Chilean counterpart, and notwithstanding his own ten years in exile, Giardinelli's is essentially a benevolent epistemology. Taking his cue from Spanish philosopher Max Aub, the Argentine writer associates this kind of trans-territorialisation with an atavistic human itinerancy. In this state of flux, Giardinelli claims, "lo único inmutable fue la literatura" [the only immovable thing was literature] (226). He goes on: "la literatura es una tierra propia, un territorio que uno lleva consigo . . . [es] el único ladrillo inmutable que hombres y mujeres tenemos para construir nuestra casa donde sea" [Literature is your own land, a territory that you carry with you . . . it is the only immovable brick that we men and women have to build our homes wherever we are] (226). Writing appears not only to promise the homecoming that de-territorialisation or migrancy disallows, but it is also an activity bound up in movement and displacement, as Giardinelli observes: "Escribimos emigrando, digo, escritura como movimiento y escritura *en* movimiento . . . Escritura como el viaje que la literatura es" [We write emigrating, that is, writing as movement and writing *in* movement . . . Writing as the journey that is literature] (226, original emphasis). These ideas echo those of Iain Chambers, for whom "writing opens up a space that invites movement, migration, a journey."[87] If Giardinelli's belated journey to the discursively overdetermined Patagonia offers limited possibilities to "reinventar lo conocido . . . desde la creación de nuevas originalidades" [to reinvent the familiar . . . from original starting points] (19), therefore, it becomes instead an opportunity to articulate the (albeit still privileged and now quite well rehearsed) theoretical proximity of travel and writing where, in the context of Latin America he avers, literature is "un imaginario territorio portátil" [an imaginary portable territory] (226).

The Argentine writer's trip to Patagonia is not only literary, however, but also historical, a journey back in time in at least one sense, in that from the very outset it entails a self-conscious process of infantilization on the part of its travelling protagonists. Although Giardinelli and his travelling companion Fernando, a Spanish academic on sabbatical from the University of Virginia, are "en edad de ser abuelos" [the same age as grandfathers], "parecíamos dos chicos haciéndonos la rabona . . . excitados como colegiales" [we were like two boys bunking off . . . excited like school kids] (15, 37). Giardinelli's assumption of this diachronic subjectivity functions on a number of possible levels. In respect of his self-fashioning as a child, and of the trip as a journey back in time, on one level the author implicitly fuels the myth of Patagonia as ahistorical or timeless, a place to which one can always travel back. Unusually and perhaps disarmingly in this case, however, the author fully implicates himself in what might have otherwise been a conventional "Orientalist" gesture and, in doing so, engineers a strategic approximation to, rather than distanciation from, the territory travelled. In addition to underscoring the nostalgic impulse of his endeavour, to at least some degree, therefore, Giardinelli might also be seen to be invoking a subject position of particular historical resonance here, one which is bound up in ideas of the journey and its narrative as a kind of *bildungsroman* or, as Juan Pablo Spicer-Escalante put it recently, a *bildungs*-travelogue.[88] Jens Andermann's reading of Moreno is useful in conceptualising this idea. Andermann conceives of Moreno's *Viaje a la Patagonia Austral*—which opens precisely with the invocation of a similar (juvenile) subjectivity[89]—as "un ejemplo emblemático de ese Bildungsroman nacional que narra la prehistoria épica como revés y legitimación de la 'madurez' finalmente alcanzada por la élite conservadora" [an emblematic example of the national Bildungsroman which narrates epic prehistory as the inversion and legitimation of the 'maturity' finally achieved by conservative elite].[90] Andermann goes on: "La evocación inicial del naturalista-niño que sueña con seguir la huella de los pioneros ilustres es, en ese sentido, un ejemplo paradigmático de construcción de un sujeto no-participante en la expansión capitalista donde su empresa se inscribe" [The initial invocation of the child-naturalist who dreams of following in the footsteps of those illustrious pioneers is, in this sense, a paradigmatic example of the construction of a non-participant subject in the capitalist expansion within which his enterprise is inscribed]. At the turn of a new millennium, Giardinelli's self-professed immaturity—like the purity of the lily mentioned earlier—functions in a context not of the consolidation of a burgeoning independent nation-state, as in the case of Moreno in the late nineteenth century. Giardinelli's anachronistic travelling persona nevertheless offers a similarly double-layered stratagem as Moreno's: here as a potential means of exculpation from collusion with state endeavours, in this case to effect the country's neoliberal transformation and entry into the so-called "New Economic Order", the prejudicial effects of which form the basis of a sustained critique throughout *Final de novela* (and to which I return in the next section).

Nevertheless, at face value at least, the travellers' posed immaturity appears to be contradicted by the modernity of their vehicle, a 1998 red Ford Fiesta. Not unlike the VW camper van which transports Cortázar and Dunlop down the Paris-Marseille *autoroute*, the Ford becomes a character in its own right in this travel book: in a humorous and overdetermined allusion to its conventionality, it is referred to throughout by the epithet Coloradito Pérez.[91] The very choice of transport—one which at first glance appears to be entirely ill-suited to the rough and often unpaved Patagonian terrain—can be seen in stark, and comic, contrast to the motor vehicles that have propelled other contemporary travelogues in the region, particularly in the anglophone tradition. Tim Cahill's *Road Fever* is an archetype in this respect, charting a macho, high-speed race with co-driver Garry Sowerby some 15,000 miles across the continent from Patagonia to Alaska in a high performance GMC truck.[92] As such, it is one of a number of other travel books which portray Latin America as an adventure playground for the contemporary traveller/travel writer, who, in embarking on such feats of derring-do, ultimately sustains an imperial logic under a different, but potentially no less insidious, guise.[93] Indeed, as Debbie Lisle notes, "[*Road Fever* is a] modern-day buddy story ... all about conquering—the elements, the bureaucracy, the landscape, the fatigue, the machine".[94] By contrast, Giardinelli's Fiesta will never provide the kind of acceleration, let alone possibly even endurance, available from a more sophisticated car such as Cahill's (although the Fiesta will in fact exceed all expectations in that respect as according to Giardinelli the travellers never change a tyre during their trip). On this level, the technological limitations of the Ford hatchback might be seen as a kind of inverse "test" for these "naïve" travellers, although the inherent satirical possibilities of the vehicle are not as fully exploited here as they are by Cortázar and Dunlop in their travel parody. Nevertheless, in that light, the Fiesta does confer on their journey the character of an "anti-adventure" in some respects, in which Coloradito clearly functions as a purposeful, democratic emblem of the quotidian (it is *not* a high performance or luxury car): for, as Giardinelli notes, "nos juramentamos a no tener prisa ni exigencias excesivas" [we pledged not to hurry or have excessive demands] (23). The professed modesty of both the mode of transportation and budget of two thousand pesos (as well as the fixed time limit of 30–40 days for the trip and its wholly peripheral route) impose certain "restrictions" on the journey, which in part go some way to fulfilling that challenge to "reinventar lo conocido . . . desde la creación de nuevas originalidades" [reinvent the already known . . . from original starting points] (19). These details also distinguish the men from most other conventional travellers, for as Giardinelli writes, evoking that time-honoured traveller-tourist dichotomy, "con una camioneta 4x4, mucho dinero y tiempo de sobra, cualquiera puede recorrer la Patagonia . . . no queríamos que nuestro viaje fuera un típico y previsible recorrido turístico" [with a 4x4, lots of money and time to spare, anyone can travel across Patagonia . . . we did not want our journey to be a typical and predictable tourist trip] (16–17). Nouzeilles's assertion that "To not be a tourist is one of the most powerful drives behind unconventional travel" is resonant here.[95] There is a further possible level of meaning in respect of the travellers' mode of transport on this journey, however. In an analogy with multiple valences, Giardinelli conceives of his Fiesta, the ordinary city "run-around", as the modern-day equivalent of the horse, "mi caballo imaginario" [my imaginary horse] (25). The invocation of this animal recalls the epic horseback journey undertaken by Swiss traveller Aimé Tschiffely in 1925 from Buenos Aires to Washington, DC.[96] Giardinelli's allusion to this tradition of continent-wide journeys by horse is at once literal and ironic. There is a clear irony at stake, as his precursor's horses—the figure of which, as Vieyra points out, in the borderlands of Patagonia "adquiría contornos míticos" [acquired mythical overtones]—throw into sharp relief the modern comfort and ubiquity of the automobile, symbol *par excellence* of a contemporary, mechanized modernity.[97] Nevertheless, in addition to the self-deprecatory effects of Giardinelli's analogy, there is also a more specific (perhaps inadvertent) literal historical allusion at work. Following his initial horseback journey of 1925, some eleven years later Tschiffely would go on to travel across Patagonia in a Ford Model A car donated to him by the North American manufacturers.[98] Thus, the automobile, in particular as well as symbolic terms, did indeed replace the horse on that epic traveller's subsequent adventures. In this respect, Giardinelli's vehicle is perhaps much less banal than it might at first appear, paying involuntary testimony to regional travelling traditions, notwithstanding the author's anxiety in respect of that very legacy.

PATAGONIAN SUBLIME

Giardinelli's imbrication in persistent discourses and tropes of travel emerges also in the "Darwinian" sense of disappointment with the Patagonian landscape which emerges at several junctures of his trip.[99] At an early stage, we learn that "la sensación dominante no es otra que la del tedio" [the overwhelming sensation is nothing other than tedium] (38), whereas later, "Lo que empieza a impresionar, por estos rumbos, es el tamaño de la monotonía" [What starts to be impressive, in these parts, is the extent of the monotony] (127). Notwithstanding the limitations imposed on the journey, Giardinelli's trajectory offers ample opportunity to experience the sublime.[100] A sighting of a dormant volcano underscores the typically dark character of the sublime encounter ("Es aterrador, esas cenizas de apariencia inocente representaban a la muerte" [It is terrifying: those ashes of innocent appearance represented death], 124), while the sight of the Perito Moreno glacier is conveyed with an equally conventional sense of astonishment at the grandeur of Nature:

> Sucede de pronto: al dar una de las tantas curvas del camino, se topa con todo el esplendor de esa pared de hielo que sólo pudieron construir los siglos y el silencio ... uno empieza a sentir que en efecto se puede ser testigo de la maravilla.
>
> [It happens suddenly: on turning one of the many curves in the road, one comes across all the splendour of that wall of ice that only centuries and silence could have built ... one starts to feel that in effect one could be witnessing a marvel.] (150)

Moreover, it is precisely Patagonia's vast and essential sublimity, its ability to throw into relief human insignificance, that Giardinelli proposes be marshalled for political ends: "¡Qué importante sería que tanto líder mundial, tanto engreído suelto, tanto pavo real y tanta prima dona vinieran a darse un baño de Patagonia! El mundo sería distinto, sin duda. Sería mejor" [How important it would be for any world leader, any random bighead, twit, or prima donna to come and bathe in Patagonia! The world would without doubt be different. It would be better] (231).

Nevertheless, throughout Giardinelli's account, the nature of Patagonia's sublimity begins to take on a particular complexion whereby the threat of annihilation derives less from the natural environment (as in Burkean conceptions of the idea) than from the incontrovertible evidence of a voracious globalisation. As Sánchez-Blanco notes, "el autor busca la argentinidad del territorio" [the author looks for the Argentine-ness of the land], and, when he finds it, "está en emergencia" [it is in crisis].[101] This, for example, on one pit stop:

> Miro el paisaje, que en la siesta parece el desierto de Arizona pero no en versión de Hollywood sino menemista. Hacia el sur la Parrilla El Caminante está cerrada, pero enfrente está abierta 'Palitos. Fast Food and Snack Bar'.

> [I look at the landscape, which at siesta time looks like the Arizona desert, not in the Hollywood but in the Menemist version. Towards the south the Traveller's Grill is closed, but opposite "Palitos. Fast Food and Snack Bar" is open.] (47)

The two eateries offer a fitting analogy of the contemporary Argentine condition. The image of the closed autochthonous restaurant, which might have offered the visiting traveller (or modern-day gaucho in Giardinelli's self-fashioning) a typical *criollo* dish of *asado* or *parrilla* [barbequed meat], is juxtaposed with an imported, albeit indigenised model of restaurant chain (its alterity signalled linguistically in its English-language subtitle), the only one of the two which is open and which depends less on the quality of its "universal" food than on the speed of its service and turnover. In metonymic form, therefore, these features crystallise the contradictory operations of Argentina's economic transformation, which, as mentioned earlier, depended precisely on the sale of national industries and a corresponding influx of trans- or multinational companies. In a later episode in Sierra Grande, once the site of one of the most important mining projects in Argentina, the traveller finds a ghost town which has been converted unsuccessfully into a tourist destination, and onto which he confers the epithet "Nuestra Comala Patagónica" [Our Patagonian Comala]. In a book in which the traveller complains of the poor quality of the country's cartographers, in a region whose toponymy is dominated by the names of European voyagers, Giardinelli's rearticulation of this place name is significant on a number of different levels.[102] First, it reinforces the "literariness" of this travelogue, as his particular characterisation of Sierra Grande alludes to the nightmarish village of the dead of Mexican writer Juan Rulfo's 1955 novel *Pedro Páramo*, about a town called Comala ravaged by a particular kind of institutionalised patriarchy. Furthermore, the analogy between the semi-feudal *caciquismo* [the cacique system] and violence of Mexico in the 1920s (the period of the so-called *cristero* wars at which Rulfo's novel is set) and the protracted corruption of Menem's presidency of Argentina during the 1990s is apposite. It is not only that Patagonia suffers from a comparable kind of geographical isolation as the Mexican author's imaginary ghost town, but also that it withers under the regime of a similarly corrupt patriarch, one "with a style of governing more suited to a monarch than the chief of a state of a republic", surrounded by an entourage that "resembled that of fifth-century Germanic warriors, stationed in one of the provinces of the expiring Roman Empire".[103] While Romero's historical analogy in relation to Menem is more atavistic even than that of Giardinelli, they function equally effectively in underscoring the endemic dysfunction of an administration in which "loyalty was rewarded with protection and impunity as far as possible."[104] As such, if the emptiness of this territory has conventionally functioned as a space onto which the traveller has projected his personal anxieties, as it does in this case to some degree, in *Final de novela* "Patagonia" also speaks to the symptoms of an entire nation in crisis.

Indeed, in contrast to Sepúlveda's largely benevolent landscape of excentrics and surrealist encounters, Giardinelli's is a geography of poverty, violence, and fascist nostalgia. To be sure, the Argentine traveller reiterates his wonder during the journey ("no cesa de asombrarme tanta belleza estéril" [so much sterile beauty doesn't cease to amaze me], 167), his comments attesting to the paradoxical quality of the sublime, in which the threat of violence can be mitigated by distance. Yet, the sources of Patagonia's sublimity in this travelogue are increasingly contemporary and political. In Los Antiguos, for example, the author encounters vestiges of "La Argentina de la impunidad" [the Argentine of impunity] (208) in the tale of a young man brutally killed in the course of a local "rite of passage". Because of the town's culture of silence and fear, the well-known perpetrators of the crime, some of them occupying positions of local office, remain unpunished. Elsewhere, with the proprietor of a hotel in Caleta Oliva and a gaucho on route 40, the author has testing encounters with some of the region's reactionary inhabitants whom he finds nostalgic for the "order" imposed by the country's former military regime. Furthermore, on more than one occasion Giardinelli's route becomes "un enorme basural" [an enormous rubbish tip] (136), while the region's cities are characterised by a "desdichada" "suciedad" [unfortunate dirtiness] (106). In this respect, the endemic rubbish in Patagonia, together with the visibility of its *villa miseria* [shanty towns] and "casuchas de chapa" [metal sheet hovels], can be seen to be testament to a particular kind of late or postmodern sublime, which, for Zygmunt Bauman, takes the specific shape of waste. For Bauman waste, in material and human forms, is "the dark, shameful secret of all production": "Simultaneously divine and satanic," he writes, waste is "a unique blend of attraction and repulsion arousing an equally unique mixture of awe and fear."[105] The littered landscape and disenfranchised population of Giardinelli's Patagonia thus bear witness to Argentina's admittance into what Bauman calls the "casino culture of the liquid modern era", which, as a corollary of its propensity to obsolescence over permanence, also "looks like a *culture of disengagement, discontinuity and forgetting*" (original emphasis).[106] In a chapter he calls "Post-Menemist Tango in Comodoro", Giardinelli sums up this idea: "La Patagonia es una cárcel abierta ... uno está en libertad pero no se puede mover" [Patagonia is like an open prison ... one is free but cannot move] (93). This statement is more than an assertion about a contentious political leadership. Redolent of Arjun Appadurai's idea that "One man's imagined community is another man's political prison",[107] Giardinelli's words attest not only to the paradoxical character of the territory he traverses—both beautiful and frightening—but also to the profound contradictions of the country's late modern experience and to the shifting significance of its landscape for this end-of-twentieth-century traveller.

PATAGONIA AS CRISIS HETEROTOPIA

In "Of Other Spaces", Michel Foucault defines heterotopia as "something like counter-sites" which "have the curious property of being in relation with all the other sites, but in such a way as to suspect, neutralise, or invert the set of relations that they happen to designate, mirror or reflect."[108] As Kevin Hetherington notes, they are effectively spaces of alternate social ordering: "sites that bring together heterogeneous collections of unusual things without allowing them a unity or order established through resemblance".[109] In his 1986 essay, Foucault identifies a distinct form of crisis heterotopia common to what he calls primitive societies: these may be privileged, sacred or forbidden spaces "reserved for individuals who are, in relation to society and to the human environment in which they live, in a state of crisis."[110] Foucault lists adolescents, menstruating and pregnant women as the "resident occupants" of these particular heterotopias, which include boarding schools and military academies. He also says that these particular sites are disappearing, gradually to be replaced by heterotopias of deviation, such as rest homes, psychiatric hospitals and prisons, for "individuals whose behaviour is deviant in relation to the required mean or norm". Among the core principles of such places in Foucault's formulation is that each society determines the function of the heterotopia in potentially myriad fashions, possibly even at the same time. Moreover, although the heterotopia is "not freely accessible like a public space" it nonetheless has "a relation to all the space that remains", which may function in terms of either illusion or compensation.[111] The examples provided by Foucault to illustrate his idea include the cemetery, garden, museum, library, colony and ship ("a floating piece of space, a place without a place . . . the heterotopia *par excellence*").[112]

Foucault's notion of heterotopia provides a suggestive model for the "postmodern" Patagonia which emerges from these contemporary travel books. The region's status as a former colony and its subsequent history might even predispose such a reading, given the parameters of heterotopia delineated by Foucault. Indeed, Nouzeilles has suggested that the idea of Patagonia as an eccentric place corresponds precisely to the heterotopia, although she prefers to link it more closely to Deleuze and Guattari's notion of this space as outside the logic of the modern state: "deserts like Patagonia are heterotopic regions that help rechannel what they call the vital, primitive energy suppressed by modernity", she writes. For anglophone travellers such as the mountaineer Gregory Crouch, whose travelogue *Enduring Patagonia* is the subject of Nouzeilles's essay, the Patagonian mountains become "a heterotopic space of deviation . . . where men can play masculine roles unavailable in modern society and have the opportunity to create alternative communities."[113] While a welcome amplification of her work on nineteenth-century travellers, Nouzeilles's conception of the region in these terms nevertheless risks perpetuating the idea of Patagonia as a "radical, outside" place, and, as such, the rather exclusive preserve of Western adventurers of the ilk of Crouch. It is for this reason that I return to the detail of Foucault's original idea which, although it may not be directly related to any particular form of landscape or geography, as Nouzeilles observes, nevertheless provides a useful paradigm in respect of the complex destination depicted in the two travel books discussed here.

While I am not suggesting that either Sepúlveda or Giardinelli belong to primitive societies, I do propose that the Patagonia of their travel books might be seen as a heterotopia of crisis, which is as much collective as it is individual, and whereby the word "crisis" takes on a particular resonance in light of the historical contexts outlined earlier in this chapter. On one level, as returning political exiles, both travellers are arguably in a state of "exception" in some ways comparable to the condition of Foucault's own (potentially problematic) list of temporarily "abject" persons. For the Chilean, there is the matter of his ideological repositioning that impels and informs the journey experience, his first to the region after expatriation. Much as "Chatwinlandia" is populated by people in his precursor's mould, Sepúlveda's Patagonia appears to provide a compensatory space of sorts, inhabited by exiles very much like himself. The journey to this site ultimately brings into focus the Chilean author's benign conception of contingent identity, the notion of what I earlier called harmonious deterritorialisation, an epistemology similar, in some respects, to Chatwin's own particular brand of nomadism. Sepúlveda's eminently translatable "reflexive autobiography" thus chimes readily not only with the aesthetics of redemocratisation but also, more broadly, with the pace of current global flows. For Giardinelli, the trip to Patagonia is predicated instead on a pathological "writerly" event, offering the opportunity for a particular form of literary tourism, in the idea of *transterración* as well as in the travelogue's metatextual form. The Argentine's journey has a more sceptical character than Sepúlveda's, however, which has to do with more than his naïve travelling persona and "ordinary" mode of transportation. That is, on repairing to this final frontier in order to assuage his writer's block, Giardinelli's Patagonia becomes a mirror which, in its vestiges of waste, violence and nostalgia, reflects a postmodern, and perhaps even neoliberal, sublime. Indeed, the Argentine writer is conscious of how such "negativity" might eventually be read in his travelogue, writing that "Ya sé la acusación que seguramente recibirá este libro ... parece en todo momento buscar el pelo en la leche" [I know the criticism that this book will surely receive ... that at every moment it seeks to find fault] (232). It is undoubtedly for that reason that he opts for such a clichéd ending both for his novel and journey account: heading for home, he writes that "Fue magnífico y valió la pena" [It was magnificent and it was worth the effort] (236). Another aspect of the heterotopia's character, however, according to Foucault, is "to create a space of illusion that exposes every real space, all the sites inside of which human life is partitioned, as still more illusory".[114] In this respect, the Patagonia of *Final de novela* is no longer an empty, utopian space at the end of the world, for as Lisle reminds us, heterotopia "are *not* romanticised spaces that exist elsewhere on the margins" (original emphasis).[115] Rather, notwithstanding its own collusion in international circuits of "literary tourism", in illuminating the region's postmodern sublimity, Giardinelli's Patagonian travelogue counters another widely circulated myth at the very core of and beyond Argentina—that of a coequal globalisation itself.

3 Spectacular Andean Adventures

> "The lands we pass through are haunted even if the ghosts do not always manifest themselves directly."[1]

It is commonplace in studies of travel writing to invoke the opening words of *Tristes Tropiques*—"I hate travelling and explorers"[2]—which have become synonymous with the problematic relationship between anthropology and travel writing. I start with the introduction to Lévi-Strauss's "seminal autobiography-cum-travel-book-cum-ethnography",[3] not for his repudiation of travelling, however, but rather for the resonance of other, less well cited statements of that section of his book for the text under consideration in this chapter. Following his uncompromising beginning to "An End to Journeying", Lévi-Strauss dismisses the role of adventure in anthropology. "Adventure has no place in the anthropologist's profession", he writes (while simultaneously affirming its place) "it is merely one of those unavoidable drawbacks, which detract from his effective work through the incidental loss of weeks or months." That statement and sentiment are also known well enough. Nevertheless, further to his portrayal of it as anthropology's negative side, Lévi-Strauss goes on to foreground the close association between adventure and visual representation. "Being an explorer is a trade, which consists not, as one might think, in discovering hitherto unknown facts after years of study," he elaborates sardonically, "but in covering a great many miles and assembling lantern-slides or motion pictures, preferably in colour, so as to fill a hall with an audience for several days in succession."[4] It is the French anthropologist's association of exploration and travelogue (in the original sense of that term, denoting a film or visually illustrated lecture about a journey) that is of relevance in what follows: a consideration of a young anthropologist's transcontinental journey, which is spectacular in more ways than one—extensive and impressive in scope and from its outset conceived as a visual spectacle.

Lévi-Strauss was concerned with "the denial of an authoritarian, ethnocentric, or pleasure-seeking role" typified by the kind of adventurers he had in mind.[5] It is perhaps unlikely, therefore, that the father of structural anthropology would at first glance have cared much for *América en bicicleta* [*America by Bike*] (2001), the account of that epic journey just mentioned. During a twelve-month period between 1998 and 1999, Argentine anthropologist and activist Andrés Ruggeri cycled some 15,000 km from Buenos

Aires to Havana in order to protest the economic blockade of Cuba and, in particular, the Helms-Burton Act, the U.S. federal law passed in 1996 which consolidated the ongoing embargo of that island.[6] The objective of Ruggeri's self-styled Latin American Tour of Solidarity was not an ethnographic one, as in his French forebear's case, but a political one: to collect signatures for a petition against the embargo, delivering it in time for fortieth anniversary celebrations of the triumph of the Cuban revolution. Not only was Ruggeri followed in this endeavour by a documentary film crew, but he also made frequent appearances on television along the way. The trip is thus complicated and potentially compromised by two issues that shape my discussion in this chapter: first, its spectacularisation and, second, its inscription within a tradition and discourse of adventure. The latter presents a problematic manoeuvre not only in the light of Lévi-Strauss's disciplinary censure but also, more fundamentally, in terms of an apparent incompatibility of that subculture of travel with the cyclist's ideological project. A further issue at stake in any consideration of Ruggeri's journey is his formal and symbolic engagement with the freight of a travelling predecessor, Ernesto Che Guevara de la Serna. Notwithstanding the ambivalence of the cyclist's intertextual relation with the revolutionary Guevara, whose image has of course been rendered in the most iconic photographs from Latin America in recent memory as well as one of its latest cinematic successes (thus adding a further layer of significance to the "spectacular" in this case), it nonetheless ensures the young Argentine's entry into a particular regional political heritage.

How, then, to conceptualise the experience of this politico (cyclist) adventurer, a figure which appears to be (re-)emerging in different guises in this and other parts of the world? In an attempt to address that question in more subtle ways than Lévi-Strauss's definition of adventure allows, this chapter will consider Ruggeri's articulation of that long-standing paradigm of travel with reference to its cultural and historical valences as well as in relation to the inescapable association with Guevara's expedition. The contemporary adventurer of Ruggeri's ilk undertakes journeys which are increasingly elemental (rather than elaborate, say, in terms of transport), extensive rather than ephemeral (with an emphasis on duration rather than brevity) but in turn also compromised by, as well as conscious of, their collusion in processes of commodification.[7] In considering Ruggeri's performance within that category, this chapter seeks to engage with, as well as to build on, the recent efforts of scholars in other disciplines and in different regions of study (such as historian Matthew Brown, anthropologists Luis A. Vivanco and Robert J. Gordon, and literary critics including Stephen M. Levin) who have separately reconsidered the significance of adventure and its narratives in ways that unsettle that baleful portrayal by Lévi-Strauss and complicate its orthodox associations. For, as Ali Behdad points out, "Travel and adventure are not static terms, and . . . it [is] necessary to discuss them within their particular historical contexts."[8] As such, and drawing on the work of Georg Simmel and Jacques Derrida, in what follows I propose that Ruggeri might be considered a "spectral adventurer", a denomination which pays tribute to the complex history of that paradigm of travel (particularly in Latin America) but which also acknowledges the haunted character of its contemporary enunciation. First, a consideration of Ruggeri's multilayered affiliations with that political and visual icon, Ernesto Che Guevara.

GUEVARA'S GHOST

With its transcontinental trajectory, a prologue by Che Guevara's former travelling companion Alberto Granado and a chapter entitled "El Che", Ruggeri's journey narrative positively encourages a comparison with that epic trip by the man who, since his death in 1967, has quite literally become a poster boy of the revolutionary (and not so revolutionary) left.[9] Guevara's 1952 expedition with Granado on a Norton 500-cc motorcycle from Buenos Aires to Caracas was recorded in a travel journal first published in 1992 as *Diarios de motocicleta: Notas de viaje* [*The Motorcycle Diaries*]. Guevara was a "disciplined diarist",[10] even as a young man, although *The Motorcycle Diaries* was not transcribed from notes until more than a year after his journey took place.[11] The popularity of the account has been unabated, however, so that it has acquired its own mythical status, as Jorge Castañeda points out: "Somewhere in the psyche of the 60s and 90s, Guevara's saga became a road book, or road movie: Jack Kerouac in the Amazon, Easy Rider on the Andes."[12] The volume was of course later adapted to the screen in a 2004 film of the same name by Brazilian director Walter Salles, featuring in the lead role the now much sought after Mexican actor Gael García Bernal (as such, this is a route whose myriad narratives have become bound up in considerable aura). Guevara, a young medical student, and Granado, his friend from Córdoba and a recent biochemistry graduate, travelled through five countries—Argentina, Chile, Peru, Colombia, and Venezuela—in eight months. At first they ride pillion of a machine nicknamed *La poderosa II* [*The Powerful One, II*], although they are forcibly dismounted after its breakdown and continue their journey by foot, bus, and boat. In the initial stages of *The Motorcycles Diaries*, the roguish pair seem intent on taking advantage of the distance from home to indulge and reinvent themselves. They freeload in a series of high-spirited, picaresque adventures and turn media celebrities of sorts when a Temuco newspaper (to which they had given an interview) reports their visit as distinguished leprology experts. Nevertheless, in addition to chronicling their high jinks, Guevara also uses the journal to denounce the endemic poverty as well as the pervasive social injustice encountered along the way (as, for example, at the U.S.-run Chuquicimata copper mine in Chile, a symbol of the foreign domination of the country's economy). His prologue attests to the journey's apparently transformative function, as well as to what we might call "Guevara's delay":[13] "The person who wrote these notes died the day he stepped back on Argentine soil. The person who is reorganizing and polishing them, me, is no longer me, at least I'm not the me I was."[14]

Notwithstanding the popularity of the travelogue even forty years after his death, opinion is split over the significance of the journey itself for Guevara's political development. Several episodes in the account have been attributed as the source of the young man's later radicalisation and have thus been read as "proto-Che":[15] these include an encounter with a Chilean Communist couple ("a living symbol of the proletariat the world over") and a stay at a Peruvian leprosy clinic, during which Guevara delivered his speech about a United America ("We are a single mestizo race with notable ethnographic similarities, from Mexico down to the Magellan straits").[16] Ricardo Piglia conceives of the young Guevara, for example, as an "essential marginal", like the Beat writers: unlike the conventional tourist or traveller, from whom he takes pains in the journal to distinguish himself, Guevara took to the road, in Piglia's view, "so as to transform himself into another."[17] Nevertheless, Geoffrey Shullenberger and María Josefina Saldaña-Portillo have illuminated the less savoury aspects of that apparent consciousness-raising in relation to Guevara's encounters with the region's indigenous peoples and cultures. Saldaña-Portillo detects vestiges of a colonialist mentality at work in the diaries, for example, diagnosing a "melancholic ambivalence towards indigenous peoples". This presents in symptoms of repulsion by living Indians and a corresponding enthrallment with their dead predecessors, which she sees as emblematic of both the "Spanish colonial subalternisation of the Indian and liberal nationalism's racialisation of *mestizaje.*"[18] Similarly, Guevara's anti-imperialist framing of Machu Picchu on the journey as a site of pan-American nationalism can be seen as another iteration of the imperialist "discovery" narrative of precursors such as Hiram Bingham, as Shullenberger points out:

> For Guevara what is discovered is not so much the site itself as the protagonist's Latin American identity ... Machu Picchu becomes in the writings of [Bingham and Guevara] the ideal ground for staging ... 'the performance of cultural purity.'[19]

For Alma Guillermoprieto, the journey is essentially nothing more than an "eight-month hitch-hiking adventure," a youthful coming-of-age trip, at the end of which, "[that] jolly and enthusiastic young man was buried forever",[20] a view confirmed by Castañeda for whom Guevara and Granado's journey was "an extended spring break, in a way." Indeed, Castañeda cautions against any attempt to ascribe Guevara's later militancy to that journey at all: "His powerful attraction to things and people different or novel is undeniable, but it goes no further than that."[21] While not disputing "a certain detachment and, occasionally, an appalling condescension [towards the poor and disenfranchised]" in *The Motorcycle Diaries*, however, Maureen Moynagh proposes a suggestive middle ground on which to conceptualise Guevara's journeys: as a form of "political tourism as . . . hybrid cultural practice".²²

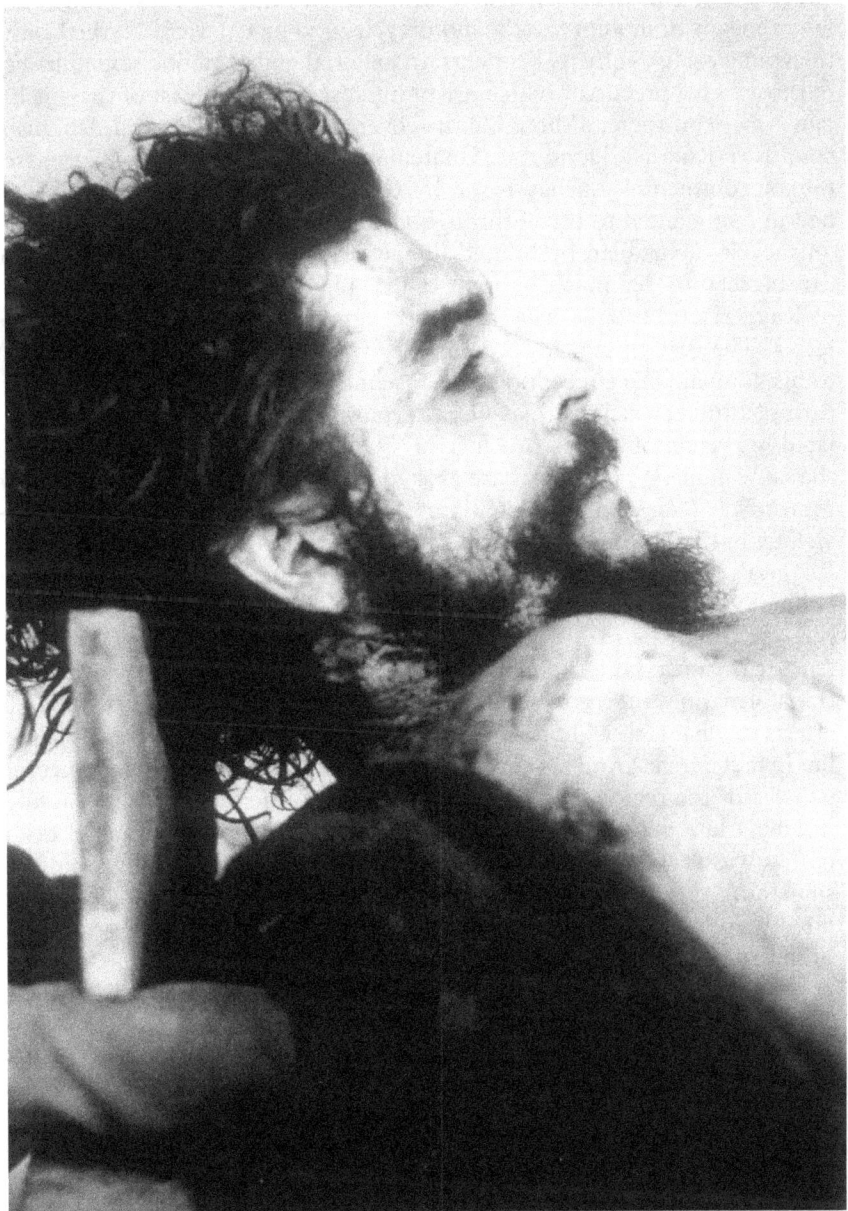

Figure 3.1 Che Guevara dead. Rex Features Ltd.

For all the difference of opinion surrounding its precise significance and impact, it is without doubt that the "legend" of that journey inevitably looms large over the young Argentine cyclist's endeavour. Ruggeri's is not nor cannot be an exact replica of his antecedent's trip, of course: historical differences aside, there are significant divergences between the two journeys, not least in terms of transportation, the bicycle being of course quite a different means of mobility to the motorcycle used by Guevara. Nevertheless, the young cyclist's efforts bear certain material and symbolic resemblances to those of his precursor which are of interest here. Not least of these is his pan-American route, although in its coverage of several Central American countries (Panama, Honduras, Guatemala, and Belize), it in fact surpasses the subcontinental journey made by Guevara and Granado.[23] Both men had in fact wanted to travel through Central America to Mexico but their journey was curtailed by limited finances: in this respect Ruggeri's route can be seen to "complete" their original plan.[24] Certain textual features of Ruggeri's travelogue have a further significant voltage in comparative terms. The very title of his account, *América en bicicleta*, alludes in part to his compatriot's conception of transcontinental solidarity, the legacy in turn of thinkers such as the Cuban revolutionary José Martí, who articulated his vision of "Nuestra América" [Our America] in an 1891 essay of the same name.[25] These ideas are evoked by Guevara in the prologue of *The Motorcycle Diaries* in his formulation of an "America with a capital A" as well as in that "United America" speech cited earlier.[26] Moreover, one of Ruggeri's book's dedications—"Todos aquellos que lucharon y luchan por la libertad de América Latina" [to all those who fought and are fighting for the freedom of Latin America]—clearly resounds with the legacy of Latin America's most famous revolutionary figure.[27] Meanwhile, the avowed transformation undergone by the cyclist in the course of his trek not only attests to what is thought to be a common outcome of the travel experience, but in fact derives from his encounters with poor, marginal, and indigenous peoples of the region. Ruggeri's claim, that "Ya no era el mismo hombre ... tenía la esperanza que fuera al menos un poquito mejor que el original" [I wasn't the same man who started this trip ... I hoped I was at least something of a better man than the one who began it] (191), is espoused directly following his involvement in grassroots political activities during Brazilian presidential elections. Ruggeri's metamorphosis is thus redolent of the change that Guevara, at the end of his South American adventure, is famously purported to have undergone in the quotation from the prologue cited earlier, thanks in his case apparently, among other things, to that visit to the leper colony. It would of course be misguided to fully equate these men's different experiences at such diverse historical moments, and the extent to which Guevara fully sympathised or identified with the poor and working classes is also debatable. Nevertheless, in contrast to the conventions of travel and exploration writing which, as Mary Louise Pratt has observed, historically "constitute the European subject as a self-sufficient, monadic source of knowledge",[28] both Guevara and Ruggeri acknowledge the heteroglossic and interactional dimension of their travel experiences.

The prologue to *América en bicicleta* by Alberto Granado is a further significant connection with Guevara, part of the symbolic and structural apparatus which confers cultural and political value on Ruggeri's travel book, albeit in complex ways. In it, Granado, whose identity is clarified in a somewhat overdetermined footnote, recommends Ruggeri in the highest terms: "si hay una obra, entre las miles que he leído, que se justifique por sí misma, es este alucinante viaje a través de los más variados paisajes" [if there is a work, of the thousands that I have read, which justifies itself, it is this illuminating trip through the most varied of landscapes] (7). Granado extols not only the text's "exactitud casi fotográfica" [almost photographic exactitude] but also the author's "memoria histórica revolucionaria" [revolutionary historical memory], although crucially, in a manoeuvre destined no doubt on some level to underscore Ruggeri's distinction, Granado underlines that "su viaje no es el del Che" [his journey is not that of Che] (7). *América en bicicleta* is no mere copy, then, is one of the implications of that endorsement, but a journey with an originality and identity of its very own. As Aaron Jaffe reminds us in his study of celebrity modernism, however, the function of the prologue is by no means always a straightforward one: "introductions are positions of enunciation and consolidation", Jaffe writes, which can be as much about the prologue writer "covertly reflecting attention back on his own reputation" as about the work being introduced.[29] In this respect, Granado's differentiation of Ruggeri's journey from Guevara's is of course potentially less complimentary, although it would appear that it is historical rather than personal differences that account for it, as Ruggeri's critical abilities are singled out, especially with regard to the media: "Y en estos momentos en que un capitalismo feroz y globalizado ha transformado los medios de comunicación en instrumentos de desinformación, donde prevalece la mentira y la corrupción, y ha convertido una profesión tan digna, valiente y necesaria, en una especie de circo romano . . . la crítica de Andrés adquiere gran vigencia" [In these times in which a ferocious and globalised capitalism has transformed the media into instruments of misinformation, where lies and corruption prevail, and has converted a formerly dignified, brave and necessary profession into a Roman circus . . . Andrés's criticism has great currency] (8). Setting the trenchant, anti-imperialist tone that is sustained throughout the rest of the volume, Granado laments the malevolent effects of the "age of the pseudo event",[30] which receive equal condemnation from Ruggeri in due course, and, in doing so, he solders the young cyclist's ideological credentials to his own. A humorous postscript to the prologue crystallises the double-edged character of this introduction, however. Granado's admission that "como Andrés Ruggeri, soy hincha de Racing desde que jugaba de centro-forward Evaristo Barrera, un cordobés" [like Andrés Ruggeri, I am a fan of Racing since Evaristo Barrera, from Córdoba, played centre forward for them] (8) is counterintuitive. On one level, in addition to the validation of the prologue itself, the alignment of Granado's personal as well as political interests with Ruggeri's (their shared support of one of Argentina's largest football clubs) confers even greater authority and prestige on the young parvenu. On another level, however, with this final flourish and apparent afterthought, which has little to do with the content of the travel book ostensibly being recommended but more to do with a popular and predominantly masculinist form of identification, Granado's concluding gesture directs attention back to his own reputation and fame: it reminds us that his allegiance and, implicitly, "authority" carry greater historical weight.[31] What we see at work in this prologue, therefore, is something of the complexity of the celebrity endorsement, which here proves to be as ambiguous as it is influential.

If, notwithstanding its ambivalence, Granado's prologue still reinforces the affiliation with the iconic Guevara (albeit by association), nevertheless it is not until the Bolivian leg of his year-long bicycle journey that Ruggeri himself addresses the inevitable comparisons between his own enterprise and that of his famous precursor. At first, in an evasive but also tactical manoeuvre, the young cyclist disavows any connection with Guevara, despite the obvious resonances and connections already mentioned:

> Muchos pensaban en primera instancia que me encontraba siguiendo el viaje del Che, algo que tuve especial empeño en desmentir. En la práctica, si bien esto no fue nunca ni mi primera ni mi principal motivación, algo de eso se metió de a poco, como por la ventana, en mi imaginación y en mi recorrido práctico. Tocar algunos de los puntos fundamentales en la vida del Che no era algo totalmente ajeno a un viaje latinoamericano de solidaridad con Cuba. Empezar en Argentina y terminar en Cuba, después de todo, no era una casualidad tan casual. No era el viaje del Che, y nunca pretendí que lo fuera. Era mi viaje, y simplemente eso, y en esta simplicidad tenían un lugar la vida y la muerte de Ernesto Guevara.

> [Many people thought in the first instance that I was following Che's journey, something I insisted on denying. In practice, if this was never my initial or principal motivation, something of that crept in gradually ... into my imagination as well as in to the journey itself. To touch on some of the fundamental points in Che's life was not totally divorced from a Latin American journey of solidarity with Cuba. To begin in Argentina and end in Cuba, after all, was not such a coincidence. It wasn't Che's journey and I never meant it to be. It was my journey and only that, and in that simple idea the life and death of Ernesto Guevara had its place.] (118)

This passage is shot through with ambivalence. At first, Ruggeri articulates a now rather conventional disinclination to identify with his travelling forebears, in large part no doubt due to a sense of belatedness. As Patrick Holland and Graham Huggan write, "contemporary travel writers realise that their own endeavours have come too late: it rests for them to emulate what others before them have achieved."[32] While some writers negotiate this dilemma through humour, Ruggeri's preferred "strategy of self-exemption" involves both a process of disavowal and, in his own self-presentation, the adoption of a particular or sometimes even different persona. I shall return to this idea shortly but what is interesting in the preceding quotation is the way in which, at the site of the Argentine revolutionary's martyrdom (and about one third of the way through the volume), Ruggeri acknowledges the increasing convergence of his and Guevara's journeys: although what that actually entails remains unclear, it would appear to comprise a reconciliation with the legacy of the hero from whom he had previously dissociated himself (prologue aside) by means of almost total erasure from the travelogue until that point. Nevertheless, this rapprochement is immediately followed by a further, more direct assertion of his own authority and legitimacy ("It was my journey"), under which Guevara is subsumed ("the life and death of Ernesto Guevara had its place"). This is a claim which, particularly in the portrayal of his own trip as a "simple idea" ("una simplicidad"), also evinces some disingenuousness, not to mention a considerable degree of superiority. The idea that Ruggeri's journey could be "simple" or straightforward is, of course, potentially reductive, even contradictory in the context of that quotation, as it effectively disregards the complex of issues at stake in the experience of travel itself as well as in the construction of its related narratives.

One way in which we can account for Ruggeri's initial reluctance to acknowledge his precursor—and for the assertion of his own journey as a more "simple idea"—has undoubtedly to do with a desire to distinguish his own political pilgrimage to protest the Cuban embargo from Guevara's "original" journey. On a material level, for example, the singularity of Ruggeri's trajectory, which is by no means the most straightforward route, is designed to enable him to stop in the greatest number of countries possible. Furthermore, from his book's inception Ruggeri emphasises the worthy and thus more superior political purpose at the heart of his endeavour: it is all about creating links between transcontinental popular movements and consciousness-raising about Cuba, as he is hosted, financed by and participates in the activities of various regional branches of the Latin American and Caribbean Continental Organisation of Students (OCLAE) along the way. Or as he puts it, perhaps echoing the title of the 1996 novel by Gabriel García Márquez (a long-term friend and supporter of Fidel Castro and Cuba), the journey is one of "solidaridad en los tiempos de neoliberalismo" [solidarity in the times of neoliberalism] (13).[33] As he passes through Vallegrande, the site in Bolivia at which Guevara literally became an icon [see Figure 3.1],[34] the motivations for Ruggeri's disavowal of Che are further elucidated as he goes on to imagine travelling as his compatriot ("un joven nacido en mi mismo país . . . ese joven de clase media y origen aristocrático" [a young man born in my same country . . . that *middle-class young man of aristocratic origin*]) might have travelled: "trataba de imaginarme la metamorfosis que llevó a Ernesto Guevara de la Serna a convertirse en el mítico Che" [I tried to imagine the metamorphosis which converted Ernesto Guevara de la Serna into *the mythic Che*] (both emphases mine, 118). Here Ruggeri's conception of his own journey as "a simple idea" appears to be bound up not only in its political motivations but also, crucially, in questions of class and fame. Thus, in contrast to the journey which formed part of the mythologisation of Guevara, Ruggeri's notion of his journey as *una simplicidad* endorses an authenticity and purity which stem from what he propounds as an even closer structural proximity to land and people in the course of his trip. This is a proximity facilitated physically by his use of the bicycle, a means of transportation chosen precisely for its accessibility, "una forma absoluta de conocer el medio, la gente, y también conocerse a sí mismo y sus capacidades" [an absolute form of getting to know the environment, the people and oneself] (10). The idea of simplicity also entails a repudiation of the fame and (distorting) lionisation of his compatriot Guevara. In other words, this characterisation of his journey is about Ruggeri's resistance to what Holland and Huggan call "the mythologies of 'exceptionality'".[35] The cyclist's claim of simplicity therefore is not just one more variant of that posture adopted to distinguish the "authentic" traveller from the vulgar tourist, although, to be sure, there is something of that dichotomy at work here: interestingly, however, one of the issues at stake in this case is class, as Ruggeri distinguishes himself as more "genuinely" *popular* (in the Spanish sense of the word, that is, of the people) than his bourgeois comrade "Che".

Further symptoms of this resistance—and more evidence of this traveller's ultimately quixotic attempt to secure a pure and unbiased travelling subject position—emerge as Ruggeri negotiates his own uneasy but necessary collusion with the media in order to raise awareness of his trip. In this respect, his choice of transportation is designed as much for its visibility as for its accessibility: "La idea era que el ciclista viajero podía con facilidad llamar la atención de los medios de comunicación" [The idea was that the touring cyclist could easily attract the attention of the media] (13). It is here that the symbolism of the bicycle as a nonmechanised form of transport functions to best effect, as it constitutes a simpler and more utilitarian means of mobility than, say, the motorcycle.[36] In contrast to the often worthy and moralistic tone he adopts elsewhere in the volume about his political activities, however, and in part perhaps because of an awareness of his intrinsic complicity in the matter, these particular symptoms of Ruggeri's unease present with a salutary strain of irony and at times self-mockery. From the outset, as he is followed by a documentary film crew (made, in the first instance, in order to help raise funds for the trip), the cyclist is quickly irked by his own "condición de estrella cinematográfica"

Spectacular Andean Adventures 57

[condition of cinema star] (23), claiming that "resignadamente me sometí a los caprichos del séptimo arte" [I submitted resignedly to the whims of the seventh art] (21). Perhaps one of the most memorable episodes of the journey in this regard, however, occurs in Brazil when Ruggeri encounters a man who claims to have seen him on television, despite the fact that at that stage he had yet to appear on local screens:

> Infinidad de veces me pasó que, a pesar de estar la gente viéndome andar por la ruta con mi bicicleta cargada, no creían que fuera verdad lo que estaba haciendo, pero si alguno decía 'sí lo vi en la TV' nadie dudaba y, si les decían que iba a Marte en bicicleta, lo hubieran creído ... Y después de todo, pocos días después salí, efectivamente, en la TV, que puede convertir en realidad hasta lo que no es.
>
> [What happened a great deal was that in spite of people seeing me cycle past with my loaded bike, they didn't believe that what I was doing was for real. But if someone said 'I saw him on TV', they didn't doubt it at all, and if they were told that I was going to Mars by bike, they would have believed that too ... And in the end, a few days later I did indeed appear on TV, which can convert into reality even something that is not.] (130)

Eschewing not only the aggrandizement afforded his revolutionary precursor, therefore, but also the reductive effects of what Guy Debord called the "society of the spectacle", Ruggeri's rather more sardonic resistance to this process of celebrification is politically expedient. Notwithstanding, the journey thus conceived as *una simplicidad*, as an attempt to establish a subjectivity outside of the corrupting logic of spectacle and celebrity, is of course a potentially futile endeavour, as Chris Rojek reminds us: "The search for authenticity is a gesture to a submerged moral world engulfed by the incessant commercialism and artificial titillation of consumer culture."[37]

SELF-STYLED HERO

The complexity of Ruggeri's association with Guevara is compounded by another ambivalence at work in this travel account in respect of its formal construction. As Granado tells us in the prologue, the young cyclist, in addition to his political activities, has also won prizes for his literary endeavours. (Guevara also had aspirations to be a writer, of course, although they conflicted with his political commitments.)[38] In fact, if, for all its equivocalness, Che's star still confers a degree of political validation on his exercise, Ruggeri gleans another kind of cultural capital precisely by means of what Jaffe, in *Modernism and the Culture of Celebrity*, calls the "textual imprimatur".[39] While clearly of quite a different historical period and literary form of production to the writers and works that interest Jaffe, *América en bicicleta* nonetheless bears certain "distinctive textual marks of authorship" that have a similar categorizing and legitimising function as those explored in that study of modernist celebrity. In this case, however, it is Ruggeri's self-fashioning as a suffering but ultimately triumphant hero and the imprimatur of adventure in his account which serve to enhance his personal aura and magnitude and thus colour the broader endeavour. The experience and rhetoric of adventure engaged by Ruggeri have nevertheless undergone some transformation from a model and discourse of high esteem to general popularity and low regard. As such, it is worth reviewing briefly the precedents of this particular subculture of travel and its related aesthetic expression, as well as its specific historical freight in Latin America, in order to evaluate its implications for this cyclist and his travel account.

The journey as adventure has a rich historical and literary tradition. As scholars such as Richard Phillips and Martin Green have pointed out, it is principally bound up in the history of imperialism as "European empires and European masculinities were imagined in geographies of adventure"[40] across the world. One of the fundamental associations of the term since the twelfth century, however, as Peter Hulme reminds us, has been economic acquisition and, as a corollary of that overlap of the colonial and the financial, risk. As an opportunity for the accumulation of wealth, adventure thus constitutes a form of consumption that is predicated on powers of acquisition and taste.[41] Although in Latin America such adventure (encompassing all three of those features) stems back to the moment of the colonial encounter, Hulme points out that "the 'pure' adventure story ... reached its apogee ... in the late nineteenth century,"[42] when there was a resurgence of adventure culture in the region during the Wars of Independence. Then, "men of all social and caste backgrounds, including foreigners, could quickly acquire honour by patriotic adventuring", a term which, as Matthew Brown, in his fascinating study of the period, writes "was defined ... for Europeans and Creoles alike as a confrontation with risk and danger, in which the obstacles posed by geography, circumstances or enemies were overcome, the adventurer finally emerging successfully to be crowned with laurels."[43] The dissemination of this "ancient and widespread subject matter"[44] has in turn been largely literary, as the history of adventure has encompassed fictional figures such as Daniel Defoe's Robinson Crusoe and Joseph Conrad's Marlow as well as the historical tales of explorers such as Christopher Columbus, Ferdinand Magellan, and Marco Polo. It is from this array of narratives, then, especially those of nonfiction, that the paradigmatic figure of the adventurer has become crystallised in what Mark Gallagher calls "male crucible narratives", where "the willingness and ability to endure extreme physical hardships" and to perform heroic deeds of national significance "often in solitude, grants men entry into a privileged space of achievement".[45]

It is not only that Ruggeri's journey adheres closely in character to the time-honoured adventure in many ways, but also that his account bears the hallmarks of its associated literature. First, our traveller is a relative novice when he embarks on his epic bicycle journey: we learn that he has undertaken one dry run in Patagonia and at the start of the trek he is still perfecting the use of automatic pedals. His amateur status on this year-long journey solo across the continent with panniers of 35 kg clearly shores up the inherent heroism of the endeavour. While the avowed objective of his journey is political, nevertheless we are also given the sense that Ruggeri is eluding constrictions of a personal, domestic nature, the escape from some local form of oppression being the more typical motivation of the literary adventurer. Notwithstanding his close involvement with student politics, for example, he tells us that these activities "me llevaron a un punto de agotamiento" [were driving me to exhaustion] (12) and, once on the move, he avers, "por fin me sentí libre" [at last I felt free] (22). Moreover, his trajectory through South and Central America, across Andes and Amazonia, takes in radically diverse conditions of topography and climate which constantly prove to be testing, as does a knee injury picked up on his Patagonian practice trip. As in the following quotation, a great deal of *América en bicicleta* deals with the challenges presented by the weather (blistering heat, strong winds or torrential rain), or what the author himself frequently calls "tortura física y psicológica" [the physical and psychological torture] (23) involved in scaling the heights of different mountain ranges or traversing other difficult terrain:

> Las condiciones para el ciclismo eran bastante malas. No había dónde refugiarse, y las gruesas gotas, ya casi columnas de agua, dolían al golpear sobre la espalda. No había otra posibilidad que soportar el diluvio, mientras miraba a los costados tratando de ver más allá de la muralla de agua, buscando algún lugar que me cubriera.
>
> [The conditions for cycling were pretty bad. There was nowhere to take refuge and the thick raindrops, almost already columns of water, hurt as they hit my back. There was no other option but to put up with the deluge, whilst I looked around me, trying to see through the wall of water, looking for somewhere to take cover.] (26)

The emphasis in this brief but typical excerpt on physicality and suffering positions the young Argentine as a modern-day Odysseus, who endures the tests and trials of the journey in a similar manner as the travellers of antiquity. Indeed, Ruggeri's narrative often appears to be as much about the kind of self-assertion of those tales of ancient wanderings as about solidarity with Cuba. As such, Ruggeri invokes his mythological and biblical predecessors in evocative and sometimes ironic analogies ("Ulysses fleeing the sirens", 219), and more than once he describes the journey as a "Calvary" (73), deploying a similarly traumatic metaphor as Gallagher's "crucible narratives", although, notably, one with more of a messianic tinge. In addition to negotiating the journey's travails, however, Ruggeri also largely embraces "la absoluta soledad de la aventura" [the complete solitude of the adventure] (60). While periodically he takes part in the activities of host organisations along the way, he equally appears to cherish his isolation, which he justifies in the following terms: "el ciclista ... sobre todo, depende de sí mismo para poder llegar" [the cyclist above all depends on himself to get there] (10). Indeed, in contrast to those ancient allusions, Ruggeri also portrays himself as the avant-garde, either as an astronaut on Mars or else an extraterrestrial on Earth, and, as in the previous quotation, he frequently refers to himself in the third person as *el ciclista* or *el pedalista* [the cyclist]. In these instances his singularity is even further enhanced as he crafts and performs a persona which, to a certain extent as with his "condition of cinema star" mentioned earlier, is not only extraordinary but pioneering. That Ruggeri overcomes his numerous battles with elements and peaks to arrive in Cuba *earlier* than his original deadline is the ultimate testament of those qualities of endurance, perseverance and, of course, masculinity. As such, he conforms closely to the normative profile of the male adventurer who, as Sidonie Smith points out, in the course of the journey "becomes even more what he is naturally understood to be".[46]

In some respects, it is precisely the young Argentine's ability to endure the many tests of his pan-American adventure that in fact serves to distinguish his endeavour further from the shadow of Guevara, who suffered physically during his own journey and throughout his lifetime from chronic asthma. Ruggeri's physical strength and resilience as a traveller thus function on one level as an index of his own difference ("It was my journey") and form part of his strategy of self-exemption from his iconic precursor. Nevertheless, in other respects, it is the elemental character of Ruggeri's solo adventure which is also significant here. As Eric Leed sees it, in modern times travel as suffering and endurance continues to signify only for the poor contemporary traveller or the pilgrim. For the latter "the once ancient sufferings of the traveller are now prized as an ascetic, disciplined freedom", writes Leed, "the stripping away of bonds to a place is analogous to a cleansing, the reduction of the purified entity to its smallest, truest dimensions".[47] While the conflation of these travelling types and a modern appropriation of austerity might in some instances seem somewhat problematic, Ruggeri's assumption of this subject position, straddling both of Leeds's subcategories, is suggestive on a number of different levels. With a total annual budget of $2,000 (U.S. dollars), Ruggeri's pilgrimage to Cuba is predicated on privation, rather than privilege: as such, suffering and asceticism are a fundamental part of the simplicity of his journey discussed earlier, although, paradoxically, they also correspond to the renowned self-sacrifice of his precursor Guevara, who left "prestigious roles in government for the solitude, discomfort, and martyrdom of the jungle".[48] In effect, however, Ruggeri's Spartan trek is an inversion of the kind of economic acquisition historically associated with the paradigm of adventure, although it certainly maintains an element of the risk which is also part of its patrimony. That is, the cyclist's asceticism (in part also a fitting form of solidarity with the embargoed island for which he is campaigning) is about redefining the gains once associated with this journey model: where historically adventure was an opportunity for wealth, its gains material or financial, for this cyclist and others of his ilk, they are now spiritual or ideological.[49] The identification of this particular adventurer, moreover, is, like Guevara, decidedly transnational, rather than more narrowly defined by national borders. As such, as Ruggeri writes at an early stage of his travel book, "La aventura se convierte en una responsabilidad, y la exigencia que ya era grande, empieza a ser total" [The adventure becomes a responsibility and the stakes, which were already high, start to become enormous] (10). This traveller's particular crown of laurels, therefore, a personal audience with Castro, provides a fitting apotheosis to a volume which is bookended by two quite different, but nevertheless closely related, regional political icons.

In many respects, then, *América en bicicleta* attests to the malleability of adventure and to the fact that, as Phillips observes, its geography (and literature) is "neither deterministic or static . . . [it] can reproduce but sometimes transgress dominant ideologies."[50] Adventure's conventional association with the national project, once motivated by a largely imperial, expansionist agenda, is mobilised in the contemporary period, alongside its longstanding democratising potential for those taking part in such journeys, as a mechanism for a transnational, oppositional politics. Formally too, in a book which evinces a similar volatility as other works of travel writing, oscillating between factual and historical commentaries and travel narrative, the adventure imprint does a great deal to shape Ruggeri's episodic account. Nevertheless, the quest model comes with a number of attendant contradictions. While certain features are reconfigured to his own political ends, it is nonetheless episodes and passages of derring-do, such as Ruggeri's dramatic struggles with the inclement weather conditions of El Niño, which predominate (meteorological systems being this hero's major adversaries, in addition to mountain ranges). A corollary of this is that Ruggeri, adventure hero *par excellence*, is constantly centre stage in the account of his journey, a position whose individualist ethic subtends the collective nature of his solidarity tour. There is, then, some disjunction between the young Argentine's conflicted "mediagenic" travelling persona, as discussed in the previous section, and his travelogue's still ultimately rather limiting imprimatur of adventure. It is interesting therefore (and maybe even indicative of his own sense of those limitations) that Ruggeri has taken to the Internet to chart his most recent politico-cycling endeavour, a year-long trip by tandem around twenty-nine countries of the southern hemisphere. Nevertheless, even these interventions into this apparently more immediate and authentic of mediums have the same tenor of dramatic *mono*logue as that of his debut, with his co-cyclist, Karina Luchetti, spared any narrative voice of her own on the Web site devoted to their project.[51] Thus, while the Internet and new media may well have democratised cultural production, as P. David Marshall has pointed out, they have also generated a new type of individualism and a "new era of narcissism":[52] Ruggeri's blog of his second, even more ambitious solidarity tour of the south speaks in some ways to the contradictions of that phenomenon.

SPECTRAL ADVENTURER

On one level, *América en bicicleta* might appear to provide sufficient evidence to validate Lévi-Strauss's indictment of adventure, which I cited at the beginning of this chapter. After all, the Argentine anthropologist and cyclist embarks on a journey not to accrue new scientific knowledge but, rather (to reinvoke Lévi-Strauss's words), to cover "a great many miles" and collect signatures, in the interests of which "motion pictures" and "slides" are purposefully assembled (some of which are reproduced as images in his book). It is that reluctant but strategic deployment of the spectacularisation of his efforts, however, which distinguishes Ruggeri from the adventurers admonished by his French predecessor. The Argentine cyclist's position also attests to the protean character of this long-standing modality of travel and to its counterdiscursive potential.[53] As such, Ruggeri's journey narrative has much more in common with the critical but hermetic properties of adventure as identified by sociologist Georg Simmel, whose 1911 essay on the subject has recently enjoyed some reappraisal in the consideration of contemporary quest narratives, than with Lévi-Strauss's.[54] Simmel claims that adventure has an *a priori* connection with the everyday but ultimately exists on an autonomous sphere: it "occurs outside the usual continuity of this life . . . it is a foreign body in our existence which is yet somehow connected with the centre."[55] Predicated on distance and differentiation, it is a mode of travel that comprises a critical departure from society, for the social and collective for Simmel could have a deadening quality.[56] Indeed, in these terms, it is fitting that Ruggeri's travel book ends not exactly with the propitious audience with the Cuban leader, but rather with a contemporaneous poem written by the Brazilian Pablo Lamarca, which serves as a sort of epilogue. Clearly written with Guevara in mind but without any apparent knowledge of Ruggeri's endeavour, "Poderosa I" is an invocation to continental solidarity through the poetic conceit of the bicycle. If, for Simmel, a remembered adventure "tends to take on the quality of a dream", the placing of Lamarca's poem after the Castro encounter ensures that, in formal as well as symbolic terms, Ruggeri's utopian trek is sealed off from the quotidian.

Simmel's conceptualisation of adventure is also pertinent in some ways to the later travel experiences of this cyclist's intertextual precursor, Ernesto Che Guevara. Ruggeri's articulation of Latin America's exceptionalism, voiced towards the end of his journey, clearly crystallises that association, especially with his predecessor's legendary utopianism, if not with the *Guerrillero Heroico*'s revolutionary violence.[57] Depicting the region in opposition to the former imperial power of Europe, Ruggeri claims that the Latin America he traverses is distinguished on the basis of: "La esperanza, y por lo tanto la diferencia, es que de este lado queremos ser distintos a lo que somos" [Hope and therefore difference, it is that we (Latin Americans) want to be different from how we are] (306). For the pilgrim-cyclist to Cuba, the invocation of the most famous global symbol of transnational solidarity and opposition is perhaps inevitable, therefore, although, as discussed earlier, "Che" serves a complex authorizing function in this instance. Guevara's 1952 trip around South America has itself been characterised as "melancholic",[58] a term employed in similarly Freudian fashion by Stephen Levin in his study of contemporary anglophone travellers.[59] To be sure, such interpretations of adventure based on psychoanalytic models of subjecthood are highly persuasive. Levin's illuminating three-part typology of the adventurer, for example, looks to have widespread uses beyond the fiction he analyses: his assessment that such narratives are "a fantasised response to the social framework of global capitalism ... [they] portray a *wish* to transform the social order" (original emphasis) is pertinent for the "nonfictional" *América en bicicleta* too.[60] Nevertheless, the "melancholic model", while useful, does not entirely account for the persistent effect of material and ideological legacies on the contemporary politico-adventurer at hand.[61] Thus, I suggest that we might ultimately describe Ruggeri's expedition and its account as spectral rather than melancholic (although I acknowledge that they are related categories).

América en bicicleta is a spectral travelogue first in a prosaic sense, in that its protagonist traverses many dark sites of the continent's ghostly geography and responds to the legacy of its bloody history. In Santiago, for example, he hails Chile as "Salvador Allende's country" (for Guevara, it was "the land of Pablo Neruda")[62] and later he makes little secret of his delight at Pinochet's arrest in London. Indeed, the account even seems to invoke at different junctures a kind of pathetic fallacy, whereby cityscapes and meteorological conditions foreshadow the prevailing historical or political climate, rather than the adventurer's own psychology. Thus, the traffic chaos of Santiago described by Ruggeri seems emblematic on the day of his arrival there, which coincides with Pinochet's swearing in as senator for life. Likewise, a grey and wet arrival in La Paz prefigures the account of a stay in which Bolivia's subordination to North American neoimperialism and its ongoing problems with the cultivation and export of coca crops predominate. One of the most powerful passages of his account of such spectral geographies, however, comes as the cyclist journeys through

Waimiri indigenous land in Brazil. This leg of the trip also testifies to Ruggeri's capacity to be an analytical and reflective traveller, as he grapples with contradictory accounts of the Indians whose territories he traverses, trying to reconcile them with his own illuminating yet unsettling encounter there. Ruggeri is ultimately reluctant to draw simplistic conclusions from it all, deciding that: "Evidentemente, había una serie de elementos que me faltaban para terminar de armar el cuadro de la situación" [Evidently, there were gaps in my knowledge that I needed to fill before getting a complete grasp of the situation] (225). Ruggeri's journey is considerably affected by the experience:

> Lo que antes era una hermosa ruta pavimentada que me permitía cruzar con comodidad la terrible jungla amazónica, era ahora un larguísimo reguero de sangre, sobre el cual estaba rodando. Las ruedas de mi bicicleta estaban teñidas de rojo y se hundían en la viscosidad de litros de vida asesinada que yo había estado usufructuando sin saberlo.
>
> [What before had been a beautiful paved road that allowed me to cross the terrible Amazonian jungle in comfort was now a huge long trail of blood on which I was peddling. The wheels of my bicycle were stained red and sinking in the viscous matter of vast numbers of murdered lives on which I had been capitalising without realising.] (226)

Just as his earlier comments attest to a discernible lack of the "authorian sureness" Debbie Lisle sees as the foundation of travel writing, which "relies so heavily on the logic of identity/difference",[63] this arresting image is in many respects indicative of the author's unsentimental depiction of these haunted sites throughout the journey.

Nevertheless it is not only in this rather loose manner that I employ a ghostly metaphor here. Ruggeri's experience is also spectral in the sense that it encompasses just the kind of ambivalent manoeuvre proposed in Jacques Derrida's conception of hauntology.[64] According to Derrida, hauntology, a new philosophical category of being conceived as an alternative to ontology, can be used to describe the status of history, in which identity is always haunted by the spectral traces of absence, loss, and death.[65] In this formulation, as Jo Labanyi lucidly summarises, "the past [is] that which is not and yet is there—or, rather, here",[66] or, as Derrida himself writes in *Specters of Marx*, "The one who has disappeared appears to still be there, and his apparition is not nothing."[67] In a book written in the wake of the collapse of communism in Eastern Europe and the Soviet Union, Derrida essentially "unpick[ed] how there is neither a beginning nor an end to history and thus Marxism, despite the supposed triumph of capitalist liberal democracy."[68] The retrieval of traces of the vanished is thus for Derrida essentially a political act: for, "anxiety in the face of the ghost," he wrote, "is *properly revolutionary*" (my emphasis).[69] Derrida's thesis in *Specters of Marx* has not been without its detractors, of course.[70] Moreover, the invocation of his ideas in the conceptualisation of ghosts of different guises by literary and cultural critics of late has engendered its own problems too. These include an erasure of the specificities of particular ghostly hauntings as well as a potentially uncritical acceptance of liminality's resistant character, as Roger Luckhurst has so splendidly illustrated: "The spectral turn reaches a limit if all it can describe is a repeated structure or generalized 'spectral process'—perhaps most particularly when critics suggest the breaching of limits is itself somehow inherently political."[71] As I hope has been evident in this chapter, Ruggeri's rather "puristic" subject position and his mobilisation of the adventure narrative are not without their contradictions. Notwithstanding, there are specific features of Derrida's thinking which prove to be pertinent in this context. One of these is the spectro-political character of his philosophy which allows for a more sophisticated conception of the cyclist's endeavour, in respect both of his journey to Cuba and the ambivalent affiliation with the iconic Guevara. What is also suggestive about Derrida's ideas here is that at stake in *América en bicicleta* is an analogous "endist" paradigm to that which informed the production of *Specters of Marx*, the work in which the French philosopher elaborates on spectrality at length. At the turn of the twenty-first century, and at the end of a decade in which Argentina, like other countries in the region, was experiencing the (in some cases ultimately ruinous) effects of a burgeoning neoliberal globalisation—the rapid privatisation of nationalised industries, the implementation of free-market development policies, huge increases in unemployment and the widespread impoverishment of vast sectors of civil society, as described in the previous chapter—Ruggeri's Latin American Tour of Solidarity is particularly timely in its symbolism, if admittedly not especially "transferable" in practical terms. That is, at a time when the Latin American left seemed long buried under the wholesale regional investment in the free market, Ruggeri's spectral adventure, apparently enthusiastically supported by activist networks throughout the region in solidarity with Cuba, attests to the possibility of resistance to the new geopolitical order. The cyclist's simple expectation, that "No es ridículo pensar en cambiar las cosas en esta sociedad" [It's not ridiculous to think of changing things in this society] (190), transpires not to be as naïve as it might sound. In more general terms, that regional opposition has indeed borne political fruit in recent years, in the form of the so-called pink tide that has seen the rise to power of various socialist presidents in Latin American countries such as Bolivia (Evo Morales), Chile (Michelle Bachelet), Ecuador (Rafael Correa), and Venezuela (Hugo Chávez), some of whom—such as Morales and Chávez—have also invoked in their political rhetoric and personae the spectre of Che.[72] Thus, while for Simmel the adventurer was "an extreme example of the ahistorical individual", a reaction to, and expression of, modernity,[73] it is in this regard that Ruggeri's spectral journey, a critique of spectacularised *post*modernity, although in some respects standing "over and above life", is, in the times of neoliberalism, thoroughly synchronic.

4 Unhomely Mexico

It is two different journeys to Latin America by women travellers of the nineteenth century, made by Flora Tristán to Peru and María Graham to Chile, which form the basis of one of the most important but curiously often overlooked interventions into the topic of travel writing and gender to date, in Mary Louise Pratt's *Imperial Eyes: Travel Writing and Transculturation*.[1] Pratt positions those two European women in counterpoint to their male contemporaries, the so-called capitalist vanguard, who flocked to the region following the dissemination in Europe of the work of Alexander von Humboldt. Less interested in nature than their precursor, these travellers adopted what Pratt identifies as an anti-aesthetic stance and a modernizing, pragmatic, and economistic rhetoric, which relied upon "a goal-directed, linear emplotment of conquest narrative".[2] By contrast, women travellers of the same period followed a distinct narratological and thematic agenda, plotting their travel narratives rather in "centripetal fashion around places of residence". Notwithstanding, social and political life were central foci of their accounts, which also showed evidence of strong ethnographic interest. Contrary to stereotype, therefore, Pratt contends, "the political dramas of Spanish America show up far more fully in the writing of these women travellers than in those of either the capitalist vanguard or the disciples of Humboldt." The so-called *exploratrices sociales* thus fused the political and the personal in the accounts of their quests in Latin America, which were not journeys of transformation or dominance of the societies they visited as much as explorations of self-realisation and "fantasies of social harmony."[3]

While attempts to determine broad thematic distinctions in travel writing on the basis of gender might ultimately prove difficult to sustain (and in any case might also be seen as a potentially reductive, even if well-meant, endeavour), what is important about Pratt's work in this area, as well as that of other scholars concerned with travel writing and gender, is the identification of enduring discursive influences and constraints which pertain to women travellers' journeys and their accounts of them.[4] For example, Pratt notes that in accordance with their greater proximity to and familiarity with the world of the interior, a product itself of prevailing cultural conceptions of femininity, interpretative analyses of the domestic realm predominate in the work of nineteenth-century women travellers such as Graham and Tristán, an observation made also of their contemporaries in other parts of the world by scholars including Sara Mills and Indira Ghose.[5] Indeed, in *Discourses of Difference* Mills identifies a critical—and subsequently much cited—paradox in the work of women travel writers during the colonial period, which she reads as a product of multiple, conflicting discourses working upon them: "It is in their struggle with the discourses of imperialism and femininity, neither of which they could wholeheartedly adopt . . . that their writing exposes the unsteady foundations on which it is based."[6] In her most recent book on the subject, *Gender and Colonial Space*, Mills has noted how this ambivalence continues to shape contemporary travel writing by women: while certain opportunities have been opened up by feminism, for example, those same avenues are often foreclosed by the affective implications of postcolonialism. As Mills sums up: "one would think this [current] freedom from constraint might enable [women travel writers] to represent themselves as being in control, but it seems also to have opened up the possibility of representing themselves as abject."[7]

It is precisely the enduring discursive ambiguity in and in respect of the work of women travellers that is the focus of the first part of this chapter. Indeed, given that, for this critic at least, women's journey narratives about Latin America have been so pivotal in the formation of conceptual and theoretical approaches to gender and travel writing, it is methodologically expedient as well as historically illuminating to return to the continent in order to consider the function of prevailing and emerging paradigms of travel there in the contemporary period. While the analysis of women's engagement with travel and travel writing has been traditionally bound up with the study of colonialism and its legacy, here I shall be concerned with the work of three contemporary women travellers in Latin America—Silvia Molina, María Luisa Puga, and Ana García Bergua—all of whom have produced travel books about Mexico during the same pivotal period of the 1990s, the decade of the so-called silent revolution.[8] My aim here is not to essentialise or homogenise the heterogeneous work of these three women travel writers, however, but rather to identify and conceptualise various compelling issues at stake in their travel production (which relate to matters of discourse rather than biology), which have hitherto received scant attention in the scholarship in this field. Indeed, it is precisely the elision of these women writers from critical discourse, an issue to which I return at greater length in the next section of this chapter, which partially accounts for their separate scrutiny here. In what follows, therefore, I shall consider and attempt to account for the striking ways in which these Mexican women writers' travel books evince degrees of that "textual turbulence"[9] which for various reasons has come to be associated with the work of women travellers.

In subsequent sections of the chapter I also explore the ways in which Molina's and Puga's books particularly speak to the fallout of Mexico's "years of crisis". As such, in contrast to prevailing assessments of their travel texts as autobiographical or else entirely inconsequential, I suggest that they are symptomatic in different ways of "a *fin de siècle* malaise in Mexico" which Roger Bartra diagnoses as "an attempt to escape from its cage of melancholy".[10] Moreover, these women writers' travelogues rest on a noteworthy *centrifugal* shift, rather than on the centripetal movement identified in the work of nineteenth-century women travellers by Pratt mentioned earlier. That is, if there is an enduring engagement in the travel writing of late twentieth-century Mexican women writers with the sociopolitical realm, there is also a marked shift in the emplotment of their "home" journey accounts, as well as, fundamentally, in their very subject positions as travellers. Far from suggesting any determinism in the relation between historical realities and cultural production, my aim in this chapter is thus in part also to foreground materiality as a condition of possibility for their journeys and travel narratives. My description of these works so far, however, should not be interpreted as an uncritical assessment of some innate oppositionality on their part to political or discursive orthodoxies. Rather, part of my agenda here is to mine the contradictions and complications of their travel texts and to underscore the ways in which travel writing offers complex maps of critical social and cultural processes. In sum, the aim of this chapter is twofold. First, to throw light on and interpret the travel writing of Bergua, Molina and Puga in a conceptual framework which takes into account questions of gender. This will address a particular critical blind spot at work in their regard as well as add to the existing scholarship in the field of travel writing and gender, in which respect there is still much work to be done on the twentieth century.[11] A second aim is to situate and evaluate these writers' travel output within appropriate material and theoretical parameters, although—and this may disappoint any Freudians whose curiosity might have been piqued by the chapter title's apparent allusion to the *unheimlich*—my approach here will not be based on orthodox psychoanalytic models. Before arriving at my theoretically grounded analyses of the travel books under consideration, I start with some necessary contextualisation.

PLUS ÇA CHANGE . . . ?

The texts under consideration in this chapter derive from a series of regional travel books about Mexico published in the mid to late 1990s, which formed part of a broader, state-sponsored enterprise towards decentralisation. Indeed, that last decade of the twentieth century constituted a period of considerable economic transformation and political fragmentation in a country which had long seen power centralised in what Daniel Levy and

Kathleen Bruhn call "regime hegemony" in Mexico City. For some six decades Mexico's ruling PRI (Partido Revolucionario Institucional [Institutional Revolutionary Party]) had provided a(n albeit sterile) form of governmental stability for the country—Peruvian novelist Mario Vargas Llosa ironically called it "the perfect dictatorship"—a situation which in Latin America was widely deemed to be exceptional.[12] Nevertheless, the 1990s saw a number of conflicts emerge between that regime and civil society at the same time as Mexico embraced and consolidated its implementation of the international trend of neoliberalism, which was in turn predicated on the reduction of state involvement in the economy, as well as in other areas of public and social life.[13] This process began under the administration of President Carlos Salinas de Gotari (1988–1994) and was continued by his successor President Ernesto Zedillo (1994–2000). On one level, as Levy and Bruhn point out, the decentralisation that occurred in Mexico over this period can be seen in a progressive sense, leading to greater electoral competition and opposition to PRI dominance as parties such as PRD (Partido de la Revolución Democrática [Party of the Democratic Revolution]) and PAN (Partido Acción Nacional [National Action Party]) grew in ascendancy. On another level, however, decentralisation also resulted from the increased influence of the United States and its neoliberal economic export based on a "smaller state, more market" model which "tends to encourage less central planning and administration of funds".[14] Thus, while decentralisation may have led to greater democratization in what had effectively been a one-party state for most of the twentieth century, it has had other, deleterious effects in the light of the wider neoliberal agenda of which it forms part.[15] As a corollary, Mexico's time-honoured exceptionalism in Latin American political history was, from the 1990s onwards, significantly called into question: as the country entered a period of uncertainty, volatility, and transition in the 1990s, a context which will become central to the readings of the travel texts which follow, it increasingly harmonized with other nations in the region in a process of "normalisation".[16]

If Mexico "enjoyed" a level of exceptionalism in political terms for most of the twentieth century, it is also likely that it will be seen to be equally remarkable by scholars of travel writing in the region for some time to come. The publishing market for travel writing in Mexico is perhaps the most buoyant in Latin America, certainly with regard to the recent (but by no means necessarily cohesive) production of a corpus of "domestic" travel writing.[17] As Thea Pitman explains in her groundbreaking work on the Mexican *crónica de viaje*,[18] throughout the twentieth century there were high levels of interest in the country in the views of foreign travellers in Mexico, which resulted in their works being translated, regardless of their respective ideologies (for example, Frances Calderón de la Barca's controversial *Life in Mexico* was translated into Spanish in 1920 and was swiftly followed by others in subsequent decades).[19] Since the 1970s particularly the printing of foreign travel writing has become "a major enterprise for Mexican publishers", with those at the vanguard typically state institutions and "the exponents of official Mexican culture: specific federal government departments, state governments, and cultural organs of [central] government."[20] Pitman suggests that the rationale for such institutional involvement in the publication of travel writing is primarily economic, given that "only the government-subsidised publishing houses can afford to publish a backdated catalogue which is unlikely to break even in terms of sales" (48). Nevertheless, there are clearly also reasons relating to the promotion of cultural and regional heritage as well as of regional and national identity that play a part in the state sponsorship and publication of travel writing, especially those volumes with a "domestic" focus.[21] Indeed various federal states such as Veracruz, Tabasco, Guadalajara, Colima, Saltillo, and Sonora have all participated in this particular trend in the production and publication of regional travel writing.[22] The objectives of some of these books have come close to propaganda at times: for example, the two volumes of the *Viajes en México* [*Journeys in Mexico*] series were first published in 1964 by the Secretaría de Obras Públicas [Department of Public Works], according to Pitman, in order to illustrate the changes that had been realised in Mexico's road network since the mid-nineteenth century.[23]

Two significant series of travel books on Mexico were commissioned in the late 1980s and mid-1990s, one in 1989 by the Mexican branch of international publishers Alianza Editorial, the other in 1994 by the Consejo Nacional para la Cultura y las Artes [The National Council for Arts and Culture] (CONACULTA), a state-run organisation formed in 1989 to replace the Ministry of Education's Department of Culture. Alianza's foray into the travel-writing market was a brief and relatively unsuccessful one, as their series, comprising only five or so books in total, foundered at an early stage due to poor sales figures. CONACULTA's intervention into the travel writing enterprise proved to be more successful, however, at least in respect of producing a sustained output and in terms of its national coverage. Formed at the beginning of Salinas de Gotari's *sexenio* [six-year term], and embracing other cultural institutions such as the National Institute of Fine Arts and the National Institute of Archaeology and History, the remit of CONACULTA is the promotion of Mexican culture in all its myriad forms.[24] Significantly, as Pitman notes, one of the primary aims of this body since its inception has been the decentralisation of Mexican culture.[25] CONACULTA's series of travel books does indeed bear out the organisation's "rationalizing" objective, with almost all of the publications in the series focusing on the diverse regions of the country, such as Campeche, Veracruz, and Huasteca, rather than on the urban metropolis of the *Distrito Federal*.[26] Nevertheless, in the only critical study to date on this series other than Pitman's, Ana Rosa Domenella identifies a crucial irony underpinning this initiative, pointing out that those authors who contributed to the CONACULTA travel-writing series are in large part from and write for a readership located in the country's metropolitan capital.²⁷ As such, these travel writers might well be conceived to some degree as interlopers or "strangers" in those "far-flung" regions they visit and write about for the series, a notion to which I shall return in my analysis of the travel texts in the next section.

CONACULTA commissioned various writers to produce books for its series from a range of authors not necessarily known previously for their travel-writing output but who had become established in other related fields or professions, such as academia, journalism, and literary fiction.²⁸ The authors' remit, as one of the commissioning editors explains, was as follows:

> Pedimos una crónica al estilo de los viajeros . . . que tenga un estilo literario, que no sea algo como estudio académico o estudio histórico; que tenga mucha soltura en el estilo, que tenga anécdotas, que sea algo fácil, agradable de leer, como para alguien que vaya a la zona en cuestión y que ello pueda ser un libro que lo acompaña en su propio viaje.
>
> [We commissioned a chronicle in a traveller's style . . . [we asked] that it should have a literary style, but not like an academic or historical study; that it have a fluidity of style, that it have anecdotes, that it be easy and pleasant to read, as if it were for someone who was going to the area in question and could be the kind of book they would take with them on their journey.]²⁹

Whatever the limitations of the series itself (a certain economy of form and a time-limited production schedule),³⁰ it is fair to say that each of the women writers under consideration here—none of whom had written any travel books previously but who, in at least two cases, were already well established for their works of literary fiction—adhere in some form to that editorial remit as well as to other general conventions associated with travel writing. Each of their volumes focuses on a different region of the country, Campeche (Molina), Michoacán (Puga), and Veracruz (Bergua), and each of them provides (albeit to varying degrees) the kind of description and information one might expect of a travel book, including details of local tourist sights, regional history, customs, and culture. As such, it is conceivable that these books would be of some use to readers as a guide on journeys to those destinations, as the series editor suggests.

The commission of CONACULTA's particular travel-writing series, therefore, is testimony to that purposeful attempt at national "democratization" to which I referred earlier, as well as to more recent endeavours to promote domestic tourism in the country. Nevertheless, in a regional context devoid both of any obvious female travel-writing precursors or indeed any prominent contemporary women travel writers at all, the participation of Bergua, Molina, and Puga in the series attests to other significant transformations in Mexico during that period. As Levy and Bruhn, among others, note, the 1990s saw declining gender differences within the population as well as important changes in the gender and makeup of the country's labour force.[31] In parallel with its political and economic transformations of the 1990s, therefore, Mexico effectively underwent a corresponding crisis in the "unifying mythos of national identity", with major shifts taking place in the cultural and intellectual sectors that were characterised above all, as Elissa Rashkin notes, "by the emergence of new media, new forms of participation and new participants", among them, crucially, women.[32] Since the 1980s, women had been entering the labour market and graduating from universities in Mexico in much greater numbers than ever before and, for the first time, activating their voices in the cultural sphere *en masse*.[33] In this context, the participation of three women writers in a state-commissioned series, which finally comprised some fourteen volumes in total, should not go unacknowledged, notwithstanding the perceptible reluctance of scholarship on Mexican travel writing to date to do so. In a broader literary and cultural tradition of travel writing in which, as Jane Robinson has pointed out, women "have rarely been *commissioned* to travel" (original emphasis),[34] it is worth recognising if only on a statistical basis the contribution of women writers to the authorship of this travel series. This is surely emblematic of the broader trend in Mexico during the period that I have been tracing here, in which, as Rashkin puts it, "voices from outside the lettered city began to gain substantial credibility and appeal".[35] If this CONACULTA series is a travel series about Mexico's regions, about decentralisation, then it is also one which bears witness to some (if albeit still limited) degree of fragmentation of the traditionally masculinist nexus of power which Angel Rama famously called *la ciudad letrada* [the lettered city].[36] Clearly, there are further issues at stake (and not necessarily ones of a positive ilk) in these women writer's collaboration with a state-sponsored attempt to map an "alternative" national cartography, to which I shall return in due course. Indeed, Molina's and Puga's travel books function in varying degrees of "complicity" with that project: in doing so, they attest to the range of "accommodations and negotiations [that operate] between state and society in Mexico", where, as Andrea Noble points out, "participation in the arena of cultural politics can of course be both hegemonic and resistant and sometimes both at the same time".[37]

Nevertheless, it is precisely the nature of the reception of these women writers' travel books by Mexicanist scholars and critics to date which crystallises one of the more general, ongoing difficulties facing the work of women travel writers, and which ultimately justifies their scrutiny in this chapter as a discrete group. A separatist view of women's travel writing has its risks, of course, and might lead to accusations of reductionism, if not of possible essentialism. For, as Charles Forsdick quite rightly states, "women's [travel] accounts are not automatically distinctive, and to reduce their reading to one wholly reliant on gender would be a denial of the diversity of the material in question."[38] While other prominent scholars in the field of travel writing, such as Patrick Holland and Graham Huggan, see the ongoing identification of connections between different women's travel narratives more cynically as a function of contemporary market forces,[39] I contend that there is still a very valid and, in fact, urgent case in this instance for a consideration of these women's travel texts as a distinct corpus. This is due to an enduring masculinist hegemony at work in this particular context as well as in literary and cultural studies more generally (to which Holland and Huggan seem oblivious) and even a residual misogyny in respect of women's literary and travel-writing output in Latin America, both of which lead to the marginalisation of their output in the critical arena. This is symptomatic, then, of what Nuala Finnegan has described as "an exhaustion with the 'gender question'", that is, "a [visible] tendency in much critical writing on the subject of Latin America . . . to erase [gender] systematically as a separate and distinct category".[40] In this chapter, my intention is not to forge artificial thematic connections between the travel texts of Bergua, Molina, and Puga on the basis of gender: indeed, as I shall illustrate, their books throw up different kinds of questions and issues, and offer different conceptions of Mexico. Rather, my aim is to illuminate and analyse a collection of travel narratives that have themselves been either elided from or inadequately conceptualised thus far in the burgeoning scholarship in this field. While I would agree with Forsdick, therefore, that women's travel accounts are not necessarily innately distinctive as a body of work, what remains a singular point of convergence—and accounts for their separate consideration here—is the nature of their ongoing critical occlusion.

In an otherwise excellent thesis on travel writing in Mexico, for example, Pitman disregards the contributions of Molina and Puga in her analysis of the contemporary *crónica de viaje* (Bergua's travelogue had yet to be published at the time of Pitman's original research project) on the basis of what she perceives as their "lack of literary quality". While there is an underlying selection bias at work in her study, as in any (my own included, of course), the implications of that manoeuvre are worth some consideration. Although some (unspecified) redeeming features of these women writers' travel books are recognised, Pitman laments that "they are all tainted by a placid and banal narrative voice", a structure which is "either overlooked or completely dull" and "contents which are superficial and/or run of the mill".[41] Such assessments, in my view, are somewhat overstated and run the risk of being unproductive. To dismiss these women writers' contributions from a discussion of the Mexican travel chronicle on the basis of their being the same ("they are *all* tainted"), or not "good enough" when measured against what is ultimately an arbitrary literary standard (the primary focus of Pitman's work being the function of a postmodernist aesthetic in Mexican travel writing), and to assert that any interest they might have is only due to their closer association with autobiography to boot, is to all too easily shore up what is a problematic elitism in the field of literary/cultural criticism.⁴² Moreover, in the context of a genre which has itself been marginalised historically, the implications of these kinds of assessments can be especially unproductive.⁴³ As Mills has argued, the critic should be concerned not with whether women's travel writing is distinct from that of male writers, "but rather with exploring the possibilities of interpreting this writing within its period and its discursive constraints."⁴⁴ The most striking difference at work in travel writing by women, Mills goes on to say, often lies not so much in the writing itself but rather in the way that it is judged and processed. For me, Pitman's assessment in that particular piece of work would seem to offer an example of just that kind of unhelpful processing.

To be sure, Pitman substantially attenuates those comments in her more recent book on *Mexican Travel Writing*, where in the conclusion she acknowledges the travel output of contemporary women writers. There (but not until the penultimate page of the book!) she accounts for their omission from that study "because they are significantly different in approach to those written by Mexican men and really merit a study apart to do them justice."⁴⁵ Let me be clear. *Mexican Travel Writing* is an important and indeed essential book for anyone interested in travel writing in Latin America. Based on extensive archival research and interviews with authors and publishers, Pitman's book not only maps out a Mexican travel-writing tradition but it also theorises the interplay between poetics and politics, proposing that "where contemporary Mexican travel writing takes on board certain aesthetic innovations associated with postmodernist literature . . . it can offer a variety of travel writing that challenges the genre's imperialist legacy."⁴⁶ As such, her work in the area is pioneering, enabling not only this discussion but no doubt those of many other scholars to come. Nevertheless, setting aside for the moment the question of how exactly women writers' travel books are "different in approach" to those of their male counterparts, Pitman's statements there raise a similar dilemma as that mentioned earlier. In the logic set up by her book, women's travel books are in effect "other" to the category of Mexican travel writing, one which is defined as an exclusively masculinist and postmodernist affair. One further aim of this chapter, therefore, is to resituate and reconceptualise the significance of the work of these women travellers in the context of a broader regional tradition and history of contemporary travel writing. It is in respect of their engagement with emerging paradigms of travel and identity that I suggest an analysis of their travel books can be more productive, and, indeed, even "postmodernist", *pace* Pitman, than any attempt to measure them up against what are ultimately subjective assessments of literary or cultural value. Indeed, if, as Pitman says, in Mexican travel chronicles of the 1980s and 1990s, the issue of national identity is typically replaced by a "postmodernist approach to identity", then these women writers' travel books have much more in common with the work of their male counterparts than she acknowledges.⁴⁷ As I shall illustrate in the following section, while their adherence to editorial or generic frameworks may well result in limited stylistic or aesthetic experimentation, each of the travel books under consideration articulates some engagement with the notion of displacement or dislocation which merits further scrutiny and thought.

It is also worth saying here that, at the other end of the spectrum, Domenella's useful article on the CONACULTA travel series fails to adequately think through the issues at stake in these travel books, although she is correct when she writes that "La marca del final de siglo está presente en la mayor parte de la colección" [the mark of the *fin de siècle* is evident in the majority of the collection].[48] Nevertheless, were critical tendencies not sufficient grounds on which to account for an exclusive consideration of the work of women travellers here, various textual features also demand examination in terms of gender. This is evident in one case especially where the woman traveller engages and contends with the intertextual nature of both travel and its writing up. In the remainder of this section, therefore, I consider Ana García Bergua's *Postales del Puerto* [*Postcards from the Port*] (1997), a travel book which evinces symptoms of a significant discursive or generic dislocation, whose foundations would appear to lie in questions of authorship.[49]

In her travel book of Veracruz, Bergua makes the customary excursions to sites of interest there such as the port, the aquarium, *los portales* (the arcades leading to the *zócalo*, or main square), and the fortress of San Juan de Ulúa. In doing so, she combines detail of encounters with locals, with recipes of regional cuisine, and evocative descriptions of the city and its inhabitants. Furthermore, quotations from the work of a range of her travelling precursors, both foreign and domestic, introduce each of the twenty chronicles or chapters of the volume (these include excerpts from Frances Calderón de la Barca, Bernal Díaz del Castillo, Fernando Benítez and Manuel Payno, among many others). These citations function, according to the author, to "conformar una visión de transparencias y matizar el presente por el pasado" [to shape a picture of transparencies and to qualify the present with the past].[50] Indeed, most of the brief chapters of Bergua's volume sustain a thematic counterpoint with the ideas laid out in their epigraphs, one of the most emblematic examples of which is the entry called "ambulantes" [street vendors]. Prefaced with an excerpt from Max Miller's *Mexico Around Me* (1937), in which that author rails against what he describes as the pest of the city's too numerous street vendors, Bergua goes on to refute the North American writer's point of view with a digression on the heterogeneity of *ambulantes* and their contribution to the city's cultural economy. These quotations at the beginning of each chapter simultaneously acknowledge Bergua's debt to as well as inscribe her within the long history of travel writing about that foundational city, "ese lugar de perpetuo tránsito" [that place of perpetual transit] (14). In addition to their structural and thematic function, therefore, which establishes a continual exchange—and another form of transit—between the different travel texts at play throughout the volume, their use is also an effective and familiar self-authorizing strategy.

Nevertheless, alongside her inscription into Veracruz's and Mexico's travel-writing heritage, what is also apparent in Bergua's travelogue is a profound ambivalence about her incursion into that very discourse and tradition. This is evinced primarily in a fascinating note of apology in Bergua's preface to her travel text, in which, without any apparent irony, the author claims that her book "no aspira más que a ser un pequeño diario de viaje al que han llegado también, por una especie de invocación, las voces de algunos viajeros de antaño" [does not aspire to be anything more than a little travel journal to which the voices of other travellers from previous eras have also arrived, by way of some kind of invocation] (9). This is a classic disavowal of authorship, and one historically associated with women writers, in which self-representation is portrayed not only as inconsequential but in fact as inadvertent. This manoeuvre is reinforced in the grammatical structures and lexical features of the Spanish. We learn, for example, that the other travellers' voices mentioned (which go on to form the epigraphs and citations in subsequent *crónicas*) "han llegado, por una especie de invocación" [have arrived by way of some kind of invocation] in an indirect, quasi-spiritual rather than deliberate manner. This abrogation of authorship is followed by a further repudiation, that "De cualquier manera no es una mirada docta sobre Veracruz" [In any case this is not an erudite look at Veracruz] but effectively "tan exterior como la de todo viajero que registra una impresión fugaz" [as much an outsider's look as that of every traveller who records a fleeting impression] (9). Here Bergua appears to recant any authority or indeed singularity, the latter a charge which in any case has been levelled at women travellers in an often dubious manner.[51] The Mexican writer does so in a self-effacing but potentially pejorative fashion, claiming that her gaze is as superficial as the next traveller's, and perhaps not even very informed. In the final sentence of the preface's opening paragraph, Bergua underscores that it is recourse to her travelling precursors that will enable her to express her affective attachment to Veracruz. This is an artful and expedient elucidation of her strategy: indeed, throughout the book, affect does indeed appear to be sublimated in what might be seen as a kind of intertextual dependency, whereby "Bergua the traveller" is largely subsumed under the sustained textual interplay. Like Bruce Chatwin (whose style in works such as *In Patagonia* "infers a calculated distance from what it portrays, but a distance that implies awareness of the self-control that ought to attend the act of representation"),[52] Bergua is thus also frequently more absent from than present as a character in her own travel narrative, although she is still very much in evidence as the shaping force behind it.

In constructing the preface and her travel text in terms such as these, however, Bergua semantically and structurally forecloses her own agency as traveller and travel writer. This foreclosure is formally reinforced in the preface's second paragraph, which consists of a list of bibliographic and personal acknowledgments, and is reiterated in a later reference in the volume to her travelling precursors, "cuyos espíritus convoco inútilmente a la hora de mancillar estas páginas y distraer los ocupados ojos del lector" [whose spirits I invoke in vain as I besmirch these pages and distract the tired eyes of the reader] (70). Clearly, such statements expressing Bergua's debt to and inadequacy in respect of existing sources of "authority", as well as her affective attachment to Veracruz, not only pay testimony to longstanding tropes in the literary fiction and travel writing of women writers of the nineteenth century. They also reveal an enduring adherence to time-honoured notions of literary femininity. As Shirley Foster and Sara Mills observe, however, the so-called apologia can be a potentially ambiguous trope, both a strategy for self-devaluation and a subversive masking gesture.[53] In this light, alongside the attempt at self-devaluation, we might also interpret Bergua's self-professed (false?) modesty as a canny acknowledgment of the limitations of her own travel text, of the very form, as well as of the series itself (a strategy employed, perhaps, to second-guess the kind of criticism mentioned earlier). Certainly, Bergua's citation of literary, historical, and travel writing sources both in the preface, in each *crónica* of the volume, and in a final bibliography, as well as the carefully crafted nature of her book, constitute a fundamental contradiction of such pretensions of humility and lack of substance.

The very title of Bergua's book—*Postales del Puerto*—synthesises the paradoxical tendency that has been identified here. On one level, the naming of the volume as a collection of postcards corresponds to the broader context of travel, tourism, and its associated discourses, and in a formal sense also foregrounds the elliptical nature of the book's *crónicas*. To some degree, Bergua reconfigures the usage of this particular touristic "genre" in the development of an occasional countertouristic theme in her volume, like Molina and Puga, lamenting the transformations that have taken place in Mexico as a result of globalisation and "las necesidades de un turismo que exige lo mismo en todas partes: un escenario prefabricado con albercas, bares, restaurant, cuartos con televisión y un trozo de playa más o menos exclusivo en la que priva el imperativo de tostarse" [the necessities of a tourism which demands the same everywhere: a prefabricated scene of swimming pools, bars, restaurant, rooms with TV and a bit of semi-private beach where sunbathing prevails] (78). Elsewhere, however, in particular in her comparisons between Veracruz and Mexico City, the author romanticises the apparently "timeless" qualities of this historic port (in "Diques" [Docks], for example, writing of the bliss of sitting on the docks, "cuando hay tanta felicidad es difícil escucharse!" [when there is so much happiness it is hard to hear yourself think!], 53). As such, Bergua falls into a similar trap as other travel writers of a "postcolonial persuasion" who, as Holland and Huggan have pointed out, effectively "remain complicit with the tourism they denounce".[54] Nevertheless, on another level, the title of Bergua's travelogue also attenuates the scope of her endeavour. The denomination of the volume as a collection of postcards—rather than, say, a travel book—implicitly situates her text in the feminised space of the "private" sphere and, indeed, within the realm of the ephemeral, and ultimately belies the evident preparation and research undertaken in the production of the text.[55] In this respect, the title converges with the diffident tone at work in the preface and elsewhere in the book. What is evident from the foreword and other features of this travelogue of Veracruz, therefore, is a fundamental inconsistency in Bergua's construction of her travel text and in her assumption of what Michel Foucault might have called the travel-writing "author-function". There is a strong impression from the outset that Bergua is an interloper of sorts, her book an uneasy incursion into a tradition and discourse of travel within which she operates with considerable contrariety and disquiet. While Pitman observes that many Mexican travel writers disavow their own authorship of travel writing for reasons relating to the genre's colonial freight, the precedents and circumscription of Bergua's endeavour in *Postales* are clearly also gendered.[56]

While Bergua's account seems to suffer from an inconsistency which is on one level eminently justifiable in the context just outlined, as well as in light of her subject position as "young" writer on the Mexican literary scene, I want to now turn to the other two travelogues in this series by more established writers, Silvia Molina and María Luisa Puga.[57] While less faithful to the conventions of travel writing and indeed to the remit of the series than Bergua's (especially in terms of their use of the CONACULTA grant that accompanied their commissions as well as in respect of the material compiled in each of their volumes), these travel texts are no less protean in character.[58] Nevertheless, their volatility may be read less as an index of an anxiety of authorship than as emblematic of the malaise of Mexico's years of crisis in which they were produced.

AUTOETHNOGRAPHY AS SCHIZOPHRENIA

In *Campeche, imagen de una eternidad* [*Campeche, Image of an Eternity*] (1996), which relies less heavily than Bergua's book on intertextuality through the use of epigraphs and citations, Silvia Molina invokes diverse and formerly divergent forms of travel discourse. Indeed, it is the coincidence of two particular modes of travel and travel writing which, to some degree, leads to the evident "instabilities"[59] of Molina's account. *Campeche* combines a personal quest for identity, in the exploration of the author's family heritage in this southeastern and largely indigenous region of Mexico, with a contemporary ethnography of the place, in which Molina (born in the capital to parents from the regional "periphery", Sonora and Campeche, respectively) asserts, "Quiero ver si me reconozco en todo esto" [I want to see if I recognise myself in all of this] (84).[60] Indeed, Molina's volume fluctuates between those two imperatives, as chapters detailing her personal memory work alternate with others which take the form of anonymised interviews with local inhabitants (including a fisherman, healer, street vendor, an archaeologist, a pizza delivery man, and a journalist) which have the appearance of the results of field work. In some respects what appears to be at stake in this volume is a realignment of discursive boundaries between formerly distinct configurations of travel and travel writing, in this case "literary" travel and ethnographic fieldwork. In this light we might well regard Molina's travelogue as a kind of autoethnography.[61] The construction and character of *Campeche* incorporates the two broad meanings of that term, in the sense that it is both an ethnography of Molina's "own" group (or, rather, her father's) as well as an autobiographical journey (to her Campechan family home) with an ethnographic interest. As such, Molina's travel book also brings into focus pertinent questions regarding the increasing permeability of boundaries between notions of home and abroad. For, as Deborah E. Reed-Danahay points out, the most prevalent theme of autoethnography in all of its configurations is that of cultural displacement: "Whether the autoethnographer is the anthropologist studying his or her own kind, the native telling his or her life story, or the native anthropologist, this figure is not completely 'at home'".[62]

In effect, Molina's journey narrative, which collates stories of repeated journeys to the region from her past and present, is predicated on a double degree of displacement: a diegetic one which corresponds to the generic precedents and formal construction of her travelogue, and another which relates to questions of selfhood. The metropolitan author's own sense of "dis-location" in this region of Mexico is established from the very outset, when she confesses that "Aunque me considero campechana, no lo soy" [although I consider myself Campechan I'm not] (19), despite her professed "cordón umbilical con Campeche" [umbilical cord with Campeche] (23). Her liminal status is also crystallised in the travelogue's opening episode, in the course of which the author presents herself as a cultural translator to her Mexican readership, although one who, significantly, is unable to communicate with an indigenous healer in his native Mayan tongue. In an inversion of the time-honoured cognitive superiority of the traveller over travellee, and in a manoeuvre not unlike Bergua's admission of her limitations as travel writer discussed earlier, Molina underscores her own ignorance and humility during this episode (as, indeed, she goes on to do elsewhere in the book): as the *h'men* reads her cards and performs a blessing, she tells us that "no sé qué hacer ni qué decir" [I don't know what to do or say] (16). At the same time, however, the author manages to set herself apart from the ordinary *chilanga*,[63] through her recounting of the *h'men*'s observation of what he calls (or she translates as) her special passion. This oscillation between self-admonishment and certitude pervades the rest of her travelogue, lending it an uneven and profoundly mercurial quality. In those autobiographical chapters dealing with episodes relating to her

Campechan family and more broadly often also to the region's cultural history, Molina's literary "travel-writing" persona is intimate, sensitive, and meditative. She describes her relationship to Campeche, for example, in terms of an "enamoramiento" [falling in love] and, in the following passage, reflects on her fetishization of a Campechan dress as a young child:

> En mi, ese vestido no sería más que un disfraz, porque el disfraz subraya lo que uno no es; enseña lo que vemos como lo distinto, lo ajeno. Y para mi Campeche era *lo otro*.
>
> [On me that dress would be no more than a disguise, because a disguise underlines what one is not: it reveals what we see as different, as alien. And for me Campeche was *the other*.] (27) [64]

In those alternate chapters where she interviews a range of the region's inhabitants, however, Molina's "autoethnographer" presents quite a different prospect altogether. Whereas in *Postales del puerto* Bergua is largely unobtrusive or absent, the traveller of these encounters is highly interventionist, probing, testing, and often correcting her respondents, above all maintaining her singularity as a strategic distancing mechanism. Furthermore, these encounters are presented largely in the form of interview scripts, in which "Molina" operates as a foil for garnering useful information or for posing questions of broader social significance, for example, concerning the effects of tourism or immigration in the region. One of the implications of this structure is, at the very least, some discontinuity of tone throughout the volume. For Molina, an established author on the Mexican literary scene who has long disavowed many of the suggested autobiographical readings of her literary fiction, the advantages of this fusion of the autobiographical and ethnographic in this journey narrative are clear.[65] That the two discourses are never fully reconciled in *Campeche*, however, attests not only to the inherent displacement at the heart of autoethnography as a genre but also to a broader pathology.

If Molina fashions a somewhat fickle travelling self on her journey to Campeche, she is equally equivocal about her views on the region in both personal and political terms. Like many migrants' offspring who might claim the identity of an inherited cultural tradition, Molina asserts ownership of Campeche before she even travels there, writing at an early stage of her travelogue that:

> Campeche es mío desde antes de conocerlo. Lo comí, lo olí, lo sentí, lo toqué, lo escuché de lejos y nadie podrá quitármelo, aunque no vuelva a ir jamás.
>
> [Campeche was mine before I even got to know it. I ate it, I smelled it, I felt it, I touched it, I listened to it from afar and nobody will be able to take it away from me, whether I return there or not.] (21)

The character of the author's affective identification with Campeche, reinforced here through the almost obsessive repetition of the object pronoun *lo* in Spanish and the series of verbs in the preterite (simple past) tense, bespeaks not only its strength but also the creative and imaginative processes implicit in the formation of such "memories". As Juan Vives Rocabert has observed, "El hijo de migrantes llega a construir un mundo imaginario relativo a ese lejano y amado país, llega a sentir que conoce a familiares y amigos a los que nunca ha visto; siente que sabe de situaciones, costumbres y leyendas nunca experimentadas y en las que no ha participado jamás" [The child of migrants goes on to construct an imaginary world in relation to that distant and beloved country; s/he goes on to feel that s/he knows relatives and friends whom s/he has never met; s/he feels that s/he knows situations, traditions, and legends never experienced and in which s/he has never participated].[66] Molina ultimately sums up this paradox in an expression of her identity as "campechana del De Efe" [Campechan from the D.F.] (124).[67] Nevertheless, the author's idealisation and "fictionalisation" of Campeche is laid bare on her most recent journey there, during the course of which, as I have already mentioned, she experiences continual problems with communication.[68] Further examples, in addition to the episode mentioned earlier, include the chapter "El pescador", an encounter which foregrounds the asymmetrical relationship of the traveller and travellee as well as a rather dubious dialectic of transcendence and immanence. The episode hinges on entirely polarised conceptions of memory, as Molina fails to comprehend a local fisherman's entreaty to forget. Molina's project is one of purposeful remembering (based on a certain degree of privilege) and is micromanaged in a similar kind of centripetal fashion as the journeys of her nineteenth-century counterparts, although, significantly, the base in this instance is the local branch of international hotel chain Ramada. Meanwhile, the angler, who has failed to catch anything from his position on the quayside all day, advocates the merits of forgetting for his own subject position and professional endeavour, both of which are predicated on stasis, or dwelling, rather than travelling. Perhaps more revealing still are the difficulties Molina encounters with Consuelo, a distant cousin who is deaf and mute, whom she almost forcibly co-opts to accompany her to the ruins at Edzná. On this particular occasion, however, Molina does reflect on her position as a traveller in Campeche:

> No sabía algo tan inmediato como comunicarme con esa mujer misteriosa y próxima . . . No sabía en absoluto quién era Consuelo, a la que había llevado arbitrariamente conmigo a ese lugar. Me daba ganas de pedirle perdón.
>
> [I didn't know anything as immediate as how to communicate with that woman who was both so mysterious and close to me . . . I had no idea who Consuelo was, whom I had arbitrarily taken with me to that place. I felt like asking her forgiveness.] (62)

To her credit, the author acknowledges that her repeated excursions with this cousin provide a fitting metaphor for her identification with Campeche (offering some degree of possible redemption too, as indicated perhaps in her cousin's "symbolic" name, meaning "consolation" or "comfort").

Molina's travelogue thus provides what might be seen as a representative example of those conflictive discursive ambivalences identified by Mills in her studies of the genre to which I referred earlier. In her work on women travel writers, Mills has consistently underscored the plausible coexistence in their work of discourses of privilege (in terms of class, race, and ethnicity) and subordination (in terms of gender). In this respect, we might well account for the unevenness of *Campeche, imagen de una eternidad* in terms of an ultimately unsuccessful convergence of these kinds of discourse, as well as of the personal/familial with the public/professional. Nevertheless, the equivocalness which imbues the travelogue, measured in Molina's personal responses to Campeche, finds a further outlet in the Mexican writer's apprehension of the region's political status. It is here that there is something more at stake than a case of generic or textual morbidity. It is worth pointing out at this juncture that the author's father, Héctor Pérez Martínez, was governor of Campeche between 1939 and 1943, and that Molina is very much a daughter of the political orthodoxy.[69] Indeed, her credentials are laid bare in the course of her travelogue, not only in reiterated references to her father's legacy but also, for example, on the occasion she is invited to a tour of the state by Ernesto Zedillo in his presidential campaign of 1994. Given the reiterated references to contemporary material contexts throughout Molina's journey as well as the volume's tonal and structural fluctuations, the instabilities at work in this text might be read further as symptomatic of an anxiety produced by those same transformations in "late modern" Mexico (which the author calls "los embates del centralismo" [the hardships of centralism]) and which are more broadly endemic in what Gilles Deleuze and Felix Guattari call capitalism as schizophrenia.[70]

Molina's hegemonic position, hinted at throughout the book, is consolidated at the very end of her travelogue, at which point the irony of her apparently exoticist title also becomes clear. Citing her own father's description of the region as "el gesto de la eternidad, lo inconmovible, lo imperecedero" [the image of eternity, what is unmovable and everlasting] (125), Molina counteracts this idea of Campeche's immanence in the cultural imaginary in terms that are potentially no less problematic than her father's. In her call for transcendence the author locates the source of this change in individual agency (as an autonomous "federal" enterprise, as it were), complaining ultimately that "Los campechanos estamos demasiados protegidos, aislados, sumergidos en nosotros mismos, en la tradición . . . añoramos el progreso, pero no traspasamos la muralla para ver allende el mar" [We Campechans are too protected, too isolated, self-absorbed, submerged in tradition . . . we yearn for progress, but we don't scale the walls in order to look beyond the sea] (124). Furthermore, the terms in which she does so are also telling, as they not only crystallise the putative ease with which such change is advocated but also reveal the dubious ideology underlying that proposition. In the course of her travelogue, Molina draws repeatedly on a feminised metaphor to describe the region: the Ciudad del Carmen of the author's childhood, for example, is "una señora educada y antigua" [an elderly and educated woman] (34). It is an associated metaphor which frames Molina's final exhortation:

> La muralla de mi tierra está enmohecida, salitrosa. Es un vestido viejo, de siglos. Creo que a Campeche le hace falta un atuendo nuevo, más suelto . . . una prenda cuyos lienzos no encierran a la gente en sí misma . . . La vida cambia, Campeche debía cambiar, dejar en el pasado su drama de soledad, de aislamiento, de señora encerrada en un corsé de piedras . . . Sueño que nos pide aflojarle las varillas que lo ciñen, romper su cíngulo de melancolía.
>
> [The walls of my land are mouldy, salty. It's an old costume that's been worn for centuries. I think Campeche needs a new outfit, a looser one . . . a garment whose cloth doesn't inhibit its people . . . Life changes, and Campeche should change, leave in the past the drama of its solitude and isolation, of a lady in a corset of stone . . . I dream that she asks us to loosen her stays, to undo the girdle of her melancholy.] (124, 126)

On one level the author's engagement with such metaphors might be seen as some indication of the gendered discourses at work in Molina's travel account (alongside even her sustained engagement with Campeche's culinary and sartorial traditions, for example, as well as with the family's female genealogy, although these are of course by no means the exclusive purview of women writers). Also at stake in the author's depiction of Campeche and its change in such terms, however, is the perpetuation of a dominant discourse of late modern consumer culture, which, as Lisa Adkins has pointed out in her work, relies upon "the sovereignty of the sign, appearance, image and style; surface, simulation and masquerade".[71] The transformation Molina calls for is expressed in terms of an easily assumed and shed identity, tantamount to the purchase of a new outfit, a process to which her own travelogue appears to adhere as she negotiates the dualism inherent in the subject position of the autoethnographer. However, as I intimated earlier, the assumption of this double identity is not a felicitous or fluid process in Molina's travel book: rather than break down the dualisms of identity, therefore, her autoethnography appears instead to reinforce them. In this light *Campeche* is not only an anxious and uneven travel text but it is ultimately a "schizoid" one, although not in the radical, revolutionary sense of Deleuze and Guattari's formulation, but rather in Fredric Jameson's more sceptical conception of the idea. Jameson associates the attributes of schizophrenia with postmodernism and late capitalism as they are forces which equally "scramble and confuse": the schizophrenic experience, in his terms, is one of "isolated, disconnected, discontinuous material signifiers which fail to link up into a coherent sequence".[72] As such, in contrast to Deleuze and Guattari's arguably more progressive notion of schizophrenia (in its "exterior limit . . . the death [of capitalism]"),[73] in Jameson's configuration, as Jonah Peretti puts it, "the schizophrenic confusion destroys the possibility of critical perspectives" and effectively reproduces and reinforces the logic of consumer capitalism.[74] Jameson's schizophrenic, I contend, provides a suggestive, if ultimately unfortunate, figure for the conception of this traveller's book. Molina's self-declared objective, at the beginning of the travelogue, about a search for identity ("Quiero ver si me reconozco en todo esto" [I want to see if I recognise myself in all of this]), is ultimately foreclosed, fragmented in confused scramble, a series of uneasy paradoxes not unlike those characterising the condition of Mexico itself at that juncture: in Bartra's terms, "a country full of modernity, but thirsty for modernization".[75]

STRANGERHOOD AS A POETICS OF TRANSITION

If Molina's travelogue attests to symptoms of a "post-Mexican" malaise, then María Luisa Puga's volume provides what might be conceived as an antidote of sorts for that pathology. Of all the books to have been produced on Mexico's regions in the CONACULTA series, María Luisa Puga's is the only one to have been written *in situ*. Originally from Mexico City, Puga relocated to Zirahuén, Michoacán (northwest Mexico) in 1985 and the pieces which make up her *Crónicas de una oriunda del kilómetro X en Michoacán* [Chronicles of a Native of Km X in Michoacán] (1995) comprise a range of texts written and published during her residence there.[76] Unlike the books of her series counterparts, however, *Crónicas* tells the reader very little about Michoacán at all, giving few details of its landscape, customs, or local "colour". Less of a conventional travelogue, then, Puga's book comprises a series of chronicles about *fuereñez*, a condition which in Mexican Spanish refers to someone who is from out of town but not a foreigner and, as such, one which implies continual displacement. Given the specificity of this term, and its lack of direct equivalent in English, I shall translate it as "strangerhood". Indeed, the two parts of Puga's travel book focus on, first, what the author calls "La fuereñez experimentada" [The experience of strangerhood], written from her own comprehension of that location, and second, "La fuereñez presenciada" [The evidence of strangerhood], in which she considers a number of other case studies of the condition in the immediate environs. In what is a much more assured volume than those of Molina and Bergua, the displacement at work in Puga's travel book is much less a symptom of the discursive unease that appears to (variously) affect the work of her contemporaries than a purposeful exploration of what might be seen as a poetics of transition.

The decision to relocate to Zirahuén is a radical one, Puga tells us in the introduction to her "travelogue", "ruralizarse voluntariamente es un paso serio" [to *ruralise* voluntarily is a serious step], and one which means that "regresar resulta imposible" [to return becomes impossible] (9).[77] Relocation to the provinces does not necessarily mean assimilation or acculturation, however, for, as she describes, although "acá nos desciudadizamos ... no nos apueblamos" [here we de-citify ourselves ... we do not village-ify ourselves]. At issue in Puga's use of neologisms such as *desciudadizar* and *apoblarse*, neither of which (like *fuereñez*) have an easy or straightforward translation into English, is that only a specific idiom can adequately describe the process of moving from Mexico's metropolitan centre to its regions: while Puga may continue to be resident in the same national territory, she has still to adopt a *sui generis* lexicon in order to capture the sense of that transition.[78] Furthermore, inherent in Puga's word play is also a strong implication of irreverence towards both the ideas and symbolic authority condensed in those very terms. The transformation of nouns such as *ciudad* [city] and *pueblo* [village] into verbs is not only indicative of the lexical malleability of Spanish but also suggests something of an underlying scepticism with regard to their ideological freight. In another context, Michael Herzfeld writes that those in opposition to official authority often find "a powerful incentive to decode and manipulate its discourse for their own purposes—a situation that makes them effective and perspicacious theorists of social and cultural life",[79] an idea that feminist theorists and critics have long sustained in this respect. Puga's use of these terms at the beginning of her travel book would appear to endorse just such a perspective. Not only does she deconstruct normative ideas and concepts that underpin the very structures of the modern nation-state, and which have particular resonance in a country such as Mexico, but she also proposes her own theory under the sign of the *fuereño* [stranger] and at a location she calls *kilómetro X*.[80]

The *sine qua non* of the *fuereño* for Puga is that "está sin estar (detenido en la frontera misma de la realidad)" [s/he is there without being there (held on the very border of reality)] (14) or, as she puts it another way, "tiene siempre dos espacios: el que dejó y el que ocupa al llegar" [s/he always occupies two spaces: that which s/he left and that s/he occupies on arrival] (24). The position of *fuereño/a* is one in fact which the author goes on to extrapolate throughout the volume, not only through her lexical choices, but also through a particular narratological strategy. Crucially, Puga shores up the application and inclusion central to *fuereñez* through her use of narrative voice; for, she writes, "somos *fuereños* casi todos" [we're practically all strangers] (9). Although it shifts throughout this diverse collection of travel texts, in several *crónicas* the author suggestively exploits the use of the relatively unusual "usted" [you] form of narrative voice as well as the more common first-person plural, "nosotros" [we]. In *Crónicas*, the "usted" [you] form functions as an effective familiarizing and universalizing mechanism, which serves to identify and assimilate the reader within Puga's discourse on transit and identity.[81] Unlike the accusatory tirade of the second-person narrator in Jamaica Kincaid's *A Small Place*, another travel book to employ this unusual "you" voice, Puga's narrator is much more benevolent.[82] Whereas Kincaid's objective is to implicate and destabilise the foreign, neoimperial, white tourist in Antigua, Puga's is not a project of explicit postcolonial retaliation, although it is a decidedly oppositional one which challenges a domestic hegemony.[83] The Mexican writer's project—a proposal for a kind of dwelling-in-transit—seeks to undermine the fixity of location and of institutional structures ("es detenerse en una tierra de nadie" [it's like stopping in no-man's-land], 24). Indeed, there is often a slippage between *usted* [you] and *nosotros* [we] voices in the space of the very same sentence in Puga's book, which encourages a further sense of collusion and complicity between narrator and reader. In the following passage, for example, the narrator imagines an anthropomorphised landscape scrutinizing the *fuereño* as s/he passes by:

> El cielo nos mira. Igual que el lago en las montañas. La neblina es el vaho de su bostezo al despertar. ¿Estás ahí?, nos pregunta amodorrado, ¿todavía no te has ido? . . . El voluminoso ganado nos mira con cálida naturalidad. Somos tan incomprensibles para ellos como cualquier hijo de vecino. Seamos lo que seamos les da lo mismo. Pasan a su lado, vacas y toros, mientras usted regula la respiración—para que el ejercicio sea efectivo—y desmienten con desparpajo aquello del rojo. No van a atacar . . . Si no molesta usted, nadie lo va a molestar.

> [The sky looks at us. As does the mountain lake. The mist is the vapour of its yawn upon waking. 'Are you still here?' it asks us sleepily, 'Haven't you gone yet?' . . . The large cows look at us with warm spontaneity. We are as incomprehensible to them as to any kid on the block. Whatever we are, it's all the same to them. They pass by you, cows and bulls, while you measure your breathing—so that your exercise will take effect—and they have the cheek to contradict that thing about the colour red. They are not going to attack. No one is interested in attacking anyone. If you don't make any trouble, no one will attack you.] (23)

Inverting the usual direction of the time-honoured "tourist gaze", this passage substantially and humorously attenuates many of the conventional (and largely pejorative) qualities associated with the figure of the stranger, particularly their encoding as anomalous or dangerous figures.[84] As the landscape and territory being traversed looks back at the traveller, the narrator sums up the indifference towards and insignificance associated with the figure of the *fuereño*, of which benevolence and recurrence are two of its distinguishing characteristics. Significantly, the shift from "nosotros" [we] to "usted" [you] at the end of that passage serves in this instance to single out any potential troublemaker who might, anomalously and foolishly, break ranks from the pacifist *fuereño* majority. Puga further normativises the experience when she sums up at the end of the first part of the book that "El fuereño tiene siempre un pie puesto aquí y otro allá. Y no se está tan mal. Es vivir como vivimos todos: de la mano del azar" [The stranger always has one foot here and another there. And it's not so bad. It's living like we all live: by the hand of chance] (65). In this formulation, then, *fuereñez* offers a largely benign position of transition and flexibility: "no es para nada fea. Es rara, eso sí" [it's not in any way bad. Although it is peculiar] (24).[85] It is perhaps not surprising, then, that elsewhere Puga employs these same terms to describe her chosen profession: "Pienso que el que escribe está siempre con un pie adentro y otro afuera" [I think that whoever writes always has a foot in both camps].[86]

Puga's configuration of location and identity in *Crónicas* is similar in some respects to other conceptions of the stranger that have gained prominence in postcolonial studies and poststructuralist theory of late. Madan Sarap, for example, describes the stranger in comparable terms as "undecidable . . . physically close while remaining culturally remote . . . standing between the inside and the outside."[87] Refugees in an era of globalisation have been cast into a similar condition which Michel Agier calls "liminal drift", and on which Zygmunt Bauman elaborates: "even if they are stationary for a time, they are on a journey never completed since its destination (whether arrival or return) remains forever and unclear, while the place they could call "final" stays forever inaccessible."[88] Puga alludes to those same globalising processes when she contextualises her *fuereño* [stranger]: as she puts it, "ya casi no hay naturales porque las circunstancias les han obligado a irse" [there are nearly hardly any natives left because circumstances have obliged them to leave] (9). Crucially, however, in Puga's work the stranger is not one who necessarily crosses national boundaries, as in Sarup's and Agier's models: rather, in this case, "el fuereño es nacional" [the stranger is national] (13). Puga's stranger, then, is domestic, territorialized, kindred, a notion supported by the use of the specific word "fuereño" itself, a term which would not necessarily be recognised or understood elsewhere in Latin America, let alone Spain. Indeed, while her thesis emerges from her own experience of living in Zirahuén, the Mexican author is at pains to affirm that it might have occurred to her in any of part of Mexico: "Estas crónicas son el resultado de un vivir así. Hubieran podido ser de Veracruz o Guerrero. Resultó Michoacán" [These chronicles are the result of living like this. They could have been from Veracruz or Guerrero. It turned out it was Michoacán] (10). Moreover, Puga largely localises the causes of the widespread displacement thematised in her book: "la basura por todos lados . . . las recónditas burguesías locales; los fraudes electorales; las vergüenzas caciquales" [the rubbish everywhere . . . the trenchant local bureaucracies; the electoral fraud; the shame of the *cacique* system] (34), a situation which nonetheless she claims "uno ama . . . por estragada que esté" [one loves . . . however devastated it is] (34). In fact, this is what precisely distinguishes this author's notion of *fuereñez* from other conceptions of the stranger—her historicisation and territorialisation of the concept in the context of contemporary Mexico, manoeuvres which in general terms tend to be elided or homogenized in poststructuralist and psychoanalytic conceptualisations of this figure.[89]

In her generally benevolent tone and positive ethics of affirmation the Mexican author's optimistic notion of strangerhood corresponds perhaps more closely than other models already mentioned to Rosi Braidotti's Deleuzian notion of nomadic consciousness. Although movement is implicit in its conception, the feminist philosopher's nomadic state signifies the subversion of set conventions rather than the literal act of travelling, for which reason it is particularly useful for thinking about the Mexican author.[90] For Braidotti, nomadic consciousness "is a form of political resistance to hegemonic and exclusionary views of subjectivity". It combines features that are usually perceived as opposing, "namely the possession of a sense of identity that rests not on fixity but on contingency".[91] "Being a nomad, living in transition," writes Braidotti, "is not fluidity without borders but rather an acute awareness of the non-fixity of boundaries. It is the intense desire to go on trespassing, transgressing."[92] In this light, Puga's notion of *fuereñez* [strangerhood] can certainly be described as rhizomatic and lateral, rather than vertical and hegemonic.[93] It is not about being in one place or another, just as nomadic consciousness "aims to rethink the unity of the subject . . . without dualistic oppositions". To be a *fuereño* [stranger], according to the Mexican writer, means to live constantly in transition—"con un pie puesto aquí y otro allá" [with one foot here and another there]. Kilometre X is the "home territory" and very symbol of that consciousness: not a determinate number, which would imply (en)closure, but a moveable figure which condenses and compels mobility in the negotiation of its very form. Indeed, the title of this "travel book" provides an indication of these same ideas. The classification of the text as a collection of *crónicas* [chronicles] signals multiplicity, rather than singularity, while Puga the author is located as just one inhabitant of *kilómetro X*, the contingent home of the *fuereño*, which in turn is territorialized in the context of Mexico through the (apparently coincidental) reference to Michoacán.[94]

Published in September 1995, *Crónicas de una oriunda del kilómetro X in Michoacán* does not only propose an abstract philosophy of permanent—and harmonious—displacement, therefore. It is also pertinent for the historical materiality to which I referred at the very beginning of this chapter. In the months before the publication of Puga's book, Mexico entered a period of political and economic transition with the election of Ernesto Zedillo to the presidency on 1 December 1994. That year had begun with the implementation of NAFTA (North American Free Trade Agreement), into which Mexico had entered with North America and Canada; the sudden, simultaneous appearance of an armed guerrilla group, the EZLN

(Ejército Zapatista de Liberación Nacional [Zapatista Army of National Liberation]) in Chiapas; followed by the murder in March of the governing party's presidential candidate, Luis Donaldo Colosio, and only six months later, the assassination of another high-ranking PRI official, Francisco Ruiz Massieu. Although the July presidential elections of that year were peaceful,[95] within three weeks of Zedillo's inauguration in December the *peso* collapsed, precipitating a serious economic crisis which also threatened the stability of the country's political system. Luis Rubio appropriately describes that time in Mexican society as one "in flux".[96] From the start of his administration, Zedillo began to radically displace the centre of gravity of Mexican politics (by, among other initiatives, devolving power from the presidency to political parties and state governors) as well as to dismantle some of the country's most traditional political institutions.[97] However, while the new structures being established were in their infancy, vestiges of older systems continued to persist, which lead to a widespread sense in the country of ongoing transition. As Rubio put it at the time: "The concept of transition implies that there is both a point of departure and a place of arrival; perhaps the biggest problem for Mexico today is the striking lack of consensus over the ultimate objectives of the current transition and . . . on what the future should look like."[98] In essence, in the midst of Mexico's then protracted and seemingly interminable period of transformation, a period Jorge Castañeda prefers to see as "una suerte de *statu quo*"[99] [a kind of status quo], Puga's proposition of a lateral, contingent *fuereñez* [strangerhood]—an expression of universal transgression and flexibility for her Mexican readers—might also be seen as a rather timely strategy for negotiating that predicament. Caren Kaplan describes Deleuze and Guatarri's rhizome "as a metaphor for politics . . . [which] constitutes an anarchic relationship to space and subjectivity, resistant to and undermining the nation-state apparatus".[100] Puga's rhizomatic *fuereñez* [strangerhood] can be seen to function in similar terms: after all, *fuereños* [strangers], Puga contends, are "ingenieros del instante" [engineers of the moment] (24) and if theirs is a poetics of transition it is one that is effectively ongoing.

Nevertheless, in that very ability to straddle borders, to move fluidly from one set of experiences to another, Puga's benign territorialized configuration of *fuereñez* [strangerhood] might in turn be seen to be rather dubious in itself. The ease encapsulated in this proposal is liable to accusations not only of sanitising or mollifying an experience which is predicated on a considerable degree of material as well as affective loss, but also of flattening out differences in a country in which sharp asymmetries of class and ethnicity continue to operate. Puga's concept has little, if nothing, to say about matters of "race", for example, in a country where approximately one third of the population is indigenous. While Puga does not ignore the inequities of life in Mexico, her universal stranger is nonetheless largely devoid of any of the trauma or anxiety which are frequently bound up in the experience of domestic and international displacement (the latter the subject of the next chapter): in this way it reveals the degree of relative privilege on which such a conception is based (Puga's was, after all, a voluntary relocation). As Sara Ahmed has observed, the turn to the stranger as a benevolent figure can create its own kind of stranger fetishism: "it invests the figure ... with a life of its own insofar as it cuts the stranger off from the histories of its determination ... and functions to elide the substantive differences between ways of being displaced from 'home.'"[101] Similarly, conceptualising Puga's ideas as nomadic might also run the risk of celebrating a perhaps now overused and idealised "emancipatory metaphor" and a utopian, "outside" space which, despite their seductive appearances, are theoretically still bound up in the legacy of colonial discourse. As Kaplan so brilliantly argues in her critique of Deleuze and Guattari: "Euro-American recourse to the metaphor of ... [the] nomad can never be innocent or separable from the dominant orientalist tropes in circulation throughout modernity", so that even "deterritorialisation is always reterritorialisation, an increase of territory, an imperialisation."[102] To some extent, Puga's purposeful Mexicanisation of strangerhood, as just discussed, absolves her from that precise accusation, although we should be wary nonetheless of its own exclusions and elisions. Puga is perhaps on more solid ground at least in her consistency throughout these *crónicas*, not only in respect of her ethics of strangerhood, however universalised, but also in terms of her insistence on the potentiality of the arts and letters (in their broadest sense) to stage encounters with otherness and difference. Indeed, the second part of her travelogue—entitled "The evidence of strangerhood"—is a sustained engagement with various local artists' initiatives and projects which, as Puga describes them, articulate and disseminate the idea that "se puede ser de otra manera" [one can be in other ways].[103] As such, Puga concludes her travelogue with the kind of thesis outlined by Bartra in his work when he writes that "the experience of a fragmented Mexico ... and the constant transgression of all borders, political and cultural, is one of the most stimulating signs in recent years."[104]

In his essay "The Mexican Office", Bartra is ultimately optimistic about the implications of postmodernity in Mexico, "even with all its bitterness". As elsewhere, he underscores transterritorialisation as a particular stimulus for intellectual creation, in which light he singles out especially the border performance art of Guillermo Gómez Peña for offering "the possibility of being Mexican without being subject to a state or territory".[105] Such a manoeuvre, however, disregards the processes of trans-, de-, and reterritorialisation at stake in the "domestic" context, in which regard Molina's and Puga's travel books offer a timely reminder that being at "home" in Mexico can entail no less a sense of displacement than being "abroad" or, indeed, between those two. As Ahmed writes, "there are always encounters with others already recognised as strangers within, rather than just between, nations."[106] Moreover, the motivations with which such "unhomeliness" is evoked in these Mexican women writers' travel texts are various. While each of the travel books explored in this chapter may have come up against its own contradictions to some degree (as does the work of Gómez Peña, of course, as we shall see in the next chapter), they nonetheless articulate paradigms of identity and transit which require and merit scrutiny in these material and theoretical contexts. The "ex-centric" movement on which they rest—a shift which, I would argue, ultimately takes questions of gender and genre into new theoretical terrain—attests as much to the specific materiality of their travel production as to transformations in Mexico's social and cultural geography during the period. Imperfect maps of a "Mexican malaise" these travelogues may be, but ones which nonetheless form part of the complex cartography of the country's experience of late modernity.

5 "Real" Ethnographies

> "I will speak of memory, and the border, and I will share some memories of the border, but I will not tell the truth. I will be lucky if I tell a story."[1]

> "The narration of migrant sorrows constitutes a political act, cast against the prerogatives of neoliberal development and the global division of labour."[2]

The two-thousand-mile-long Mexico-U.S. border has been thematised in a vast array of works of literary fiction, poetry, art, film, theory, and music from both sides of the line. In such works it has been variously conceptualised as a historical wound, a den of sexual licentiousness, an Edenic paradise, and, in the decade of the 1990s, as a privileged theoretical site. As José Manuel Valenzuela Arce points out, "podemos identificar algunos ejes importantes donde se establecen las metáforas y posicionamientos analíticos sobre la frontera, como la ruptura, la pérdida, la traición, el puente, el muro de contención, los intersticios, la transnacionalización o los rizomas" [we can identify some important axes on which metaphors and analytical positions on the border have been based, including rupture, loss, betrayal, bridge, containment, interstices, transnationalisation, or rhizomes].[3] In the past decade, however, scholars in disciplines such as anthropology, cultural, and literary studies have become increasingly sceptical of some of Valenzuela's list of concepts. The propensity to speak of the border and its associated figure of the migrant as figurative tropes rather than as material referents, for example, has meant that "with the border as a dramatic prop, immigrants [have] become symbols in a battle of images."[4] The suspicion about this development appears to be shared by writers and filmmakers of border narratives of late, who in different ways can be seen to be restoring the materiality of that border and undocumented migrants' experience of crossing it to the sometimes theatrical landscape of the region's cultural production.[5] The travel texts considered in this chapter, Rubén Martínez's *Crossing Over: A Mexican Family on the Migrant Trail* (New York: Picador, 2001) and Luis Alberto Urrea's *The Devil's Highway* (New York: Bay Books/Little, Brown, 2004), chart notorious cases of recent failed border crossings; in what follows they are located within this broader cultural shift as well as within material changes in migratory behaviour.[6] Although they speak to such transformations, however, these travel books self-consciously appeal to the fictive in their avowed attempt to tell true stories. Indeed in their imperative and strategic processes of fictionalisation, they not only allow for an encounter with what Lacan calls the Real, but they also illuminate the political possibilities of mourning in a landscape which is literally and symbolically spectral. Drawing on Judith Butler's recent work on vulnerability and mourning, this chapter argues that it is in the journey narrative's long-standing engagement with and ambivalence in respect of "fiction"—alluded to in the first epigraph—that the political voltage of *Crossing Over* and *The Devil's Highway* can be appreciated. In effect, then, like the category of thanatography ("writing about death") to which they owe some debt, these travel accounts are at once both morbid *and* generative.

While more extensive studies of border culture have adopted a welcome transnational perspective in respect of their primary material, as Debra Castillo and María Socorro Tabuenca Córdoba point out, when dealing with this region, "it is important to take both sides—the United States and Mexico—into consideration *or* to be specific about which side one is going to talk about or study" (my emphasis).[7] My focus on these particular authors, therefore, both of whom, notwithstanding their respective affiliations with El Salvador and Mexico, live, work, and publish primarily north of the border, does not seek to privilege their travel narratives in English over the corresponding output in Spanish south of the border. In any case, Martínez's and Urrea's identities, locations, and output in fact complicate precise distinctions between north and south, as do the particular routes of the journey narratives at hand and their bilateral processes of preparation.[8] My concern with these authors' travel books, then, is not about questions of cultural hegemony or spatial limitations. The following analysis rests on the unique character of their travelogues, which speak to specific border traumas in ways which do not find a direct correlate in the fictional Spanish-language travel narratives of, say, Luis Humberto Crosthwaite or Rosario Sanmiguel.[9] A further significant issue which accounts for their selection is that Martínez and Urrea have each attracted critical attention for the assumption of autoethnographic subject positions in their border narratives, an approach which, although valid, has its limitations. In addition to their journey accounts' singular character, the critical reception of these authors' work to date also exposes the limits of some of the interpretative tools in travel-writing studies in the context of Latin America. One of the aims of this chapter, therefore, is to shift the emphasis in the scrutiny of Martínez's and Urrea's work away from the question of positionality in order to consider other less well studied but equally compelling features of their travel texts. Insofar as they illuminate the possibilities of collective mourning, I suggest that Martínez's and Urrea's journey narratives might be better served by the term "ethico-fictive ethnographies", a categorisation which takes a more complete account of the contexts in which they operate. My objectives here are thus consonant with recent attempts by scholars such as Maureen Moynagh, Bill Ashcroft, and Peter Bishop to provide complex yet suggestive political readings of contemporary travel texts in other (largely anglophone) regions of the world.[10] In addition to providing a fuller understanding of these particular journey narratives, therefore, my aim is also to engage in broader questions relating to what Bishop calls "the limitations imposed by western-centric interpretive and defining frameworks," while being attentive "to the emergence [in travel writing] of new postcolonial forms and narrative multiplicities."[11] To begin my discussion I turn to some necessary introductory detail regarding the texts' composition and critical reception.

BORDER TOURISTS?

Both Rubén Martínez and Luis Alberto Urrea have written extensively on the Mexico-U.S. border and on transnational migration in a number of different formats. A creative writer and journalist, Rubén Martínez is the son of a Mexican father and Salvadoran mother, editor of *L.A. Weekly* and frequent contributor to CNN and other media outlets. His first book, *The Other Side: Notes from the New L.A., Mexico City, and Beyond*, captures a strong and often impassioned sense not only of his ambivalent residence in the United States ("my home is L.A. and L.A is an anti-home")[12] but also of his permanent dislocation as a serial border crosser. Although he might count himself a member of similar cultural circles as Guillermo Gómez Peña (whom he credits in the "Acknowledgments" sections of both *The Other Side* and *Crossing Over*), Martínez's conception of the transnational experience is not as felicitous as that of the self-styled *cyber-vato*, say, in *The New World Border* (a work to which I shall return in more detail later), as suggested in the following passage:

> I have lived both in the North and the South . . . trying to be South in the South, North in the North, South in the North and North in the South . . . I must be much more than two. I must be North and South in the North and South.[13]

What is striking here is Martínez's strong sense of contingency, the admission of his own perpetual flux when confronted with questions of identity-in-transit.

Similar questions inform his 2001 work *Crossing Over: A Mexican Family on the Migrant Trail*, which takes the death of three Mexican migrants from the same family in a road accident in Riverside County, California, as its point of departure. In April 1996, Benjamín, Jaime, and Salvador Chávez and five other men were killed, and nineteen injured, when a truck in which they were travelling with their *coyote* (human smuggler) crashed following a high-speed pursuit by the Border Patrol. The incident had been overshadowed by the emergence a few days earlier of video footage similar to that of the Rodney King affair, which depicted Riverside police beating a group of unarmed Mexican migrants by the side of a freeway. Martínez's journeys to sites associated with the victims of that border traffic accident (the locus of their deaths in Temecula, Riverside County, their hometown of Cherán, Michoacán, and their intended destination as agricultural workers of Watsonville, California) shape Martínez's journey in "the[ir] ghost steps across the border" to accompany other Chávez family members who, despite their recent loss, try the same crossing at a later date. In effect, then, in what the author calls "an appointment with the dead",[14] Martínez "goes native" over a period of two years, assuming a life in Cherán in order to contract the services of a local *coyote*. In this respect the book's title resonates as much with the migrants' transnational crossing as with the author's own temporary and, of course, voluntary transformation into a clandestine border crosser. In two parts, the book pays testimony to Martínez's process of acculturation in that provincial village and provides an account of the experience of transnational Mexican migration and settlement in the United States. In premise and structure, therefore, it has certain affiliations with ethnography, as the author takes up residence in the town's only modest hotel, befriends the grieving family, consults townsfolk, and attends the local fiesta, while he waits for an opportune moment to "travel". Chapter titles—which are largely either prosaic, as in Book One ("Home", "Fiesta", "Harvest"), or toponymic, as in Book Two ("Warren, Arkansas", and "St. Louis, Missouri")—reinforce the account's apparent proximity to this "factual" discourse.

Luis Alberto Urrea's border travelogue, *The Devil's Highway* (2004), also builds on a sustained body of work about this region, much of which is based on the author's personal experience. Born in Tijuana to a Mexican father and American mother, Urrea worked as a relief worker in that city before dedicating his career to writing, in the course of which he has produced memoir, short fiction, poetry, novel, and travelogue.[15] In one of his earlier books of "nonfiction", Urrea contends that "If, as some have suggested lately, I am some sort of 'voice of the border,' it is because the border runs down the middle of me. I have a barbed-wire fence neatly bisecting my heart."[16] Urrea's invocation of that fence metaphor—entirely fitting in its *homage* to Gloria Anzaldúa, of course—might seem somewhat melodramatic. Nevertheless, it is effective in symbolizing the extent of his creative engagement with what he calls, in the subtitle of his debut work of *Across the Wire* based on firsthand experience working with the residents of a Tijuana dump, "life and hard times on the border". His later, Pulitzer-prize nominated *The Devil's Highway* re-creates the May 2001 desert border crossing of twenty-six undocumented Mexican migrants. The journey became a *cause célèbre* as a result of its tragic outcome: their *coyote* lost his way and led fourteen of the men to their deaths. "It was," Urrea writes in forthright fashion, "the big die-off, the largest death-event in border history."[17] Charting the border crossing of a group of Mexican "walkers" (many of them former coffee farmers from Veracruz) from Sonora into Arizona, this journey narrative was researched over the course of a year's interviews with figures involved in the debacle from either side, including survivors, mediators, and rescuers, as well as consultation of the extensive documentation related to the affair. Indeed, the book's dedication, to "the dead and . . . those who rescue the living", underscores its "bifocal" intentions. Not an account of a personal journey, therefore (unlike Martínez's travelogue), or one even that Urrea has completed in person, the book marks a departure of sorts as it implies a markedly different subject position as editor and compiler of a journey narrative in which he is ostensibly not a protagonist.

Both Urrea's and Martínez's incursions into the migrant border (crossing) narrative to date have led to the reiteration of long-standing questions relating to travel and power.[18] Although the criticisms levelled at Urrea in this respect relate to an earlier work, rather than to *The Devil's Highway*, they are worth considering here in brief for their relevance to the broader methodological issue I want to address in this section. José David Saldívar extols the virtues of *Across the Wire*, Urrea's account of migrants in Tijuana, in "smuggl[ing] across the U.S.-Mexico border line a discrepant cosmopolitan world that has never been acknowledged by either Mexico or the United States".[19] Nevertheless, he takes Urrea to task over two issues in respect of that book. Saldívar describes how Urrea "cast[s] himself as a positioned geocultural subject" whereby he poses as a sort of countertouristic guide to the border city: "Part travel writer, part observer participant and 'official translator' of the crew of Baptist relief workers he joins," he writes, "[in *Across the Wire*] Urrea documents the heroic struggle of the newly arrived Tijuanans who are largely invisible to the swarms of U.S. tourists who only 'do' the Avenida Revolución."[20] One of the ironies that emerges from this "autoethnographic" position, however, as José Pablo Villalobos has observed, is that the success of Urrea's first book not only encouraged travel-writing aficionados to read his second volume but also to visit the fabled city of Tijuana itself,[21] persuaded no doubt by the author's heady dispatches from that place which, for Saldívar, evoke "the hallucinogenic excitement [of the border], the military structures of eroticism, the intensities and 'rushes' that feel like euphoria".[22] As such, inadvertently, "Urrea too attracts tourists to the sites he puts on the border map for all to see."[23] It is not only, however, that Urrea's first border travelogue has that unwitting outcome (and attests to the long-standing complicity between travel writing and the tourist industry it purports to deplore). Saldívar also sees the author's affiliation with a Baptist charity (for which he works on the Tijuana dump) as a form of "imperial complicity" and he admonishes the writer's failure to acknowledge or explore the issues of power traditionally bound up in the positions of missionary and travelling ethnographer. As a result, for Saldívar, *Across the Wire* ultimately comes up short in terms of its author's failure to be self-reflective.

Rubén Martínez has been taken to task on similar charges in respect of *Crossing Over*. Although praised for his articulation in that book of "new forms of belonging and cultural citizenship", Martínez has also been rebuked for the evident chasm that opens up between the undocumented subjects of his journey narrative and his own "middle-class American" privilege. This privilege, it has been claimed, is emblematised in the Blazer SUV in which he is depicted at various junctures of the book, as well as in the absolute freedom of mobility across the border in both directions he enjoys. Indeed, for María Antonia Oliver-Rotger, Martínez's "ethnographic account of a 'multi-locale' community"[24] also reproduces time-honoured binary oppositions (for example, between a local stasis and a cosmopolitan dynamism) typical of the conventional travel book.

To be sure, many of these criticisms are eminently valid, as there are clearly issues of inequality at stake in the relationship between these authors and the voiceless, in this case undocumented, subaltern subjects who are their objects of "study". The implications of this kind of asymmetry have been debated at length in anthropology, as well as eloquently conceptualised by postcolonial theorists, most notably perhaps by Gayatri Spivak, while in the context of Latin America, they have been considered at length with particular regard to *testimonio*.[25] Nevertheless, in this case, that these authors' "auto-ethnographic" positions are deemed to be based on such a conventional metropolitan-subaltern dialectic (an approach which has been extremely valuable in more general terms in revealing travel writing's complicity with imperial or other hegemonic enterprises) seems to me to be rather a blunt and limited instrument with which to unlock their travel texts. That is, an apprehension of these writers as ethnographers in the conventional sense of that term can be reductive as it fails to take into account not only their "transnational" identities but also the kind of identificatory processes at work in their travel texts. Moreover, a fixation with—and to a certain extent, predetermination of—authorial power in this manner may well turn our attention away from other features of these works which disrupt generic conventions and unsettle orthodox epistemologies. Let me be clear: I am not proposing that we ignore or discount the issues of power at stake in respect of author and subject matter in this context, for these writers are indeed "enmeshed in a world of enduring and changing power inequalities".[26] Nor am I suggesting that Martínez's and Urrea's "transnational" identities in some essentialist way exempt them from the implications of such power relations. Nevertheless, in my view, an exclusive and conclusive focus on these issues in their travel books within conventional critical parameters *is* unsatisfactory (I am not sure, for example, how far I can endorse Saldívar's damning accusation of Urrea's "imperial complicity": it seems to me just a little more complicated than that). Furthermore, this approach can also divert our attention from the potentiality of certain rhetorical and structural features of the category of travel writing (never a straightforward form in any sense) for specific political and ethical ends. After all, as James Clifford and George Marcus remind us, even the inequality at stake in power relations in ethnographic work "is complex, often ambivalent, potentially counter-hegemonic."[27]

Exercised by a similar dilemma, Bill Ashcroft has recently suggested a number of ways in which the contemporary travel writer might "escape the urge to *possess* that knowing entails" and thus shift the emphasis in travel writing away from an aggressive form of knowledge acquisition (such as that of traditional ethnography, for example) to a mode of reflection.[28] First, Ashcroft reminds us that a discourse of the literary in fact allows for the transcultural encounter to be realized, while he also admits to the power of an engagement or metaconversation with discourse itself. Second, he contends that bearing witness to events of a political nature, its attendant risks notwithstanding, "can avoid the pressure of knowing", precisely because it offers the intimacy of identification:

> It might indulge in rage and resentment, but the affect of such identification disempowers the witness ... [s/he] may, by identifying with the witnessed subject and the witnessed trauma, reconcile a history of unequal power relationships.[29]

Significantly, Ashcroft cites Latin American *testimonio* as a form of witness writing *par excellence*, predicated as it is on the kind of trauma which provides the occasion for witnessing. Ashcroft ultimately proposes that it may not be as the result of any theoretical development that the power relationship between observer and informant will be destabilised in travel writing but in fact because of globalisation itself: "For in a globalised, diasporic world, travel may not be a movement between subjectivities, but the very means by which subjectivity is established."[30] Maureen Moynagh's work on the political tourist's archive is also useful for thinking through this dilemma relating to power, knowledge, and travel. Moynagh concedes that political tourists of the ilk of photographer Susan Meiselas (and those so splendidly examined in her book-length study *Political Tourism and Its Texts*) are often implicated in discourses which effectively contradict their projects, especially in the sense that travellers "collect and produce knowledge about 'others' that is used to affirm their own sense of their project and, ultimately, themselves."[31] For Moynagh, however, it is significant that the works of such travellers constitute an archival practice that records "political events" and that they attest to the tourists' "ongoing affective engagement with the struggles they have witnessed". Thus their work combines the affective and the informative, "striving for a power that is both, indeterminately."[32]

It is in the present context, then, that Moynagh's particular conception of the political tourist proves to be suggestive: for both Martínez and Urrea have constructed and contributed to—in inadvertent as well as systematic fashion—a particular archive of work which speaks to the phenomenon of undocumented migration from Mexico and Central America to the United States. While the events of their border travel narratives are not of exactly the same order as, say, the Nicaraguan or Cuban revolutions witnessed by Moynagh's selection of tourists, nonetheless their travelogues' thematization of political issues (to the extent that these border debacles are a product of ongoing geopolitical arrangements) is unquestionable. Nevertheless, there is more at stake than these authors' travel texts bearing witness to border catastrophes in the sense that Ashcroft describes. There is evidence from the quotations cited earlier from Martínez ("I must be North and South in the North and South") and Urrea ("the border runs down the middle of me") that it is indeed mobility in the globalised era which constitutes their subjectivity, as Ashcroft suggests, although of course their positions contrast starkly with the protagonists of their travel books for some of whom mobility leads to death. Through the mobilization of the travel narrative, however, and, especially, by means of their appeal to the fictive, Martínez's and Urrea's books encourage processes of affective identification—a quality which is central to Ashcroft's and Moynagh's proposals—which open them up to possible political and ethical interpretations. In order to fully contextualise those readings in theoretical terms, a short detour to consider material processes of migration as well as shifting cultural conceptions of the border is necessary.

MIGRATION, MOURNING, AND TRAUMA

The history of Mexican migration to the United States is long and tumultuous. Indeed, today's border region (stretching between the Gulf of Mexico and Baja California, a territory originally populated by Mexica or Aztec peoples) has been a magnet for migrants from many cultural and linguistic traditions.[33] At certain junctures—for example, following the signing of the Treaty of Guadalupe Hidalgo in 1848, in the aftermath of the Mexican Revolution and, later, during the Second World War when the dearth of a native labour force led to the foundation of the so-called *bracero* programme of 1942–1964—Mexican migrants have been welcomed and received legally in the north. The revolution of 1910 provoked a mass exodus of Mexicans of all social classes over the border as a result of its sustained violence. A subsequent wave of migration occurred under the *bracero* programme, allowing an estimated 4.5 million Mexicans to migrate north in order to participate in seasonal agricultural work. This bilateral agreement inadvertently provoked a large influx of illegal immigration also, as it "obviated the need . . . to comply with bureaucratic procedures that were both time-consuming and cost-incurring", with the result that "[l]ess scrupulous employers, willing to hire undocumented workers, also served to profit insofar as they could get away with paying lower wages."[34] Following an economic downturn in the 1950s, however, the U.S. government implemented a series of deportations as part of Operation Wetback in an attempt to bring such illegal immigration under control.

During the last three decades of the twentieth and the early years of the twenty-first centuries, the flow of migrants from the south seeking better economic and sometimes political opportunities has not ceased.[35] Nevertheless, the border itself has been increasingly strengthened in this period and, as such, its crossing has become considerably more perilous for those travelling without documents. The 1986 Immigration Reform and Control Act (IRCA), for example, contained several provisions which have had far-reaching effects on Mexican migration to the United States. Whereas on the one hand it offered an amnesty to long-term undocumented residents settled in the north and a legalisation programme specific to agricultural workers, on the other hand IRCA also criminalised the hiring of undocumented workers and allocated greater resources to the Border Patrol for enforcement. Following further fortification by the Clinton administration under Operation Gatekeeper in 1994, a number of official and unofficial interventions took place along the border which included Operation Hold the Line in El Paso, Operation Safeguard in Arizona, and Operation Rio Grande in McAllen.[36] The effects of IRCA, however, as Jorge Durand and Douglas Massey have illustrated in their pioneering work on the Mexican Migration Project, have been entirely counterproductive. Until its implementation, Mexican migratory behaviour had been characterised by its circular nature.[37] Its most common motivation, according to Durand and Massey, is (and remains) related to home acquisition, whereby migration is conceived as a strategic form of compensation for missing and failed mortgage markets in that country. The more recent militarization of the border following IRCA, however, Durand and Massey point out, "has [now] lowered the likelihood of Mexicans returning home" at all. Meanwhile, IRCA's increased resource allocation means that the Border Patrol, with a budget of over $1.3 billion a year, is now the largest arms-bearing branch of the U.S. government next to the military.[38] The border has thus engendered what Saldívar calls "a military machine of low-intensity conflict",[39] and been "plastered with a veritable alphabet of militarisation (USAF, CIA, DEA, DoD, FBI, INS)": it has even been constructed in part with recycled fibreglass left over from Operation Desert Storm.[40] In 2005, a further bill—HR4437—was passed by the U.S. House of Representatives to criminalise all undocumented workers and to construct a 700-mile border fence between the two nations. Although the Secure Fence Act is the only provision of this more recent bill to have been signed into law, the transformation of Mexican immigration in the United States from "a circular movement of workers affecting three states into a national population of settled dependents scattered throughout the country" is now complete.[41]

That U.S. immigration policy has fundamentally altered the normative trajectory of many Mexican migrants into settlement rather than return is not only significant in socioeconomic and political terms: it has also had profound psychological implications. In consequence, the effects of transnational displacement on Mexican migrants have inevitably been conceptualised in psychoanalytic terms. Ricardo Ainslie, for example, contends that the immigrant experience represents "a special case of mourning", which is predicated on the loss of loved ones and places following geographic dislocation. Ainslie employs Donald Winnicott's idea of the "potential space", "an intermediate area of experiencing that lies between fantasy and reality ... a space pivotal in the management of ... separation and dislocation",[42] to theorise certain spaces (such as the Chinatowns or Little Italys which proliferate in urban locations across the globe or, in his case, the flea market of La Pulga in Austin, Texas) where immigrants have sought to re-create lost worlds.[43] While such an account might fail to take into consideration how long-term, transnational connections might transform the mourning process,[44] more permanent migrants could well be susceptible to a related neurosis, precisely as a result of their inability to return home. As the stricter enforcement of border controls has engendered a 500 per cent rise in migrant fatalities since the mid-1990s, tales of disappearance and death on the border have inevitably been on the increase. As such, as Alicia Schmidt Camacho points out, stories of loss and death are the *sine qua non* of the contemporary border experience. In fact, Camacho argues, "undocumented status might [itself] constitute a melancholic condition for migrants in the U.S." For those for whom the option of return to Mexico has been foreclosed, the idea of home may well take on the qualities of a lost object, the absence of which, in Freudian terms, threatens the "integrity of the border crosser's personhood", engendering related feelings of guilt and distress.[45] Ainslie's depiction of the migrant experience as a process of mourning and Schmidt Camacho's emphasis on its melancholic character are both important studies of undocumented migrants with therapeutic and symbolic value. For the purposes of this study, they have a particular thematic currency, reminding us of the (habitual rather than exceptional) psychic trauma—in addition to physical harm—incurred in border crossing at this site as well as others. These psychoanalytical studies also have a theoretical resonance for my discussion. Whereas in melancholia, bereavement consists in not letting go and involves, "due to the incorporation of the object in order to preserve it ... *the loss of the self*" (original emphasis),[46] by contrast in mourning, in letting go of what has previously given meaning to the world, there is the possibility of a changed or different future. It is precisely a form of this process—what Wendy Wheeler calls "the healthy mournings of something we might call *post*modernity"—which is at stake in Martínez's and Urrea's travel texts.[47] In what follows, therefore, rather than focus on the psychological implications of migration, I want to consider how these journey narratives of border trauma might provoke productive and collective processes of mourning by means of certain formal and thematic features. My reading of these books and the context in which they operate is thus also informed by psychoanalytical frameworks, although not in the purely Freudian sense in which the work of Ainslie, Schmidt Camacho, and other travel/writing scholars in related areas have been invested to date.[48] Rather, I first invoke Lacan, whose notion of the Real provides a useful way of looking at the symbolic functions and cultural conceptions of the border to date, a brief survey of which I now consider.

The Mexico-U.S. border—constituted for over 1,200 miles by the Rio Grande and elsewhere by little more than a barbed-wire fence[49]—bisects an area in which cultural and linguistic hybridity are thrown into relief by the proximity of two countries and (at least) two cultures determined and sustained by their asymmetrical relationship. The border region is thus a contact zone in every sense of Mary Louise Pratt's term, one which has been adapted for use in this particular context by Saldívar as the "*transfrontera* contact zone".[50] A corollary of the border's multicultural history and identity (one which encompasses not only "Hispanic" and "Anglo" but, as mentioned earlier, also a significant number of indigenous cultures and histories) is its polyvalency. As Claire Fox observes, it "is a place where urban and rural, national and international spaces simultaneously coexist, often in complex and contradictory ways."[51] While the border region has undergone significant shifts in respect of its identity and geography throughout history,[52] the borderline itself has been variously imagined in a range of different cultural and historical texts, the affective trajectory of which has been traced by Valenzuela. As he points out, in the wake of the U.S.-Mexican War and the 1848 Treaty of Guadalupe Hidalgo the border underwent a process of metaphorisation as a form of "ruptura" [rupture] from the newly independent but seemingly also impotent Mexico and later, following the selling off of its territories (under the Gadsden purchase), as a profound "pérdida" [loss].[53] This loss (of land and citizens) threw into relief the newly postcolonial country's sense of uncertainty and was not long afterwards attributed a greater degree of corporeality in the form of the metaphor of the scar or wound.

This particular strain of vocabulary has been significantly reconfigured in recent decades. In her 1987 work *Borderlands/La frontera*, something of an *ur* text in border studies, Gloria Anzaldúa appropriates that traumatic terminology in the development of her own embodied theory and subjectivity of *mestiza* consciousness. Famously, she configures the border as "a 1,950 mile-long open wound/dividing a pueblo/running down the length of my body/staking fence rods in my flesh/splits me splits me".[54] Notwithstanding her tendency to essentialise U.S.-Mexico relations as well as to perpetuate a somewhat dubious modern-premodern dichotomy in that work, Anzaldúa's image of the "borderlands" has served, particularly in the north, "as a popular locus for discussion of the breakdown of monolithic structures",[55] including paradigms of ethnicity, gender, and sexuality. Indeed, as Javier Durán points out, thanks to Anzaldúa, "la frontera, the borderlands, ha llegado a reemplazar a Aztlán como el paradigma simbólico referencial más importante del chicanismo actual" [the frontier, the borderlands, has supplanted Aztlán as the most important symbolic paradigm in today's Chicano politics].[56] Like his radical feminist counterpart, Guillermo Gómez Peña has also invoked the border as a "privileged site of operations."[57] For the post-Mexican multimedia performance artist, the border and borderlands are everywhere: "Everyone is now borderígena", he says in the trademark Spanglish of his post-literary hypertext *The New World Border*, "meaning a native of the great border region".[58] Gómez Peña's revised global cartography is a utopian one, an imagined end of century geography in which no centres remain and there are no "others". His post-national configurations of the border and the migrant have in turn been validated by various critics and theorists such as Homi Bhabha, Sergio Gómez Montero, and Nestor García Canclini, who have in different ways (rather unquestioningly) endorsed his ideas.[59] Bhabha, in *The Location of Culture*, for example, cites Gómez Peña in support of his notion of hybridity and "in-between" spaces, describing the performance artist's work as inventive and interventionist, part of "an insurgent act of cultural translation".[60]

While on one level Anzaldúa's and Gómez Peña's conceptions of the border might be theoretically seductive, their universalist thrust has a potentially pernicious normalising effect. Indeed, a number of writers from north and south have begun to show signs of frustration with the kind of theorizing undertaken (and widely appropriated) during the 1990s, as a result of which the border became "the trope *du jour*—of the postmodern condition".[61] As George Yúdice, in *The Expediency of Culture*, laments, "'the border culture' . . . has become susceptible to poaching by the ubiquity or 'border crossing' of capital or transnational artists", whom he accuses of "not do[ing] enough justice to the specificity of place".[62] The migrant voice in Gómez Peña's work, for example, is a highly articulate and privileged one, which has been widely re-cited, as mentioned, in what Eduardo Barrera calls a "quasi-incestuous relationship [that] becomes a circuit that excludes primary referents".[63] Nevertheless, it is not only that Gómez Peña's and others' deracinated representations effectively erase the physical frontier as well as the flesh-and-blood migrant, as Castillo and Tabuenca Córdoba and others have noted, but also that they run the risk of entrenching colonialist practices, by subordinating if not silencing artistic expression produced on the Mexican side of the border.[64] Moreover, as Pablo Vila astutely observes, in an exhaustive critique of the border theories of Anzaldúa, Gómez Peña, Emily Hicks, and Renato Rosaldo, the very idea of *crossing* borders requires some caution and potentially some modification, as "the fragmentation of experience can lead to the *reinforcement* of borders instead of an invitation to cross them" (my emphasis).[65] Whereas the idea of an elastic or expansive borderlands is also attractive, given that the Mexican migrant—confronted by pervasive obstacles of "race" and gender wherever s/he goes—continually faces crossing the border "even if s/he is in Chicago",[66] Vila further advises against the homogenization of that line. "It is one thing," he sums up, "to write about the metaphor, but quite another to cross it daily."[67]

What becomes evident from this necessarily abbreviated overview of the border's myriad cultural and symbolic formulations is that it appears to operate in concert with an experience of the Real. According to Jacques Lacan, the Real is the unknown that is located at the limit of our symbolic universe. It is that which cannot be known: a "traumatic otherness that cannot be represented or incorporated by the subject in language."[68] The Real both precedes and comes after the Symbolic: "it is that which resists symbolization absolutely."[69] A paradoxical concept, the Real upholds but at the same time undermines our social reality, remaining the same but becoming transformed within the Symbolic. As a limit place to the Symbolic and the Imaginary, therefore, the Real is implicitly associated with trauma and anxiety: as Dylan Evans describes, "It is this character of impossibility and of resistance to symbolisation which lends the real its essentially traumatic quality."[70] The Real also has associations with the body "in its brute physicality", as a "traumatic kernel at the core of subjectivity".[71] Indeed, for Slavoj Žižek, "*on account of its traumatic/excessive character, we are unable to integrate it into (what we experience as) our reality, and are therefore compelled to experience it as a nightmarish apparition*" (original emphasis).[72] In popular culture, Žižek claims, the anxiety associated with the Real can present as a particular form of traumatic recurrence: as a return of the dead.[73] One frequently cited instance of the Real is AIDS, which has been variously conceived as a form of divine retribution, a punishment for homosexuals, or as plot to stem population growth in Africa: "explanations [which] circle around the same brute fact of the disease which carries on regardless of the reasons attributed to it."[74]

The Mexico-U.S. border—indifferent, as one might expect, to the often conflicted attempts at its representation (as Martínez has it at the end of *Crossing Over*, "there is no border: the line is an idea")[75]—would seem to offer another persuasive example of the dimension of the Real. It occupies a literal and symbolic position of liminality, of course, in respect of the imaginaries of the two countries it bisects, yet its historical "persistence" has that paradoxical quality of sustaining and undermining their geopolitical positions and associations. Moreover, the affiliations of the border with trauma are many, whether in the form of the regular fatalities that occur at its crossing or as a result of the drug-related violence of recent years, or the inflated hysteria with which it is regularly depicted on CNN's *Lou Dobbs Tonight*. In this light, Martínez's and Urrea's travel books can be read as more than part of a counterdiscourse to that postmodern theorizing both of this site and of the figure of the migrant described previously. On one level, they confer, along with other examples of this more recent corpus of border texts, another, particular symbolic function on the Mexico-U.S. border in the history of its continually shifting signification: that of a site of "dark travel" which has engendered a sub-genre of "thana"-travel narratives (travel accounts about death).[76] On another level, however, in retracing the fatal border crossings of undocumented migrants, these morbid travelogues bring into focus a landscape that is both literally and symbolically spectral. In effect, they offer an encounter with the Real, speaking to its traumatic return in the form of what Martínez calls the migrants' "ghost steps".

ETHICO-FICTIVE ETHNOGRAPHIES

The strategy which allows for that encounter in Martínez's and Urrea's travel texts and which constitutes the source of much of their affective and political power is their appeal to the fictive. This strategy also has a particular provenance in generic terms. Indeed, the mediation of fact and fiction is one of the central and more notorious features of travel writing's famed hybridity. According to convention, travel writing brokers a highly ambivalent encounter between the two as "writers avail themselves of the several licences that are granted to a form that freely mixes fact and fable, anecdote and analysis."[77] In the most extreme cases, of course, travellers' tales have been seen to be equivalent to lies.[78] Indeed, for Debbie Lisle, the combination of fact and fiction in the travel book cannot be divorced from the legacy of colonialism and its separation of knowledge into academic and popular forms of information. Lisle dismisses purely "literary" engagements with the formal, aesthetic, and stylistic elements of travel writing as "depoliticising because they fail to take account of how both form and content are complicit in wider discourses of power."[79] She suggests that the "discourse of literary genre" in fact works against any transgressive potential in travel writing's ambivalent relation to fact and fiction, as it is arrested by its positioning within a hierarchy of literature. Whereas on one level accounting for her own study's preferred lack of sustained engagement with the formal properties of its selection of travel books, on another level Lisle's position—as a political scientist—seems overly categorical in its refusal to allow for a broader and more subtle consideration of form in contexts beyond the anglophone tradition with which she engages (like other critics, she cites *Los autonautas de la cosmopista* by Julio Cortázar and Carol Dunlop as a laudable example of the countertravel parody).[80] In this concluding section, I want to reconsider the role of fiction in Martínez's and Urrea's travelogues. My aim is to illustrate how the "fictive" in a broad sense operates expediently and tactically in their narration of border traumas. Indeed, I argue that we might ultimately read their works as "ethico-fictive ethnographies", a term I invoke to take account both of the issues of positionality discussed earlier in this chapter *and* their travelogues' deployment of figurative discourses within a broader philosophical context.

While less obviously dependent on certain figurative strategies in its narrative composition than Urrea's thana-border-travelogue, Martínez's

Crossing Over nevertheless speaks to the *centrality of the fictive* in travel of this particular kind and at this particular site in a number of different ways. In what is on one level a claim to personal legitimacy in the endeavour, and in what Oliver-Rotger describes as "a long flashback",[81] like other travel writers Martínez makes intermittent recourse to autobiography at certain junctures of his account of the journeys of undocumented Mexican migrants. For Dennis Porter, of course, such a combination in the travelogue of exploration in the world with self-exploration is a marker of the most interesting travel books, enabling "a dialogic encounter with others".[82] Yet in *Crossing Over* this self-exploration is invariably undertaken secondhand and involves processes of invention that are resonant of what Marianne Hirsch calls "postmemory". Postmemory is distinguished from memory, according to Hirsch, by "generational distance and from history by deep personal connection": it is a particular form of memory "because its connection to its object or source is mediated not through recollection but through *an imaginative investment and creation*" (my emphasis).[83] Thus, Martínez's journey south from Los Angeles to Mexico, we learn at the beginning of *Crossing Over*, retraces the road trips of his father as "a pudgy teenager with slicked-back hair . . . devour[ing] the nocturnal landscape from the cramped cab of a 1948 Ford double-axle truck" (24) selling American knickknacks with his own travelling salesman father in the early 1950s. For Martínez's "wide-eyed" father, "Mexico was a grand adventure" (24). The trip to Cherán for the author himself, therefore, constitutes a process of "swimming against the tide, drawn by memory", to a Mexican town which he sees as "somehow, a more radical version of what I grew up with back in Los Angeles, in between the Old World . . . and the New" (30). This is not only about legitimacy, therefore, but about a telescopic process of identification whereby Martínez invokes and extrapolates on the "wanderlust" of his own migrant precursors. This is elaborated most clearly towards the end of the book:

> I see Mexicans pour into Los Angeles, I see them on the banks of the Mississippi in St. Louis. I see their brownness, I see my own . . . when they are denied their Americanness by US immigration policy, I feel that my own is denied as well. They are doing exactly what my father's parents and my mother did. They are doing exactly what all Americans' forebears did. (217)

There is a considerable level of justification to Martínez's process of identification here, which is certainly part of the normative coding of interventions into the contemporary cultural politics of the Mexico-U.S. border. Nevertheless, although apparently blind on some occasions to the implications of his presence in Cherán (in one instance portraying himself as "the eternal peacemaker" when his very presence as a visiting journalist stokes existing animosity between a Chávez family member and a rival crew of *norteños*,

[67]), on others he acknowledges the limits of his identification as well as its adverse affects: "I did not live what the migrants lived," Martínez confesses, "but I saw a bit of what they saw" (17).[84] Later, when accompanying Raúl Tapia to work in Warren, Arkansas, where he has lived for decades and where his family are "hurtling into the middle class" (228), Martínez admits that his presence patently reinforces the structures of power between employer and employee: "I start to regret the interview . . . suddenly the old man who's challenged the cops and held his own in cantina brawls is the obedient help" (233). Such incidents attest to this traveller's capacity for a certain degree of self-reflexivity.

If Martínez's postmemorial interventions are predicated on processes of elaboration and invention, what also becomes evident in *Crossing Over* is the myriad ways in which the firsthand migrant experience is inexorably invested in different forms of storytelling. For example, the serial undocumented border crosser is compelled to create an assemblage of aliases in order to escape detection from the Border Patrol, as Martínez describes in the case of Rosa, who makes several attempts to cross:

> Today she was María. Later she'd become Julia, Rita, Iris, and Alejandra. Names she remembered from magazines: movies stars, rock singers. Names of people she'd fantasized being. Names of people that in some way, she was becoming. (180)

In this context fictive processes are not only tactical but multilayered: even the alias has its own imaginative provenance as it is mediated through various forms of popular culture. In *The Devil's Highway*, Urrea identifies a similar phenomenon and the resulting difficulty in deciphering the identity of *coyotes*, who are known only by their code names. The smuggler in his case, for example, was known by at least three different aliases: Rooster Boy, on account of his distinctive haircut, Chuy, a boyhood moniker and a diminutive of Jesús (in one of those instances in which fact is stranger than fiction, he shares with the eponymous son of God the same birthday and the dubious biblical association of leading men into the desert), as well as Méndez, a pseudonym of his own adoption, and his girlfriend's surname. Nevertheless, it is not only that the identity of the border crosser rests on processes of fictionalisation. Storytelling skills, points out Martínez, are also their central preserve, whether for the prodigal migrant like Wense, who, in retelling the outcome of his earlier crossings, "casts himself as a hero" in "an adventure to add to Cherán migrant lore" (148), or the survivors of Urrea's desert disaster, who on their rescue in a slightly different context became "paid professional narrators . . . Like all good bards, they embellished and expanded their narratives" (187). Here, the fictive has in the main to do with strategies of survival and expediency, and is a central part of the journey experience, rather than about the kind of aesthetic privilege assumed by Lisle. Notwithstanding, Martínez's own recourse to certain figurative analogies to portray particular aspects of the migrant experience in the course of his account is striking as well as fitting. In an encounter with the Tapias in their home in Wisconsin, for example, he describes how the journey from "poverty in Cherán" to "American comfort and mobility" seems "to have taken place in the span of an MTV video jump cut" (228). Similarly, on Rosa's detainment on the border she is led to the Border Patrol's headquarters' "high tech surroundings . . . a surreal jump-cut from the mountain terrain she'd just hiked through" (180). These visual metaphors are deployed in both instances to convey something of the chasm but also speed of difference (in terms of landscape, culture, language) which inform border crossings at this site. To be sure, such comparisons have a tendency to familiarise as much as derealise: in doing so, they speak to the paradox of postmodernity, whose pervasive virtualisation leads to the irony that, as Žižek puts it, "we begin to experience 'real reality' itself as a virtual entity."[85]

If *Crossing Over* speaks to the operation of the fictive in the contemporary border crossing experience more generally, *The Devil's Highway* flaunts in formal terms that undecidability between fact and fiction that has long authorised but also troubled travel writing in the eyes of readers and critics. Notwithstanding its classification as "current events" on the back cover (and the flyleaf listing of the author's other border travelogues as "nonfiction"), the book evokes a panoply of literary devices and fictional rhetorical strategies. The title, despite appearing to be predicated on what to the uninitiated might seem a metaphorical allusion, in fact refers to the particular section of the desert in Pima County (spanning the Growler and Granite Mountains) at which the migrant protagonists of this journey narrative crossed into the United States. In time-honoured fashion, the book's subtitle, "A True Story", functions to mitigate any possible figurative interpretation of the book's name and content. The epigraph (song lyrics from an Arizona rock band The Sidewinders) and some of its chapter titles ("A Pepsi for the Apocalypse", "Bad Step at Bluebird"), however, derive self-consciously from the creative imagination, while the acknowledgments and index sections at the back of the book confer on the account the conventional apparatus of (academic) nonfiction.

The prefatory "Author's Note" is a further critical yet ambivalent feature of the volume's paratextual apparatus. On one level it enumerates the many material sources of Urrea's account ("Border Patrol reports, sheriff's department reports, legal documents, testimonies and trial documents, correspondence, and many hours of taped interrogations and confessions" [xv]) and on another level, it lays bare its fictional obligations. "Where actual words are known, they are presented as straight dialogue", we learn, although the vast majority of exchanges, shown without quotation marks in the text proper, are presented as "possibilities based on recollections and inferences from the recorded testimonies" (xvi). Explicit as he is about the inevitability and expediency of such strategies in the preface, however,

Urrea is also keen to draw attention to his work as craft and labour. In contrast to the Mexican author Ana García Bergua, therefore, who, as we saw in the previous chapter, makes apparent light of her learning in the preface to her travel book, for even first-time readers of his work, Urrea leaves no doubt as to the kind of legitimacy he wields in respect of the subject matter. In doing so, he inserts himself into a long-standing but *sui generis* travel-writing tradition, evidence of which we have also seen elsewhere in this study. The idea of endurance (and to some extent travail) on which *The Devil's Highway* rests is underscored in quantitative as well as qualitative terms: not only is the book based on a year's research and travel undertaken by the author, but it "consumed four leather-bound notebooks of about 144 pages each" (xvi). This reference to what appears to be both an idiosyncratic and anachronistic form of writing equipment (of an indeterminate but actually quite specific length!) points to the level of weight and durability afforded the material gathered by Urrea: the traveller's leather-bound books connote a more significant and prestigious shelf life, say, than the easily erasable and potentially fragile electronic documents of a laptop computer. The use of high-quality notebooks, moreover, alludes not only to the particular tools of the gentleman traveller (as, for example, in the contemporary "nomadic" tradition of Bruce Chatwin's moleskins mentioned in Chapter 2) but also to the eccentricity which characterises the variations of that figure in the anglophone travel-writing tradition especially.[86] For the Mexican American author to assume this particular mantle is a subversive gesture in some respects in a journey narrative about *homo sacer*,[87] which is essentially devoid of the kind of cosmopolitanism normally associated with the persona of the leisured, eccentric journeyman. Indeed, in a final effort to sustain the preface's transparency, Urrea concludes with an attempt to shore up his authority. While admitting that the book is not an account of a journey of his own design, nonetheless in the final paragraph he assures the reader of his intimacy with its route, the time of year as well as the meteorological conditions under which it took place.

The concluding paragraph of Urrea's preface might be read as an iteration of the traveller's conventional assertion of cognitive superiority, dependent as it is on the repetition of "I know . . . I know . . . I know" (xvi). To be sure, there is an anxiety about epistemology at work here. Nevertheless, it is in fact only one of two explicit occasions in *The Devil's Highway* in which the first-person narrative voice is employed (the other being the extensive "Acknowledgments" section at the book's end which elaborates in greater detail on the personal and print sources consulted in the course of the book's composition). For obvious reasons, this journey account—like large parts of Martínez's—is narrated primarily in the third-person narrative voice. At times it is the perspective of the "objective", omniscient narrator that is inferred, in a narrative punctuated by verbs in the perfect conditional tense and conjectural turns of phrase such as "it seems likely". At others, the narrative is focalised in free indirect discourse through the different points of view of a range of characters involved in the affairs from both sides of the line.[88] Indeed, it is largely due to the pervasive use of free indirect discourse, in addition to its "postmodernist" fragmentary and sometimes even nonlinear structure, that Urrea's *The Devil's Highway* reads at times like a work of contemporary narrative fiction.

Narrative focalisation not only "enhances the polyvocality of the text by bringing into play a plurality of speakers and attitudes",[89] however, but it encourages multiple and sometimes conflicting processes of identification with various figures, particularly in Urrea's thana-travel book. For example, there is the case of the coyote on the morning of the "walkers'" departure:

> It is easy to imagine Méndez's morning. Oh, shit, the alarm clock's going off too early. Six o'clock. Last night was Friday, party night. Dancing with Celia. Drinks. Cigarettes and laughter, up too late with the gang. Too late, too tipsy to make love. (98)

Or elsewhere, the migrants as they rage and despair whilst getting increasingly lost in the desert:

> It was that goddamned Méndez: no, it was this evil desert. No, it was the pinche Mexican government that picked the homeland apart ... No, it was the Migra, it was the gringos, it was the US government and its racist hatred of good Mexican workingmen just trying to feed their children! They themselves were the fools. (134)

This multiplicity of perspectives is especially effective when it is used to lay bare the difficulty of establishing truth at critical junctures of the border crossing, such as when the coyote leaves the migrant walkers, ostensibly to fetch water. This episode is related over several pages in *The Devil's Highway* using direct and reported speech, free indirect discourse, and even an excerpt from the U.S. Department of Justice INS investigation report, as in the following passage:

> Méndez called them together.
> Or they called Méndez to their meeting.
> Méndez told them they were doomed if he did not go find help.
> He told them he could make it to water, and possibly to help. It would be better if he went alone: he could move quicker.
> No, he took his partner.
> All right, then two were better than the big group. Two definitely had a better chance.
> Those two chicken shits planned the whole time to book out of there and save their asses.

"Real" Ethnographies 111

> Or the members of the group told Méndez he had to save them and go alone to find water. And then, at the last second, he said he'd take Lauro.
> He was afraid Lauro might die soon without help.
> They pressed their money on him and asked him to get water, to get a vehicle and a driver.
> Or he demanded money to save them.
> Or he extorted money so he'd have funds for himself after he saved himself and left them to die.
> They said, 'Take all we have.'
> Or he said, 'Give me all you have.'
> They collected seventy dollars.
> They collected ninety dollars.
> Or they collected two hundred dollars.
> Or he stole three hundred dollars.
> The money confuses more than the terrain, more than the hyperthermia. Versions of the dollar amount, and what the dollars implied, never end. (151)

The democratising quality of this narratological strategy is further buttressed by the use of the second-person narrative voice at other key junctures of both travel accounts. As in other instances of the "you" voice discussed in this study, the second-person narrator interpellates the reader in direct and unvarnished fashion. Indeed, in *The Devil's Highway*, the reader is enjoined to assume a plethora of different subject positions which are likely to be unfamiliar and potentially even anathema, as, say, in the case of the Border Patrol officer: "You're not a border guard, you're a beat cop. Your station chief urges you not to hang out in small-town restaurants, not to frequent bars . . . Liberals don't like you. Conservatives mock and insult you" (23). Critically, over several grim and graphic pages, the second-person narrative voice also calls upon the reader of this travel account to occupy the most hazardous of places in the desert, that of the migrant undergoing the six stages of hyperthermia leading to death:

> You piss in your hands, or in whatever container you might have. You try not to dribble a single drop, and you lament all the priceless piss wasted on the desert floor . . . Proteins are peeling off your dying muscles. Chunks of cooked meat are falling out of your organs, to clog your other organs. The system closes down in a series. Your kidneys, your bladder, your heart. They jam shut. Your brain sparks. Out. You're gone. (128–129)

In this respect, Emile Benveniste's suggestion that the second person "assumes or calls up a fictive person" is apposite.[90] The narrative persona is doubly fictive in this particular instance, because to write about dying or death presupposes a radical departure from fact in itself. As Ivan Callus writes in respect of (auto)thanatography, "its distance from fact and the realisable are assumed ... literature has its credibility and credulity strained before (auto)thanatography."[91]

The "fictive" in a broad sense thus looms large in Martínez's and Urrea's travel books but not, as Lisle suggests, "because it is positioned as an ideal that the travelogue can never achieve."[92] Rather, it is implicated in an essential and enabling range of functions. First, it is an inherent part of the process of recall of Martínez's narrative "I" who frames the account of the Chavezes' border crossing story through postmemory, primarily as a means of identification. The experiences of undocumented border crossers themselves (both migrants and *coyotes*) as detailed in these travelogues are also heavily invested in imaginative processes. To write about and from the perspective of death, moreover, as do both writers in the course of relating these border disasters, presupposes a necessarily fictive narrative voice. The very nature of these journeys and their outcomes compels them to certain creative obligations, then, which, rather than point up their accounts' lack of "authenticity" and thus "failure" as travel books, have an affective charge which opens them up to political and ethical interpretations.

Judith Butler's recent work is useful in conceptualising what is at stake here. In *Precarious Life: The Powers of Mourning and Violence*, a book written in the aftermath of and as an engagement with the fallout of the attacks of 9/11, Butler proposes that the recognition of our corporeal vulnerability can be a basis for new forms of sociability and political community. "Loss has made a tenuous 'we' of us all," she writes, meaning that "each of us is constituted politically in part by virtue of the social vulnerability of our bodies."[93] Vulnerability can yield an experience of humility and dependence whereby we can forge connections with others who are at risk of violence.[94] Butler contends that mourning can have a collective political, rather than a privatising, function, therefore: it can become "a resource for politics ... by which we can develop a point of identification with suffering itself."[95] Although *Precarious Life* emerged as a response to a very specific act of violence in recent history, the ideas Butler explores in that book may have wide application, not only because of their unquestionable interdisciplinary relevance, but also because of the book's "radically distinct vocabulary [which] demonstrates the extent to which there has been a near fatal exclusion from public debate in recent years of solidaristic and compassionate values."[96] Butler's Levinasian inspired critique has not been without its critics, however, and it is precisely for its own universalist assumptions that it has been taken to task. While acknowledging her attempt to create a positive ontology from loss, Malini Johar Schueller advises caution in thinking about the uses of vulnerability as Butler proposes, for "a recognition of this vulnerability will not eliminate the problem that some vulnerabilities are more vulnerable than others, that some vulnerabilities matter more than others." As Schueller writes, "vulnerability shouldn't become a competitive sport, but it cannot simply be an equalizer either."[97] In a discussion of a corpus of travel narratives which seem to be restoring the materiality of the border and the flesh-and-blood migrant to a landscape from which arguably the "human" had until recently been emptied out, it might seem peculiar to recur to a theoretical framework which has in turn been problematised for its own insensitivity to "particular striations". Nevertheless, while mindful of their shortcomings, I contend that Butler's ideas still have currency and application to the process of thinking through the affective implications of the travel books at hand. While vulnerability may have its problems as a global politics, in this specific context (in which the inequalities of the global system are thrown into such sharp relief), there are details of Butler's thinking which have a particular pertinence. Indeed, although her emphasis on vulnerability and the "face" have attracted most notice to date, relatively little attention has been paid to her emphasis at the beginning of *Precarious Life* on the narrative dimensions of understanding acts of violence. Butler notes how in explaining the events of 9/11 the first-person point of view was shored up to the exclusion of accounts that might otherwise have decentred it. She underscores the need to emerge from such a unilateral narrative perspective in order to understand our positions as global actors and to consider the ways in which our lives are profoundly implicated in those of others. Butler writes: "The ability to narrate ourselves not from the first person alone, but from, say, the position of the third, or to receive an account delivered in the second, can actually work to expand our understanding of the forms that global power has taken."[98]

Butler's ideas about the political possibilities of heterodox narrative perspectives, together with her reconceptualisation of vulnerability and mourning, in my view, offer a suggestive framework within which to conceptualise the broader implications of the thematic and formal properties of Martínez's and Urrea's travel books. In addition to their currency in the context of a form which has historically rested on the surety, authority, and cognitive superiority of the first-person narrator, Butler's proposals also allow us in this instance to move beyond more conventional psychoanalytical approaches to narratives of migration such as those mentioned earlier. Both *Crossing Over* and *The Devil's Highway* seek to narrate particular traumas that have occurred as a result of recent increases in border enforcement. In doing so, on a narratological, thematic, and symbolic level, Martínez's and Urrea's travelogues effectively decenter the narrative "I" that has long been operational in conventional journey accounts.[99] As such, they test the boundaries of traditional definitions of travel writing such as Jan Borm's, whose admittedly tentative delineation of the travel book in any case also seems to hint at the fragility of its parameters: "*Any narrative characterised by a non-fiction dominant that relates (almost always) in the first person a journey or journeys that the reader supposes to have taken place in reality while assuming or presupposing that author, narrator and principal character are but one or identical*" (original emphasis).¹⁰⁰ Moreover, the affective implications of such strategies in these travelogues—multiple processes of identification and the assumption of a plurality of different subject positions—have a broader political resonance. One of Butler's principal points is that the failure to tell accounts of violence from positions beyond that of the first person means that others cannot be included in processes of mourning: "They cannot be mourned because they are always already lost." This leads to a derealisation of the Other which means that "it is neither alive nor dead, but interminably spectral."¹⁰¹ It is through recourse to fictive processes that the undocumented migrants' border experiences and fatalities can be enunciated in Martínez's and Urrea's travel accounts. In their processes of naming and reclaiming the identities of the dead migrants and in their narrative constructions of those border crossings, therefore, these travel books gesture towards the possibility of collective mourning in the way that Butler suggests: repudiating a generalised melancholia which prohibits grief for the Other, they suggest in their very forms that "we develop a point of identification with suffering itself."¹⁰²

These travelogues' appeal to the fictive, then, a discourse with which travel writing has long had an ambivalent relationship, not only allows for an encounter with the "Real" but is also the source of their affective and political voltage. Although of course the reader may never achieve a comparable level of experience as that of the flesh-and-blood migrants on this trail, *Crossing Over* and *The Devil's Highway* are unambiguous in their insistence that their deaths be mourned. Moynagh contends that political tourists belong to a particular category of traveller who seeks to participate in or manifest solidarity with a political struggle taking place elsewhere in the world. For Martínez and Urrea, however, the border struggle is not "away" or "abroad" but very much at "home", yet they are as equally engaged in "affectively resonant processes of identification and affiliation across international borders and boundaries of cultural difference" as their more conventionally "distanced" political tourist counterparts.¹⁰³ Moreover, if their "ethico-fictive ethnographies" can contribute to "something like a transnational literacy" (as Moynagh suggests can be the result of the work of political tourists), then it might well be worth risking their contradictions too. And whereas, as Clifford suggests, there are no neutral or uncontaminated terms or concepts with which to talk about travel or, indeed, its narratives, the "ethico-fictive" modifier at least brings to bear a sense of the implications (and complications) of these books' operations within formal and epistemological contexts.¹⁰⁴ It also brings into focus the expediency of the reformulation of certain interpretative tools in the study of travel writing of Latin America.

Afterword

"We are not all . . . 'on the road' together."[1]

An endist paradigm has long haunted travel, its writing, and even to some extent more recently its study. Evelyn Waugh's 1946 announcement ("I do not expect to see many travel books in the near future")[2] is one of the most renowned statements of the form's imminent demise, while the idea of "entropology" from Claude Lévi-Strauss (whose abhorrence of adventure framed the discussion in Chapter 3), relating to what he perceived as travel's final recourse, also persists in memory. Indeed, Patrick Holland and Graham Huggan conclude their study with a discussion of a recent rearticulation of that "revulsion from travel", which appeared in a *Guardian Weekly* debate in the mid-1990s, the same time period that has been under consideration in this book. The contributors to that debate, Holland and Huggan point out, counselled "stay[ing] home, because there is nowhere left to go, because travel is essentially futile, because 'correct' people do not travel"[3] while they conveniently (for some of them were "tourists with typewriters") recommended the travel book as a "purer" and more acceptable form of journey for the new millennium. Thea Pitman, meanwhile, observes a singular tendency in Mexico to abnegate the existence of travel writing at all, a manoeuvre she sees as "signal[ling] the informed, postcolonialist, nature of some contemporary Mexican writers' practice of the genre."[4] In turn, in his inaugural lecture as professor of English and travel writing studies at Nottingham Trent University, Tim Youngs's sardonic recollection of a colleague's dismay that he was writing *another* book on the subject crystallises a perception outside travel-writing studies, if not of the form's impending termination, certainly of the lack of sustainability of its field of study. Nevertheless, Youngs's and others' dismissal of such obituaries are timely and entirely in keeping in the face of the overwhelming evidence to the contrary.[5] That I too am resistant to those terminal assessments goes without saying. Nevertheless, in light of the foregoing it seems fitting to conclude my own study with a recent episode which has announced a putative end of global proportions and which has echoes of the questions explored in preceding chapters.

During the final weeks of bringing this book to completion, an acquaintance knowingly asked whether I had any plans to travel to Mexico. When I offered what I thought would be a disarming "unfortunately not" (for I was on to his insinuation), he countered: "What do you mean, 'unfortunately not'? What about Mexican swine flu?!" In March 2009, Mexico did indeed experience a high number of acute cases of respiratory infection; by mid April a U.S. laboratory had reported two human cases of "swine flu" and on 25 April the World Health Organisation declared the outbreak of the virus in North America a "public health emergency of international concern". Before the month was out, the International Health Regulations emergency committee recommended a change from pandemic influenza phase 4 to phase 5, a position that was revised on 11 June when the WHO invoked phase 6 and announced the first pandemic of the twenty-first century.[6] At the time of writing, seventy-four countries across the world had reported over 94,000 cases of the virus: of those, the United States and Mexico had by far the greatest number of infected inhabitants and deaths (170 and 119, respectively, of a total of 429 mortalities worldwide), although the reporting of statistics in Mexico has been inconsistent and was called into question at an early stage.[7] In the wake of the outbreak, Mexican President Felipe Calderón called for a five-day shutdown of Mexico City, a measure which led to a ban on collective public gatherings, the closure of shops, restaurants, and even churches.[8] As many commentators remarked, drawing on an analogy of the kind we saw in the previous chapter, scenes in that city were reminiscent of cinematic or video-game representations of "post-apocalyptic" worlds (Danny Boyle's *28 Days Later* [2002] and Paul Anderson's *Resident Evil* series [2002–2007] being the most frequently cited and germane comparisons in that respect) (see Figure A.1). Elsewhere, in the outbreak's infancy, notwithstanding that "evidence shows that border screening is an ineffective means of control",[9] France called upon Europe to ban flights to Mexico and, while she rejected that plea, EU health commissioner Androulla Vassiliou advised that travellers forego all but essential trips to that country and to the United States. Indeed, many international airlines cancelled scheduled journeys to Mexico. Meanwhile, the Obama administration in Washington was lobbied about (but discounted) the question of shutting the border with its southern neighbour (a timely reminder, consonant with my argument in Chapter 5, that, as Andrea Noble puts it, "the border's metaphorical status must always be anchored in and set against an understanding of its material reality").[10] Staying at home in this case was not about the topos of exhaustion which so preoccupied those *Guardian* writers of the 1990s, therefore, but rather the attempted but at times ill-judged preservation of well being.

I refer to this episode not to trivialise what in 2009 became a worldwide scare with real dangers to health and life at stake, for the consequences of this strain of disease are serious and hypothetically terminal in physical and economic terms. Although it is not yet known how the outbreak will develop, it is likely that more people will contract and die from the H1N1 strain of influenza in different countries and at different junctures, for, as Michael Barrett points out, "it remains to be seen whether technological

Figure A.1 A deserted Mexico City metro after the 2009 flu outbreak. Rex Features Ltd.

advances have provided the tools to allow us to intervene" as the virus spreads in coming months.¹¹ Furthermore, for a country already hit hard by the global recession and by an escalation in its protracted and violent drugs war along its border with the United States, the flu became more than a public health issue; it quickly exacerbated Mexico's economic concerns. During its temporary quarantine, Mexico City's mayor, Marcelo Ebrard, put the losses to the country's economy (of which tourism accounts for some 8%) at $88 million per day: with the Banco de México already forecasting a fall in GDP of up to 4.8 per cent in 2009 in the light of the global financial crisis, the outbreak was estimated to take out up to a further 0.8 per cent of GDP.¹² Nevertheless, the virus, its fallout, and my friend's immediate "stigmatization" of Mexico also bring into focus a number of issues relating to globalisation, travel, and Latin America that are pertinent to the concerns of this study.

On one level, the spread of this recent flu virus says a great deal (that we perhaps already know) about globalisation. Its rapid diffusion is a result of both its highly contagious character and the world's ever-increasing interconnectedness. That the first victims of the illness to be diagnosed in Britain were a Scottish couple who returned from their honeymoon in Cancún, for example, attests not only to that resort's ascendency to the status of the "new Acapulco" but also to the place of Mexico's Yucatán as a destination currently in vogue in Western Europe for a particular kind of niche travel, the wedding journey. As such, it speaks to the country's continued function as a host for foreign travellers embarked on ever more multiform versions of those paradigmatic journeys to/in the region mentioned in Chapter 1. Nevertheless, "swine flu" potentially puts paid to what, for all its possible problems, might have been a more benign image of this site in a continent in which, in the Western geographical imagination, excess, extreme otherness, and anachronism prevail (and where the more anticipated health risk for the foreign visitor might have been a temporary bout of "Montezuma's revenge"). The flu outbreak might thus consolidate Mexico's fame in travel mythology as a dark and dangerous destination (and, to be sure, there was some inference of that in my friend's provocation). That that more recent exchange reinforces the associations of the episode which opened this book (see pp. 1–2) is a reminder of the obstinacy of myths associated with (travel to) Latin America in the period of neoliberal globalisation, "a contemporary moment of hyper-imperialism and intense conflict between the global North and global South."[13] As we have seen in preceding chapters, contemporary "writer-travellers" of this region engage, contest but sometimes, as result of their internalisation, uphold such myths in what is an uneasy and often compromised practice and form of narrative. In this respect, they are like many of their much heralded "postcolonial" counterparts in other parts of the world, whose oppositional stance to conventional modes of travel, as Holland and Huggan observe, "provides a further alibi for travel writing while still depending on its traditions and its—not least, commercial—cachet."[14] As Paul Smethurst argues, however, while acknowledging the urgency of subversion and of "writing back", "simply seizing the form of travel writing is already a significant step towards establishing postcolonial travel writing."[15] It is precisely the ambivalent interplay between varying degrees of accommodation and negotiation that makes contemporary travel writing of the sort analysed in this book so compelling and worthy of study.

For all the interconnectedness of the world, its allegedly smooth flows of global capital, and the ease (for some, like those Scottish honeymooners) of crossing boundaries and time zones at will, the fallout of and reactions to this outbreak of flu have also underscored another, contradictory side of global processes. If myths are obstinate (but as we have seen, for example in relation to the "emptiness" of Patagonian territories in Chapter 2, also malleable), asymmetries of power seem especially obdurate at present. To the extent that Mexico did not stockpile the same reserves of antiviral drugs as countries in Western Europe and the United States, which claimed to be well prepared for the emergency, the mortality statistics of the flu episode testify to persistent inequalities in the global "free" market economy.

Furthermore, what also transpired in the wake of this outbreak was a particular recrudescence of the local which, as Stuart Hall has observed, "is often a response to globalisation."[16] Indeed, evidence of that resort has been seen throughout this study where, for example in Chapters 3 and 4, indigenised and politicised forms of adventure and strangerhood are invoked by travellers as contestatory positions to the new neoliberal hegemony. The "reach for groundings" in the flu episode, however, presented as rapid attempts by countries across the world to close down the possibility of contact with the flu source in Mexico, manoeuvres which have also been accompanied by a war of and over words. In addition to the calls for the closure of borders and a cessation in air travel, therefore, a battle over what to call this strain of influenza commenced which had insinuation and cultural stereotyping at its core. As Howard Markel and Alexandra Stern have noted, "epidemics always have scapegoats",[17] especially during economic downturns, and, as Barrett points out, "some depressingly predictable examples of infection bigotry have emerged" in this case.[18] The so-called Mexican swine flu is a misnomer on many levels: it is in fact a hybrid assortment of the H1N1 influenza virus from avian, swine, and human strains. Moreover, there is as yet no evidence that the virus emerged from pigs; flu cannot be transmitted through meat; and, in any case, diseases do not have nor do they discriminate between national identities.[19] Nevertheless, in the wake of the spread of this virus across the world, several Asian governments banned imports of Mexican pork, while Egypt carried out a mass cull of its own pigs.[20] Israel's deputy health minister, meanwhile, declared that "swine flu" was an offensive term because it referred to animals considered unclean in Jewish and Islamic faiths: as such, he announced, no doubt to the consternation of Mexicans, that they would call it "Mexico flu".[21] It is worth pointing out, however, that historically Mexico has not been entirely innocent in this kind of blame game. In the 1930s, the Chinese were attributed as the source of a disease outbreak in that country, an episode of "Sinophobic fever" which culminated in the expulsion of Chinese residents from the northern state of Sonora. In 2009, the governor of Veracruz, in a desperate attempt to defend his own state from accusations of being the source of the recent virus, claimed that the strain had originated in "Asia, in China; it came from there, from American visitors and surely from Mexico City and the state of Mexico. It is not associated with the pork industry in the Perote Valley."[22]

These attempts to denominate and disown the virus attest to the readiness of different nations and regions to resort to protectionism and xenophobia, particularly at moments of crisis in the "global community". They also bring into sharp focus the politics in which language is invested. That issue has been one of this study's enduring concerns in respect of the vocabulary of travel in Latin American geographies, in which neocolonial context the recalibration of critical terminology relating to the operation of an inherited narrative form is so necessary. Drawing on a range of theoretical tools, this book has sought to reach for an appropriate language and methodology with which to speak of the complex experiences of and journey accounts by contemporary travellers of Latin America. While Janet Woolf is sceptical of the point of "tinkering with the vocabulary of travel" (to accommodate women in her case), because she sees it as still *"the wrong language"* (original emphasis),[23] I contend that there is much benefit to be had from modifying well, perhaps even, overused terms and concepts in the context of the kind of historically, regionally, and theoretically grounded readings that have been undertaken in this book.

Contemporary Travel Writing of Latin America has been concerned not only with the "politics of mobility" in the region (of which the flu outbreak has been so resonant) but also with its form, for I agree with Debbie Lisle that the "formal aspects of travel writing cannot be divorced from its content."[24] While the material considered in preceding chapters has been largely orthodox in its presentation (that is, taking the form of published books), there has been evidence too of some incipient transgressions in this respect. For example, Mempo Giardinelli's metafictional travel book (Chapter 2), Luis Urrea's "postmodernist" travelogue, and Rubén Martínez's collectivist "photo-travel text" (Chapter 5) in different ways test the boundaries of the "genre" (and of that conversation between fact and fiction), while spectral cyclist Andrés Ruggeri's more recent departure from the book to the blog mentioned in Chapter 3 is also a significant development. Indeed, even Lisle allows that "by embracing the dissolution of sanctified literary boundaries and by encouraging the dissemination of the journey metaphor into other cultural forms, the travelogue can become a more meaningful site for current debates about mobility, location and belonging."[25] My exclusive focus on a particular form of written travel narrative in Latin America, therefore, has not intended to supersede consideration of its many other expressions in the region. These include photographs, films, installations, *retablos*, music, and Web sites, all of which do and will continue to provide a rich source of material for other research in this field and whose burgeoning global reach (and further analysis of which) might lead to some demythologisation of those persistent fictions about Latin America. Indeed, a recent piece of news from Bolivia regarding one of its most fabled tourist attractions is instructive in this regard. The San Pedro prison in La Paz, once notorious for its inmates' violence and drug habits and a long-standing draw for international tourists, many of whom apparently "deemed it better value than the Inca citadel [of] Machu Picchu", has now barred travellers from paying to visit, eat, and take drugs there. After years of turning a blind eye to "bizarre practices which had become the stuff of lore", the authorities were forced into the crackdown, significantly, after tourists uploaded a video of their prison visit to YouTube in February 2009, events which are testimony not only to some regional resistance to exploitative forms of tourism but also to new and ever more accessible forms of journey account.[26] It is in this respect also, in terms of the travelogue's ongoing capacity to mutate (like myths and viruses), that the terminal paradigm I have invoked here can once again be thwarted, notwithstanding the progress of the "Mexican swine flu" or any temporary injunction on travel to that part of Latin America.

Notes

NOTES TO CHAPTER 1

1. Arjun Appadurai, *Modernity at Large: Cultural Dimensions of Globalisation* (Minneapolis: University of Minnesota Press, 1996), p. 64.
2. Dennis Porter, *Haunted Journeys: Desire and Transgression in European Travel Writing* (Princeton, NJ: Princeton University Press, 1991), p. 3.
3. Dean MacCannell, *The Tourist: A New Theory of the Leisure Class* (1976) (Berkeley: University of California Press, 1999), p. 1.
4. Mabel Moraña, Enrique Dussel, and Carlos A. Jáuregui, eds., *Coloniality at Large: Latin America and the Postcolonial Debate* (Durham, NC: Duke University Press, 2008), p. 2.
5. Maureen Moynagh, *Political Tourism and Its Texts* (Toronto: University of Toronto Press, 2008), p. 7.
6. James Clifford, *Routes: Travel and Translation in the Late Twentieth Century* (Cambridge: Harvard University Press, 1997), p. 39. As Clifford notes, in essence travel is "an inclusive term embracing a range of more or less voluntarist practices of leaving 'home' to go to some 'other' place" (p. 66). I am also sympathetic, however, to Clifford's rejection of apparently more "neutral", theoretical terms such "displacement" and "nomadism" as well as his observation that in any case "there are . . . no neutral, uncontaminated terms or concepts. A comparative cultural studies needs to work, self-critically, with historically encumbered tools" (p. 39).
7. Clifford, *Routes*, pp. 38 and 91.
8. Jason Wilson, "Travel Literature", in Verity Smith, ed., *Encyclopedia of Latin American Literature* (Chicago: Fitzroy Dearborn, 1997), p. 803.
9. Mary Louise Pratt, *Imperial Eyes: Travel Writing and Transculturation* [1992] (London: Routledge, 2008), p. 3.
10. Porter, *Haunted Journeys*, p. 10.
11. Cited by Jason Wilson in Alexander von Humboldt, *Personal Narrative of a Journey of the Equinoctial Regions of the New Continent,* abridged and translated with an introduction by Jason Wilson and a historical introduction by Malcolm Nicolson (London: Penguin 1995), p. xxxix.
12. Roberto González Echeverría, *Myth and Archive: A Theory of Latin American Narrative* (Cambridge: Cambridge University Press, 1990), p. 102. Echeverría also notes that "The discovery and conquest of America gave rise to a great deal of travel literature, much of it concerned, even if at times incidentally, with scientific reportage" (p. 100). He underscores the literary quality of scientific travellers' accounts, however, describing their authors as "powerful writers", their stories "fraught with dangerous and droll adventures", p. 104. Indeed, Echeverría's own concern is precisely with illustrating

the powerful influence of scientific travel writing on Latin American literary fiction and narrative more generally.
13. Echeverría, *Myth and Archive*, p. 105.
14. Neil L. Whitehead, "South America/Amazonia: The Forest of Marvels", in Peter Hulme and Tim Youngs, eds., *The Cambridge Companion to Travel Writing* (Cambridge: Cambridge University Press, 2002), pp. 122–138 (at p. 122).
15. For a diverse selection of these works, see Stephen Greenblatt, *Marvelous Possessions: The Wonder of the New World* (Chicago: University of Chicago Press, 1991); Angela Pérez Mejía, *A Geography of Hard Times: Narratives about Travel to South America, 1780–1849*, trans. Dick Cluster (New York: State University of New York Press, 2004); and, for a counterargument to Pratt, Matthew Brown, "Richard Vowell's Not-so-Imperial Eyes: Travel Writing and Adventure in Nineteenth-Century Hispanic America", *Journal of Latin American Studies*, 38 (2006), 95–122.
16. Michael Kowalewski, "Introduction: The Modern Literature of Travel", in *Temperamental Journeys: Essays on the Modern Literature of Travel* (Athens: University of Georgia Press, 1992), pp. 1–16 (p. 1). Nevertheless, the number of studies on twentieth-century travel writing in other regions of the world is growing. These include Charles Forsdick, *Travel in Twentieth-Century French and Francophone Cultures: The Persistence of Diversity* (Oxford: Oxford University Press, 2005); Thea Pitman, *Mexican Travel Writing* (Bern: Lang, 2008), and Loredana Polezzi, *Translating Travel: Italian Travel Writing in English Translation* (Aldershot, UK: Ashgate, 2001), as well as, in the anglophone tradition, Debbie Lisle's *The Global Politics of Contemporary Travel Writing* (Cambridge: Cambridge University Press, 2006).
17. Steve Clark, ed., *Travel Writing and Empire: Postcolonial Theory in Transit* (London: Zed Books, 1999), p. 3.
18. Polezzi, *Translating Travel*, p. 1.
19. Hulme and Youngs, eds., *The Cambridge Companion to Travel Writing*, p. 1.
20. See, for example, Susana Cerda, "Placing Oneself in Conflict Zones: Gabriel García Márquez, Jorge Ibargüegoitia, and Juan Villoro" (unpublished doctoral thesis, University of Warwick, 2008) and Cristina Sánchez-Blanco, "Mempo Giardinelli y la percepción de la región patagónica a través de la experiencia de un viaje: De la construcción literaria del espacio natural y universal de la 'modernidad' a la literatura de viajes contemporánea social y local" (unpublished doctoral dissertation, University of Cinncinati, 2005). Other recent studies on travel writing in/about Latin America include Miguel A. Cabañas, *The Cultural "Other" in Nineteenth Century Travel Narratives: How the United States and Latin America Described Each Other* (Lewiston, NY: Edwin Mellen, 2008); Ingrid E. Fey and Karen Racine, eds., *Strange Pilgrimages: Exile, Travel and National Identity in Latin America, 1800s–1990s* (Wilmington, DE: Scholarly Resources, 2000); Jacinto Fombona, *La Europa necesaria: Textos de viaje de la época modernista* (Rosario, Argentina: Beatriz Viterbo, 2005); and Mónica Szurmuk, *Women in Argentina: Early Travel Narratives* (Gainesville: University of Florida Press, 2000).
21. Lisle, *The Global Politics of Contemporary Travel Writing*, p. 42.
22. Tzvetan Todorov, "The Journey and Its Narratives", in *The Morals of History*, trans. Alyson Waters (Minneapolis: University of Minnesota Press, 1995), pp. 60–70 (at p. 68).
23. Paul Theroux, *Fresh-Air Fiend: Travel Writings 1985–2000* (Boston: Houghton Mifflin Harcourt, 2000), p. 355.

24. See, for example, Iain Sinclair, *Lights Out for the Territory* (London: Penguin, 1995) and *London Orbital* (London: Penguin, 2003), Jorge Macchi, *Buenos Aires Tour* (Turner/MUSAC, 2004), and Hector Perea, *México: Crónica en espiral* (Mexico City: CONACULTA, 1999). For more on Macchi's installation see Eva-Lynn Jagoe, "Buenos Aires and the Aesthetics of Defamiliarization", *Journal of Latin American Cultural Studies*, 17, no. 3 (2008), 299–315.
25. Clifford, *Routes*, p. 85.
26. Kowalewski, *Temperamental Journeys*, p. 12.
27. Pratt, *Imperial Eyes*, p. 226.
28. Paul Fussell, *Abroad: British Literary Travelling between the Wars* (Oxford: Oxford University Press, 1980), p. 202.
29. Forsdick, *Travel in Twentieth-Century French and Francophone Cultures*, p. vii.
30. Gareth Williams, *The Other Side of the Popular: Neoliberalism and Subalternity in Latin America* (Durham, NC: Duke University Press, 2002), p. 2.
31. Thea Pitman, "Mexican Travel Writing: The Legacy of Foreign Travel Writers in Mexico, or Why Mexicans Say They Don't Write Travel Books", *Comparative Critical Studies*, 4, no. 2 (2007), 209–223 (at p. 209).
32. Pratt, *Imperial Eyes*, p. 7.
33. Pratt, *Imperial Eyes*, p. 12.
34. Pratt, *Imperial Eyes*, p. 225.
35. Pratt, *Imperial Eyes*, p. 242.
36. Wilson, "Travel Literature", p. 803.
37. Shannon Marie Butler, *Travel Narratives in Dialogue: Contesting Representations of Nineteenth-Century Peru* (New York: Peter Lang, 2008).
38. Butler, *Travel Narratives in Dialogue*, p. 7. She observes further that those scholars who do look at the travelogues of Latin American travellers "tend to choose for their corpus those narratives that involve Latin Americans' travels abroad to Europe and/or the U.S." (p. 7).
39. Porter, *Haunted Journeys*, p. 19.
40. For more on this, see Chapter 5.
41. Attempts at such an endeavour might ultimately prove to be futile, if not dubious: for, as Patrick Holland and Graham Huggan suggest, a "formal approach to travel writing risks running aground on definitional inconsistencies." In *Tourists with Typewriters: Critical Reflections on Contemporary Travel Writing* (Ann Arbor: University of Michigan Press, 2000), p. 10.
42. Fussell, *Abroad*, p. 202. What distinguishes travel books from guide books, for Fussell, is their inclusion of an autobiographical narrative, a determination which is akin to Porter's description of the nonfictional travel book as one which "combines explorations in the world with self-exploration" (Porter, *Haunted Journeys*, p. 5).
43. Holland and Huggan, *Tourists with Typewriters*, p. 8.
44. Jan Borm, "Defining Travel: On the Travel Book, Travel Writing and Terminology", in Glenn Hooper and Tim Youngs, eds., *Perspectives on Travel Writing* (Aldershot, UK: Ashgate, 2004), pp. 13–26 (at p. 13).
45. Borm, "Defining Travel", p. 17.
46. As Glen Hooper and Tim Youngs point out, however, even this aspect of Borm's definition is "a complicated matter since ideas about non-fiction change over time". "Introduction", *Perspectives on Travel Writing*, pp. 1–11 (at p. 4).
47. For more on the term, see Pitman, *Mexican Travel Writing*, pp. 32–37.
48. Stephen M. Levin, *The Contemporary Anglophone Travel Novel: The Aesthetics of Self-Fashioning in the Era of Globalisation* (London: Routledge, 2008).

49. In respect of the volume's spatial organisation, I take my cue from existing and eminently useful studies of travel writing in other cultural traditions such as those of Holland and Huggan (*Tourists with Typewriters*), Hulme and Youngs (*The Cambridge Companion to Travel Writing*), and David Scott (*Semiologies of Travel: From Gautier to Baudrillard*, Cambridge: Cambridge University Press, 2004), all of which are organised at least in part around different geographical sites or zones. None of them, however, other than in brief or very general terms, consider Latin America in any sustained detail, other than as a "host" site or destination for Anglo or Francophone travellers such as Bruce Chatwin, Henri Michaux, and others.
50. Although not concerned with travel writing as such, I am thinking here of Krista A. Thompson's recent study of visual touristic images of Jamaica and the Bahamas in *An Eye for the Tropics: Tourism, Photography and Framing the Caribbean* (Durham, NC: Duke University Press, 2006).
51. Thomas Perreault and Patricia Martin, "Geographies of Neoliberalism in Latin America", *Environment and Planning A*, 37, no. 2 (2005), 191–201 (at p. 191). As Perreault and Martin observe, "Because of its seemingly omnipresent character" (as an economic orthodoxy now promoted by the IMF and World Bank) "neoliberalism in practice eludes simple identification" so that it is perhaps better to think of "multiple, often contradictory neoliberalisms, that emerge from a diversity of political contexts and generate a range of effects" (pp. 192, 194).
52. Indeed, as Kurt Weyland points out, not all Latin American countries embraced neoliberalism at once: many new democratic regimes in the region postponed structural adjustment, fearing that it would provoke social and political unrest and put the survival of democracy in peril. Chile was one of the earliest of the continent's incipient neoliberal regimes, as "radical market reforms were pushed through [there] but by dictator Augusto Pinochet with the force of arms." See Kurt Weyland, "Neoliberalism and Democracy in Latin America: A Mixed Record", *Latin American Politics and Society*, 46, no. 1 (2004), 135–157 (at p. 136).
53. Perreault and Martin, "Geographies of Neoliberalism in Latin America", pp. 198, 197.
54. Weyland, "Neoliberalism and Democracy in Latin America", p. 151.
55. Weyland, "Neoliberalism and Democracy in Latin America", p. 142.
56. Williams, *The Other Side of the Popular*, p. 8.
57. Williams, *The Other Side of the Popular*, pp. 2, 12.
58. Francine Masiello, *The Art of Transition: Latin American Culture and Neoliberal Crisis* (Durham, NC: Duke University Press, 2001), p. 3. Masiello observes that given Argentina's particular path to democracy, blighted by government corruption, cover-ups and lies, it is no wonder that the mask represents neoliberal democracy's face, "stressing a state-driven theatricality at a time when government has so much to hide and citizens are forced to dissemble in order to comply with the consensus" (p. 4).
59. Masiello, *The Art of Transition*, p. 17.
60. Without essentialising or exoticising the primary travel texts considered in the following chapters, and notwithstanding my reservations about "literary" associations, there are some suggestive correspondences with Deleuze and Guattari's delineation of the category of minor literature in their regard. Deleuze and Guattari propose three main characteristics of minor literature: "the deterritorialisation of language, the connection of the individual to a political immediacy, and the collective assemblage of enunciation." Gilles Deleuze and Felix Guattari, *Kafka: Toward a Minor Literature* (1975), trans. Dana Polan (Minneapolis: University of Minnesota Press, 1986), p. 18.

Notes   125

61. Williams, *The Other Side of the Popular*, p. 1.
62. Another (very different) landmark study to mention in this respect is George Yúdice's *The Expediency of Culture: Uses of Culture in the Global Era* (Durham, NC: Duke University Press, 2003), which considers culture as a complex phenomenon, "located at the intersection of economic and social justice agendas", and how "as an expedient [it has] gained legitimacy and displaced or absorbed other understandings of culture" (pp. 17, 1).
63. As Moraña et al. point out, "The general resistance to postcolonial theory in Latin America is due, in part, to the perception that the concept of neocolonialism should replace that of postcolonialism, which seems to imply—at least in some interpretations of the prefix *post*—that colonial times have passed." One of the other difficulties in adopting postcolonial theories in the context of Latin America lies in their elaboration "mainly in American academe in reference to decolonisation processes that took place, for the most part, after World Wars I and II" (Moraña et al., eds., *Coloniality at Large*, pp. 13, 5).
64. Moraña et al., eds., *Coloniality at Large*, p. 15.
65. Paul Theroux, *The Old Patagonia Express: By Train through the Americas* (New York: Washington Square Press, 1980), p. 416.

NOTES TO CHAPTER 2

1. "La Pampa y el Desierto (que es como se llamaba antiguamente a la Patagonia) son nuestra tierra literaria por antonomasia." Mempo Giardinelli, *Final de novela en Patagonia* (Barcelona: Ediciones B, 2000), p. 17.
2. See Fernanda Peñaloza, "Appropriating the 'Unattainable': The British Travel Experience in Patagonia", in Matthew Brown, ed., *Informal Empire in Latin America: Culture, Commerce, and Capital* (Oxford: Blackwell/Society of Latin American Studies, 2008), pp. 149–172 (at p. 159, n15).
3. Ernesto Livon-Grosman writes that "la literatura de viaje de la zona conserva un grado de especifidad tal que es posible leer estos textos como parte del imaginario argentino, a pesar de que las lenguas en las que fueron escritos no sean siempre el castellano" [the travel writing of the region has such a high degree of specificity that it is possible to read these texts as part of the Argentine imaginary, in spite of the fact that the languages in which they were written are not always Spanish]. "Lo abierto y lo cerrado: el espacio patagónico en la literatura de viaja, *ciberletras*, 5 (2001), http://www.lehman.cuny.edu/ciberletras/v05.html (accessed 21 July 2004). See also his book-length study *Geografías imaginarias: el relato de viaje y la construcción del espacio patagónico* (Rosario, Argentina: Beatriz Viterbo, 2003).
4. See Chris Moss, *Patagonia: A Cultural History* (Oxford: Signal, 2008), p. 90.
5. Peñaloza, "Appropriating the 'Unattainable'", p. 159. Peñaloza notes that, as opposed to Welsh towns, natural sites were in fact named by Argentine explorers who believed that British travellers "should be honoured for their contribution to the knowledge of the area and its inhabitants."
6. Quoted in Moss, *Patagonia: A Cultural History*, p. 213.
7. In respect of such well-trodden territories, Holland and Huggan claim that contemporary travel narratives can only attempt to recapture them through recollection, parody, revision or occasionally refutation. In *Tourists with Typewriters: Critical Reflections on Contemporary Travel Writing* (Ann Arbor: University of Michigan Press, 2000), p. 67.
8. Hernán Santiváñez Vieyra, "La Patagonia a traves de sus viajeros", *Revista de Occidente*, 218–219 (1999), 141–153 (at p. 141).

9. Paul Theroux, *The Old Patagonia Express: By Train Through the Americas* (New York: Washington Square Press, 1980), p. 416.
10. Moss, *Patagonia: A Cultural History*, p. x.
11. Eva-Lynn Jagoe, *The End of the World as They Knew It: Writing Experiences of the Argentine South* (Lewisburg, PA: Bucknell University Press, 2008), p. 12.
12. Jagoe, *The End of the World as They Knew It*, p. 15.
13. Jens Andermann, *Mapas de poder: Una arqueología literaria del espacio argentino* (Rosario: Beatriz Viterbo, 2000), p. 108.
14. Jagoe, *The End of the World as They Knew It*, p. 15. The experience of the South is thus "always a readerly one", she writes (p. 203).
15. Gabriela Nouzeilles, "Patagonia as Borderland: Nature, Culture and the Idea of the State", *Journal of Latin American Cultural Studies*, 8, no. 1 (1999), 35–48 (at p. 39).
16. Jagoe, *The End of the World as They Knew It*, p. 18.
17. Moss, *Patagonia: A Cultural History*, p. 277.
18. Moss, *Patagonia: A Cultural History*, p. 251.
19. Indeed, in terms of Moss's assumption of a lack of a local travel writing tradition, it is also worth noting that Buenos Aires–based publisher Sudamericana recently launched a series of "domestic" travel books, one of the first volumes of which—on the subject of beaches—has been penned by the much respected and fêted Argentine author Alan Pauls, *La vida descalzo* [*Life Barefoot*] (Buenos Aires: Sudamericana, 2006). The other volume published in this series to date, at the time of writing, is Edgardo Cozarinsky's *Palacios plebeyos* [*Plebeian Palaces*] (Buenos Aires: Sudamericana, 2006). I am grateful to Nick Caistor for bringing this series to my attention.
20. Nouzeilles, "Patagonia as Borderland", p. 35.
21. As Iparraguirre elaborates: "La mirada europea era incapaz de proveer a estos grupos humanos de un mínimo lugar de pertenencia simbólica" [The European gaze was incapable of providing these (indigenous) groups with a minimum place of symbolic importance]. In "Patagonia: historia y ficción, Documento histórico y novela: una experiencia de escritura", *Páginas de Guardia*, 1 (2006), 101–116 (at p. 107).
22. The region only became strategically important to Argentina and Chile in the late nineteenth century when both countries sought to colonise the wilderness of their respective territories. For more on the history of the dispute over the region between the neighbouring countries, see Richard O. Perry, "Argentina and Chile: The Struggle for Patagonia 1843–1881", *The Americas*, 36, no. 3 (1980), 347–363.
23. Vieyra, "La Patagonia a traves de sus viajeros", p. 146.
24. Livon Grosman, "Lo abierto y lo cerrado", n.p.
25. See Nouzeilles, "Patagonia as Borderland", p. 37.
26. As Vieyra writes, "Moreno busca institucionalizar la inmensidad y demostrar que la Patagonia era un lugar digno de ser colonizado. Advierte a sus conciudadanos sobre sus potencialidades económicas" [Moreno sought to institutionalise the immense region and demonstrate that Patagonia was a place worthy of colonisation. He highlighted to his compatriots its economic potential], in Vieyra, "La Patagonia a traves de sus viajeros", p. 147. However, as Nouzeilles observes, "the fact that Moreno's text was oriented towards the future should not diminish the performative efficiency of his writing. Writing about Patagonia was in itself a symbolic way of taking possession of its space and its inhabitants on behalf of the state", Nouzeilles, "Patagonia as Borderland", p. 38.
27. Iparraguire, "Patagonia: historia y ficción", p. 109.

28. Nouzeilles, "Patagonia as Borderland", p. 36. As she points out elsewhere, it is in fact since the 1980s especially that Patagonia has begun to feature more strongly in the imagination of the adventure traveller. She attributes this in part to travellers such as Yvon Chouillard, who founded the Patagonia brand of outdoor clothing. See Gabriela Nouzeilles, "Touching the Real: Alternative Travel and Landscapes of Fear", in John Zilcosky, ed., *Writing Travel: The Poetics and Politics of the Modern Journey* (Toronto: University of Toronto Press, 2008), pp. 195–210 (at p. 204).
29. Daniel Buck, "Sequels to a Patagonian Journal", *Americas*, 52, no. 5 (2000), 6–13 (at p. 13).
30. Nicholas Shakespeare, *Bruce Chatwin* (London: Vintage, 2000), p. 537.
31. David Taylor, "Bruce Chatwin: Connoisseur of Exile, Exile as Connoisseur", in Steve Clark, ed., *Travel Writing and Empire: Postcolonial Theory in Transit* (London: Zed Books, 1999), pp. 195–211 (at p. 196). For Taylor, Chatwin's work is characterised in large part by an "aestheticist posture" and in his treatment of the many exilic characters he meets in Patagonia, for example, there is a deliberate erasure of the apparent reason for displacement: "The Chatwinian convention is to elide particularity ... [His technique] is disconcertingly reductive of persons, who are divested of contextualising discussion or life-narrative", p. 202.
32. Taylor, "Bruce Chatwin: Connoisseur of Exile", p. 196.
33. See Manfred Pfister, "Bruce Chatwin and the Postmodernization of the Travelogue", *Literature Interpretation History*, 7, nos. 2–3 (1996), 253–267 (at p. 259). Indeed, for Moss, "[the English author] invented Chatwinlandia, not Patagonia" (Moss, *Patagonia: A Cultural History*, p. 266).
34. Pfister, "Bruce Chatwin and the Postmodernization of the Travelogue", p. 262.
35. Taylor, "Bruce Chatwin: Connoisseur of Exile", p. 204.
36. Paul Magee, *From Here to Tierra del Fuego* (Urbana: University of Illinois Press, 2000), p. 8.
37. As Francine Masiello describes: "The Chilean 'miracle', sociologists have told us, sparkles from the gloss of consensus, a concerted effort—until the recent detention and release of Pinochet—to 'forgive and forget.' Argentine democracy, by contrast, has taken a more fitful path, with five aborted coups between 1987 and 1992 and a continued tradition of public protest, where citizens, ready to denounce government corruption, are answered by cover-ups and lies." Francine Masiello, *The Art of Transition: Latin American Culture and Neoliberal Crisis* (Durham, NC: Duke University Press, 2001), p. 4.
38. The effects of these were striking: inflation decreased, the budget was balanced, and "the restoration of the country's financial credibility abroad facilitated the renegotiation of the foreign debt and new international loans." Gabriela Nouzeilles and Graciela Montaldo, eds., *The Argentina Reader: History, Culture, Politics* (Durham, NC: Duke University Press, 2002), p. 474.
39. Notwithstanding their success, some union leaders opposed these free market reforms as they went against the tradition of Peronism, which had long been a standard bearer for the import-substitution model. See James McGuire, *Peronism without Perón: Unions, Parties and Democracy in Argentina* (Stanford, CA: Stanford University Press, 1997), p. 216.
40. Unemployment rose to 35% in some areas (Nouzeilles and Montaldo, *The Argentina Reader*, p. 474).
41. Luis Alberto Romero, *A History of Argentina in the Twentieth Century*, trans. James P. Brennan (University Park: Pennsylvania State University Press, 2002), p. 320.

128 Notes

42. Kurt Weyland, "Neoliberalism and Democracy in Latin America: A Mixed Record", *Latin American Politics and Society*, 46, no. 1 (2004), 135–157 (at p. 136).
43. Michael J. Lazzara, *Chile in Transition: The Poetics and Politics of Memory* (Gainesville: University Press of Florida, 2006), pp. 17–18. What was later given the name "neoliberalism" was first introduced to Chile by a group of economists influenced by the Chicago School just two years after the 1973 coup. Although perceived by some as a particularly radical and misguided reform, its success was deemed to be worthy of emulation, as Marcus Taylor describes: "Proponents soon referred to it as the 'Chilean model' and claimed that it provided a blueprint for other countries to follow." *From Pinochet to the "Third Way": Neoliberalism and Social Transformation in Chile* (London: Pluto Press, 2006), p. 2.
44. José Joaquín Brunner, "Notes on Modernity and Postmodernity in Latin American Culture", in John Beverley, José Oviedo, and Michael Aronna, eds., *The Postmodernism Debate in Latin America* (Durham, NC: Duke University Press, 1995), pp. 34–54 (at p. 48). For more on Brunner's work, see Hernán Vidal, "Confronting the Catastrophes of Modernity: The Cultural Sociology of José Joaquín Brunner", in Anny Brooksbank Jones and Ronaldo Munck, eds., *Cultural Politics in Latin America* (Basingstoke, UK: Macmillan, 2000), pp. 158–184.
45. Brunner, p. 48. Martín Hopenhayn claims that "This collapse has given rise to a certain sense of existential bereftness, of having been orphaned ... the much-debated end of ideologies is ... an absence of any prospect of personal 'redemption' through a revolutionary movement, or of any possibility of 'contexualising' a personal project with reference to a national one." Martín Hopenhayn, "Globalisation and Culture: Five Approaches to a Single Text", in Brooksbank Jones and Munck, eds., *Cultural Politics in Latin America*, pp. 142–157 (at p. 152).
46. Beck cites as an example of this context the conflict over technology policy: "In the conflicts over nuclear power plants or reprocessing facilities ... employers and labour unions, the supporters of the traditional technology consensus, have been forced into the spectators gallery. The conflicts are now carried out directly between the state power and citizens' protest groups, and therefore in a *completely changed social and political scenario* and between agents who at first glance seem to have only a remoteness from technology in common". In *Risk Society: Towards a New Modernity*, trans. Mark Ritter (London: Sage, 1992), p. 202 (original emphasis).
47. Sepúlveda has lived for some years also in Gijón, Spain, where he has established book festivals dedicated to Latin American fiction and crime fiction. Since his relocation to Europe he has achieved considerable international success with his own novel-length fiction, which has also been widely translated. This includes *Un viejo que leía novelas de amor* (Barcelona: Tusquets, 1994 [1989]) [*The Old Man Who Read Love Stories*, trans. by Peter Bush, London and Chicago: Arcadia, 2002] and *Mundo del fin del mundo* (Barcelona: Tusquets, 2004 [1991]) [*World at the End of the World*].
48. Luis Sepúlveda, *Patagonia Express* (Barcelona: Tusquets, 1995), p. 11. All translations of this text are from Luis Sepúlveda, *Full Circle: A South American Journey*, trans. Chris Andrews (Melbourne: Lonely Planet, 1996). Page references to the English edition are given in square brackets.
49. Pfister, "Bruce Chatwin and the Postmodernization of the Travelogue", p. 260.
50. Casey Blanton, *Travel Writing: The Self and the World* (New York: Twayne, 1997), p. xiv.

51. Theroux, *The Old Patagonia Express*, p. 416.
52. For more on this idea see Joy Logan, "'Discovering the Real': Travels in Patagonia", *Romance Studies*, 21 (1992), 63–70.
53. Holland and Huggan maintain that the detached stance of the nomad-individualist is at the heart of Chatwin's "special" appeal: "this is Chatwin the blond flirt . . . using travel as a come-on. Do you want me? Or do you want to be me?" In *Tourists with Typewriters*, p. 169.
54. Michael Cronin, *Across the Lines: Travel, Language, Translation* (Cork: Cork University Press 2000), p. 33.
55. Miguel Angel Quemain, "'No soy un escritor chileno': Entrevista con Luis Sepúlveda", *Quimera*, 121 (1993), 20–24 (at p. 21).
56. Tim Youngs, "Punctuating Travel: Paul Theroux and Bruce Chatwin", *Literature and History*, 6, no. 2 (1997), 73–88 (at p. 74).
57. The unrest in Chile in the early 1970s also looms large over Chatwin's journey in *In Patagonia*. For example, whilst in Gaimán, at the heart of Welsh Patagonia, Mrs Jones, on hearing that morals "back home" are down, tells him: "And they're down here too. All this killing. You can't tell where it'll end." Bruce Chatwin, *In Patagonia* (London: Vintage, 1998 [1977]), p. 29.
58. Indeed, it is significant that environmental concerns such as the deforestation of the Amazon region, an issue on which Sepúlveda cements his friendship with Captain Palacios in Chapter 10, and dolphin hunting, the subject which frames his anecdote of Panchito Barría in Chapter 6, also feature as a backdrop to the adventures in this part of the book.
59. We might note that in their affiliation, as in the encounter with Carpintero, Sepúlveda and Palacios's collaboration marks another salient feature of late or reflexive modernity, the establishment of new kinds of community, which effectively transcend geographical boundaries. For more on this phenomenon see Roland Robertson, "Glocalisation: Time-Space and Homogeneity-Heterogeneity", in Mike Featherstone, Scott Lash, and Roland Robertson, eds., *Global Modernities* (London: Sage, 1995), pp. 25–44 (at p. 31).
60. This is complemented by other references made to such concerns elsewhere in Sepúlveda's work, as well as by further biographical details. For example, he has written an eco-crime novel, *Yacaré*, which is concerned with the same subject of the illegal hunting of endangered crocodiles and his 1989 novel *Mundo del fin del mundo* is similarly concerned with illegal whaling (Sepúlveda himself has also worked for Greenpeace in the past).
61. Sepúlveda has also won a number of literary prizes for his fiction. For more on this see John Hassett, "Luis Sepúlveda: *Nombre de torero, Patagonia Express, Historia de una gaviota y del gato que le enseño a volar*", *Chasqui*, 26, no. 2 (1997), 149–151 (at p. 149).
62. There is some debate about the terms used to describe the region. As Catherine Davies points out, "South America" is used as a geographical term to distinguish the part of the American continent south of Central America (that is, south of the Panama Canal) whereas "Latin America" is a widely used term, deriving from French imperial discourse, which, as Davies puts it, is effectively "a misnomer". Carlos Fuentes famously proposed that the most accurate term to describe the entire region is "Indo-Afro-Iberoamerica". For a succinct summary of that debate, see Catherine Davies, ed., *The Companion to Hispanic Studies* (London: Arnold, 2002), pp. 1–4.
63. Not long afterwards, of course, in 1997, Michael Palin would go on to publish a travel book of the same name as Sepúlveda's English translation, based on a BBC series about a journey around the Pacific Rim.
64. Personal communication with Janet Austin (commissioning editor, Lonely Planet), 9 December 2002.

65. The details of the episode entail a confrontation between farmhands and Indians led by the Spanish anarchist Soto and the army at Jaramillo station. The soldiers opened fire precipitously and, as a result, hundreds of insurgents were shot beside graves they had been forced to dig themselves.
66. For more on the commodification of ethnic autobiographies, see Graham Huggan, *The Postcolonial Exotic* (London: Routledge, 2001), pp. 155–176.
67. See Nicholas Murray, *Bruce Chatwin* (Bridgend, UK: Seren Books, 1993), p. 43.
68. Huggan, *The Postcolonial Exotic*, p. 15.
69. Brennan charts a tendency in Third World literature of recent decades (1980s and 1990s) to capture a large market because, he argues, "the perceived collapse of activist options drove a huge number of the disenchanted into the compensations of books at a time when Western governments were busy retaliating against decolonisation and the progressive social legislation launched by [earlier eras] . . . Politics was in the large part what its audience was hungry for." In *At Home in the World: Cosmopolitanism Now* (Cambridge: Harvard University Press, 1997), p. 200.
70. Huggan, *The Postcolonial Exotic*, p. 15.
71. Michael Cronin, *Translation and Globalisation* (London: Routledge, 2003), p. 121.
72. Andrew Graham-Yooll, "Light at the End of the Tunnel: The New Writers of Latin America", *The Antioch Review*, 52, no. 4 (1994), 566–579 (at p. 566).
73. Brennan, *At Home in the World*, p. 184.
74. For more on Polanski's film version see Bernard Schulz, "Lo difuso de la política en la versión cinematográfica de *La muerte y la doncella*", *Revista chilena de literatura*, 56 (2000), 127–134.
75. Catherine Boyle, "Violence in Memory: Translation, Dramatization and Performance of the Past in Chile", in Brooksbank Jones and Munck, eds., *Cultural Politics in Latin America*, pp. 93–112 (at pp. 103–105).
76. Nelly Richard, *Residuos y metáforas: Ensayos de crítica cultural sobre el Chile de la transición* (Santiago: Cuarto Propio, 1998), p. 71.
77. Cronin, *Across the Lines*, p. 123.
78. Giardinelli, *Final de novela en Patagonia*, p. 52. All further references to this edition will be given in parentheses after quotations in the text and all translations are my own. Catalan publisher Ediciones B established the Premio Grandes Viajeros in conjunction with Iberia Airlines in 1998.
79. Holland and Huggan, *Tourists with Typewriters*, p. 206.
80. Eric Leed, *The Mind of the Traveller: From Gilgamesh to Global Tourism* (New York: Basic Books, 1992), p. 7.
81. Giardinelli is the author of several novels including *Luna Caliente* [*Sultry Moon*] and *Santo Oficio de la Memoria* [*The Holy Office of Memory*] (for which he won the Rómulo Gallegos prize) and volumes of short fiction. In 1996 he founded a cultural and educational organisation in his native Chaco, a tropical region in the country's northeast. See www.fundamgiardinelli.org.ar. For a detailed bibliography of his work and a video interview, http://www.audiovideotecaba.gov.ar/areas/com_social/audiovideoteca/literatura/giardinelli_bio2_en.php (accessed 14 November 2008).
82. Cristina Sánchez-Blanco, "Mempo Giardinelli y la percepción de la región patagónica a través de la experiencia de un viaje: De la construcción literaria del espacio natural y universal de la 'modernidad' a la literatura de viajes contemporánea social y local" (unpublished doctoral dissertation, University of Cinncinati, 2005), p. 2.

83. Ali Behdad, *Belated Travellers: Orientalism in the Age of Colonial Dissolution* (Durham, NC: Duke University Press, 1994), p. 3.
84. Also worthy of mention here is Adrian Giménez Hutton, who in 1998 meticulously retraced the Englishman's route in order to test the veracity of *In Patagonia*. In the course of his journey Hutton attempts to interview various residents (or their descendants) who had met the English writer and takes photographs of similar scenes as those captured by Chatwin, which are included in his own volume, *La Patagonia de Chatwin* (Buenos Aires: Sudamericana, 1999).
85. Julio Cortázar and Carol Dunlop, *Los autonautas de la cosmopista: un viaje atemporal Paris-Marsella/Les autonautes de la cosmopiste ou un voyage intemporel Paris-Marseille* (Buenos Aires and Paris: Muchnik/Galliard, 1983).
86. Loredana Polezzi, *Translating Travel: Contemporary Italian Travel Writing in English Translation* (Aldershot, UK: Ashgate, 2001), p. 210.
87. Iain Chambers, *Migrancy, Culture and Identity* (London: Routledge, 1994), p. 10. The convergence between travel and writing is predicated, for Chambers, on the fact that "[writing] starts from known materials—a language, a lexicon, a discourse, a series or archives—and yet seeks to extract from the limits of its movement, from the experience of transit, a surplus, an excess, leading to an unforeseen and unknown possibility."
88. Juan Pablo Spicer-Escalante, "Time Is Money: Eduarda Mansilla's Gendering of Modernity in *Recuerdos de viaje*", Women Travellers in Latin America seminar, Centre for Travel Writing Studies, Nottingham Trent University, 26 November 2008.
89. It begins: "Niño aún, la lectura de las aventuras de Marco Polo, de Simbad el Marino y de las relaciones de los misioneros en la China y el Japón publicadas en los *Anales de Propaganda Fide*, hecha en alta voz en el refectorio del colegio, despertó en mí un vivo deseo de correr tierras" [As a child, reading aloud in the school canteen the adventures of Marco Polo, Sinbad the Sailor and of the missionaries in China and Japan published in the *Anales de Propaganda Fide*, stirred a nascent desire in me to visit other lands]. Francisco P. Moreno, *Viaje a la Patagonia Austral 1876–1877*, estudio preliminar de Raúl Rey Balmaceda (Buenos Aires: Sol/Hachette, 1969 [1879]), p. 27.
90. Andermann, *Mapas de poder*, p. 122.
91. Pérez is as common a surname in the Hispanic world as, say, Smith in the English-speaking domain.
92. Tim Cahill, *Road Fever: A High-Speed Travelogue* (London: Fourth Estate, 1992).
93. A slightly different complexion of contemporary anglophone adventure in the region is represented by Redmond O'Hanlon, the title of whose *In Trouble Again: A Journey Between the Orinoco and the Amazon* (London: Penguin, 1989) gives a sense of the character of his journey there. Indeed, Holland and Huggan describe O'Hanlon as "The Benny Hill of the tropics" who "careens around the train forests of Borneo and Brazil with an almost demented enthusiasm". See Holland and Huggan, *Tourists with Typewriters*, pp. 78–81.
94. Debbie Lisle, *The Global Politics of Contemporary Travel Writing* (Cambridge: Cambridge University Press, 2006), p. 96.
95. Nouzeilles, "Touching the Real", p. 197.
96. Tschiffely's journey was recorded in his book *Southern Cross to Pole Star* (London: Heinemann, 1933). The South American leg of Tschiffely's journey was more recently retraced by the British adventurer James Greenwood, the account of which was published as *No Guns, Big Smile: South America by Horse* (London: Pelham Press, 1992).

132 Notes

97. Vieyra, p. 150.
98. Tschiffely's later journey was published as *This Way Southward: An Account of a Journey through Patagonia to Tierra del Fuego* (London: The Book Club, 1941). In a travelogue which begins with a visit to his old equine friends, Mancha and Gato, from the first epic ride he accounts for his switch to a motorised form of transport. Although not abandoning the saddle completely ("I proposed to make side-trips to the interior of the Andes on horseback or foot"), he confesses that: "I have had my full share of long-distance riding. Now I leave the field to others, wishing them all the luck I have had", *This Way Southward*, p. 49. With the Ford at his disposal, Tschiffely completed his trip to Tierra del Fuego and back without a single breakdown.
99. Famously, at the end of his journey on board the *Beagle*, Darwin wrote that "The plains of Patagonia frequently cross before my eyes; yet these plains are pronounced by all wretched and useless. They can be described only by negative characters; without habitations, without water, without trees, without mountains ... The plains of Patagonia are boundless, for they are scarcely passable, and hence unknown: they bear the stamp of having lasted, as they are now, for ages, and there appears no limit to their duration through future time." *The Voyage of the Beagle: Journal of Researches into the Natural History and Geology of the Countries Visited During the Voyage of HMS Beagle Round the World, Under the Command of Captain Fitz Roy, R.N.* (Chatham, UK: Wordsworth Classics, 1997), p. 477.
100. There is a vast literature on the sublime, which as a concept has been conceived in different and sometimes contradictory ways throughout history. For an overview of writing on the idea, see Peter de Bolla, *The Discourse of the Sublime: Readings in History, Aesthetics and the Subject* (Oxford: Basil Blackwell, 1989), and *The Sublime: A Reader in Eighteenth-Century Aesthetic Theory*, ed. Andrew Ashfield and Peter de Bolla (Cambridge: Cambridge University Press, 1996). For more on the sublime in nineteenth-century travellers' accounts of Patagonia, see Fernanda Peñaloza, "Ethnographic Curiosity and the Aesthetics of Othering: Nineteenth-Century British Representations of Argentine Patagonia" (unpublished doctoral thesis, University of Exeter, 2004).
101. Sánchez-Blanco, p. 3. She goes on: "Es una Patagonia decadente y empobrecida que nada tiene que ver con aquella que va buscando el turista que visita esta tierras ... las llanuras son símbolo del fracaso del progreso que auguraban futuros mejores para las tierras patagónicas [It's a decadent and impoverished Patagonia which has nothing to do with that which is sought by the tourist visiting the region ... the plains are a symbol of the failure of the progress which augured a better future for Patagonian lands], pp. 4–5. In a later, short article on the eve of Nestor Kirchner's assumption of the presidency in 2003, Giardinelli returned to this theme, writing, in the light of the Peronist's own former governorship of the Patagonian state of Santa Cruz, that "todos somos patagónicos" [we are all Patagonians]: "ese límite final de nuestra misma geografía ... está en emergencia como nunca pero a la vez— ojalá—en vísperas de una extraordinaria oportunidad" [that final limit of our geography ... is in crisis as never before but at the same time—let's hope—on the threshold of an extraordinary opportunity]. "Todos somos patagónicos", http://www.todoteca.com.ar/modules.php?name=News&file=print&sid=48 (accessed 25 July 2007).
102. Maps are of course deeply implicated in a colonial history of cartography. For more on this see J. B. Harley, "Deconstructing the Map", in John Agnew, David N. Livingstone, and Alisdair Rogers, eds., *Human Geography: An*

Essential Anthology (Oxford: Blackwell, 1996), pp. 422–443; and Andrew Thacker, "Journey with Maps: Travel Theory, Geography and the Syntax of Space", in Charles Burdett and Derek Duncan, eds., *Cultural Encounters: European Travel Writing in the 1930s* (Oxford: Berghahn, 2002), pp. 11–28.
103. Romero, *A History of Argentina in the Twentieth Century*, p. 297.
104. Romero, *A History of Argentina in the Twentieth Century*, p. 297.
105. Zygmunt Bauman, *Wasted Lives: Modernity and Its Outcasts* (Cambridge: Polity, 2004), p. 22.
106. Bauman, *Wasted Lives*, p. 117.
107. Arjun Appadurai, "Disjuncture and Difference in the Global Cultural Economy", in Mike Featherstone, ed., *Global Culture: Nationalism, Globalisation and Modernity* (A Theory, Culture and Society Special Issue) (London: Sage Publications, 1990), pp. 295–310 (at p. 295).
108. Michel Foucault, "Of Other Spaces", trans. Jay Miskowiec, *Diacritics,* 16, no. 1 (1986), 22–27 (at p. 24). Foucault distinguishes between two distinct configurations of space: utopia and heterotopia. Utopia are sites with "no real place" which present "society in a perfected form".
109. Kevin Hetherington, *The Badlands of Modernity: Heterotopia and Social Ordering* (London: Routledge, 1997), p. 43. Hetherington's point is that heterotopia is a pertinent concept for conceptualising modernity itself as a process of social ordering that encompasses both freedom and control. "Modernity is defined by the spatial play between freedom and control," he writes, "and this is found most clearly in spaces of alternate ordering, heterotopia" (p. 18).
110. Foucault, "Of Other Spaces", p. 24.
111. Using the example of a mirror, Foucault suggests that it can function as both utopia and heterotopia. As a "placeless place" and in opening up an "unreal, virtual space . . . behind the surface" it has a utopian function. Foucault, "Of Other Spaces", p. 24.
112. Foucault, "Of Other Spaces", p. 27.
113. Nouzeilles, "Touching the Real", pp. 201, 207.
114. Foucault, "Of Other Spaces", p. 27.
115. Lisle, *The Global Politics of Contemporary Travel Writing*, p. 190. In the heterotopia, as Lisle explains, "the perfectly ordered utopian ideal is never closed off from alternative mappings that take place within the very boundaries that the authorial vantage point marks out", p. 189.

NOTES TO CHAPTER 3

1. Dennis Porter, *Haunted Journeys: Desire and Transgression in European Travel Writing* (Princeton, NJ: Princeton University Press, 1991), p. 12.
2. Claude Lévi-Strauss, *Tristes Tropiques*, trans. John and Doreen Weightman (London: Penguin, 1992), p. 17.
3. Peter Hulme, "Travelling to Write (1940–2000)", in Peter Hulme and Tim Youngs, eds., *The Cambridge Companion to Travel Writing* (Cambridge: Cambridge University Press, 2002), pp. 87–101 (at p. 92).
4. Lévi-Strauss, *Tristes Tropiques*, pp. 17–18.
5. Porter, *Haunted Journeys*, p. 267. A contemporary example of such a traveller in the anglophone tradition is provided by Patrick Leigh Fermor, who sums up the tenor of his mountaineering trips to Peru and Bolivia with the Andean Society in the early 1970s thus: "Pleasure is the watchword and it tinges all our doings with comedy and charm." In *Three Letters from the*

Andes (London: John Murray, 1991), p. 6. Fermor is one of a number of contemporary travellers who, for Patrick Holland and Graham Huggan, use "their travel writing . . . as a means of confirming their identities and consolidating their status as imperial national subjects". *Tourists with Typewriters: Critical Reflections on Contemporary Travel Writing* (Ann Arbor: University of Michigan, 2000), p. 15.

6. Named after Senators Jesse Helms and Dan Burton, who sponsored it, the act extended the existing embargo to apply to foreign companies trading with Cuba.
7. A paradigmatic example in this respect, and something of a "classic" of contemporary travel writing, is Robyn Davidson's *Tracks* (London: Picador, 1980), the account of her solo journey by camel across the Australian desert, which was covered by *National Geographic*. In relation to Ruggeri's route, other anglophone cyclists who have been drawn to the transcontinental South American sojourn include Rupert Attlee, *The Trail to Titicaca: A Journey through South America* (Chichester, UK: Hindon/Summersdale Press, 1997), and Anne Mustoe, who followed the "Che Trail" by bike in *Che Guevara and the Mountain of Silver: By Bicycle and Train through South America* (London: Virgin Books, 2007). See also http://www.annemustoe.co.uk. (accessed 9 August 2007)
8. Ali Behdad, "The Politics of Adventure: Theories of Travel, Discourses of Power", in Julia Kuehn and Paul Smethurst, eds., *Travel Writing, Form and Empire: The Poetics and Politics of Mobility* (London: Routledge, 2009), pp. 80–94 (at p. 81).
9. The history of Che imagery was recently commemorated in an exhibition at the Victoria and Albert Museum in London. *Che Guevara: Revolutionary and Icon* (7 June–28 August 2006) took as its starting point the 1960 portrait of Guevara photographed by Alberto Díaz Korda, which is possibly the most reproduced image in the history of photography. For more, see http://www.vam.ac.uk/vastatic/microsites/1541_che/ (accessed 20 August 2007) and the exhibition catalogue edited by Tricia Ziff, *Che Guevara: Revolutionary and Icon* (London: V&A Publications, 2006). As Maureen Moynagh points out, however, the consumption of the image of Che "has a great deal more to do with a willingness to accept the status quo than it does with a desire to transform the world." In *Political Tourism and Its Texts* (Toronto: University of Toronto Press, 2008), p. 138.
10. Alma Guillermoprieto, "The Harsh Angel", in *Looking for History: Dispatches from Latin America* (New York: Vintage, 2001), pp. 73–86 (at p. 75).
11. The journal was transcribed and published by his widow Aleida March. It was first published in English in 1995.
12. Jorge Castañeda, *Compañero: The Life and Death of Che Guevara*, trans. Marina Castañeda (New York: Alfred A. Knopf, 1997), p. 46. As Moynagh observes, "The book . . . was ultimately published because of who Ernesto Guevara later became rather than because of any intrinsic interest it may hold—although it is certainly not devoid of intrinsic interest." Moynagh, *Political Tourism,* p. 151.
13. This is an obvious reworking of the phrase "Darwin's delay", which has been coined to describe the twenty-three year gap between Charles Darwin's return from the voyage of the *Beagle* in 1836 to the publication of the *Origin of the Species*, based on material accrued during that trip, in 1859. The delay has been attributed in part to Darwin's fear at the heretical nature of his ideas about evolution. "Guevara's delay" was due to rather more prosaic concerns: the need to sit examinations in order to complete his medical degree.

He returned from the journey with Granado in July 1952 and sat final exams in April 1953. For more on the chronology of events, see Jon Lee Anderson, *Che Guevara: A Revolutionary Life* (New York: Grove Press, 1997), pp. 71–99.
14. Ernesto "Che" Guevara, *The Motorcycle Diaries: A Journey around South America*, trans. Ann Wright (London: Fourth Estate, 1996), p. 12.
15. The phrase is from Moynagh, *Political Tourism*, p. 151.
16. Guevara, *The Motorcycle Diaries*, pp. 59, 135.
17. Ricardo Piglia, "Ernesto Guevara: The Last Reader", *Journal of Latin American Cultural Studies*, 17, no. 3 (2008), 261–277 (at p. 267).
18. See María Josefina Saldaña-Portillo, "'On the Road' with Che and Jack: Melancholia and the Legacy of Colonial Racial Geographies in the Americas", *New Formations*, 47 (2002), 87–108 (at p. 106).
19. Geoffrey Shullenberger, "That Obscure Object of Desire: Machu Picchu as Myth and Commodity", *Journal of Latin American Cultural Studies*, 17, no. 3 (2008), 317–333 (at p. 327).
20. Guillermoprieto, "The Harsh Angel", pp. 75, 76.
21. Castañeda, *Compañero*, pp. 44, 54.
22. Moynagh, *Political Tourism*, p. 17. She continues: "As a cultural practice that foregrounds social and cultural contradictions, not least the axes of power that produce inequality, even as it strives to overcome them through its promotion of social transformation, political tourism offers at minimum an exemplary instance of the workings of modernity. Its utopian impulse toward social transformation—its effort to imagine across nations, ethnicities, classes and genders—however much it remains caught in the contradictions that produce modernity in the first place, is nonetheless valuable at a juncture when those divisions seems more entrenched than ever" (p. 174).
23. Tricia Ziff notes that "There is now even an activity holiday called the Che Trail that follows his revolutionary journey", in *Che Guevara: Revolutionary and Icon*, p. 13.
24. Granado was soon afterwards offered a job near Caracas while Guevara caught a ride home on a plane run by a family friend. See Anderson, *Che Guevara: A Revolutionary Life*, pp. 92–93.
25. See José Martí, "Nuestra América", in José Martí, *Ensayos y crónicas*, ed. José Olivio Jiménez (Madrid: Muchnik, 1995), pp. 117–126.
26. Guevara, *The Motorcycle Diaries*, pp. 12, 135.
27. Andrés Ruggeri, *América en bicicleta* (Buenos Aires: Ediciones del Sol, 2001), front matter. Until otherwise indicated, all references to this work are given as page numbers in parentheses in the text and all translations are my own.
28. Mary Louise Pratt, *Imperial Eyes: Travel Writing and Transculturation* (London: Routledge, 1992), p. 136.
29. Aaron Jaffe, *Modernism and the Culture of Celebrity* (Cambridge: Cambridge University Press, 2005), p. 109.
30. Chris Rojek, *Celebrity* (London: Reaktion, 2001), p. 18.
31. Barrera, who hailed from the same province of Córdoba as Granado, was a striker for Racing during the 1930s and one of the club's highest scoring players.
32. Holland and Huggan, *Tourists with Typewriters*, p. 7.
33. The novel is *El amor en los tiempos del cólera* [*Love in the Time of Cholera*].
34. The second most famous shot of Guevara is the photograph taken by Freddy Alborta after the Argentine's execution, his prostrate body cleaned up and displayed by Bolivian military officers. It is this photograph that has consecrated the Christ-like image of Guevara.

35. Holland and Huggan, *Tourists with Typewriters*, p. 123.
36. Historically the bicycle has long had a utilitarian value. See David V. Herlihy, *Bicycle: The History* (New Haven, CT: Yale University Press, 2004).
37. Rojek, *Celebrity*, p. 161.
38. As Piglia points out, "the politician triumphs when the writing fails", p. 265. It is thus as a reader that Piglia ultimately conceptualises the revolutionary: "isolated and sedentary amidst the march of history, counterpoised to politics—the reader who perseveres quietly in the deciphering of signs and makes meaning in isolation and in solitude, and, in any given situation, does so through the force of his own determination, outside every context", "Ernesto Guevara: The Last Reader", p. 277.
39. Jaffe, *Modernism and the Culture of Celebrity*, p. 1.
40. Richard Phillips, *Mapping Men and Empire: A Geography of Adventure* (London: Routledge, 1997), p. 3. See also Martin Green, *Dreams of Adventure, Deeds of Empire* (London: Routledge and Kegan Paul, 1980).
41. See Luis A. Vivanco and Roberto J. Gordon, eds., *Tarzan Was an Eco-Tourist and Other Tales in the Anthropology of Adventure* (Oxford: Berghahn, 2006), p. 20.
42. Peter Hulme, *Colonial Encounters: Europe and the Native Caribbean, 1492–1797* (London: Methuen, 1986), p. 183.
43. Matthew Brown, *Adventuring Through the Spanish Colonies: Simon Bolivar, Foreign Mercenaries and the Birth of New Nations* (Liverpool: Liverpool University Press, 2006), pp. 7–8.
44. Paul Zweig, *The Adventurer* (London: Dent, 1974), p. 7.
45. Mark Gallagher, *Action Figures: Men, Action Films and Contemporary Adventure Narratives* (New York: Palgrave Macmillan, 2006), p. 35.
46. Sidonie Smith, *Moving Lives: 20th Century Women's Travel Writing* (Minneapolis: University of Minnesota Press, 2001), p. 62. By contrast, the female adventurer "un-becomes the feminised woman and becomes other to herself".
47. Eric Leed, *The Mind of the Traveller: From Gilgamesh to Global Tourism* (New York: Basic Books, 1992), p. 10.
48. David Kunzle, "Chesucristo: Fusions, Myths, and Realities", *Latin American Perspectives*, 35 (2008), 97–115 (at p. 100). In *The Motorcycle Diaries*, the young Guevara complains repeatedly of hunger throughout the journey, in the early stages capitalising on his and Granado's appearance in the press as a means to supplement their freeloading.
49. Other politico-cyclists have been attracted to the pan-American route. Frenchman Aissa Fetouaki, for example, cycled around nine different countries in the subcontinent for charity (see http://www.lanacion.com.ar/02/01/16/dg_366936.asp, accessed 9 August 2007).
50. Phillips, *Mapping Men and Empire*, p. 5.
51. See http://elmundoentandem-proyecto.blogspot.com/ (accessed 14 July 2008).
52. P. David Marshall, "New Media—New Self: The Changing Power of Celebrity", in P. David Marshall, ed., *The Celebrity Culture Reader* (London: Routledge, 2006), pp. 634–644 (at p. 637).
53. This is hinted at in Paul Zweig's description of the adventurer "as a darkly anti-social character", a formulation which suggests the inherent possibility of transgression and dissent in its associated narratives. See Zweig, *The Adventurer*, p. 7, and also Phillips, *Mapping Men and Empire*, p. 116.
54. See Vivanco and Gordon, eds., *Tarzan Was an Eco-Tourist*.
55. Georg Simmel, "The Adventurer", in *On Individuality and Social Forms* (Chicago: University of Chicago Press, 1971), pp. 187–198 (at p. 188).

56. Simmel goes on to associate the adventurer with three other social types: the artist, the gambler, and the stranger. "This extreme example of the ahistorical individual" in his words is, like those others, a reaction to and expression of modernity ["he is a man who lives in the present . . . is not determined by the past . . . nor does the future exist for him"], "The Adventurer", p. 190. As Aram A. Yengoyan points out, however, adventure is not simply the reversal of the social or there simply to critique the social: "what Simmel is asking is how social forms can be altered to create context(s) that are fragmentary and through which adventure may be enhanced", in "Simmel and Fraser", in Vivanco and Gordon, eds., *Tarzan Was an Eco-Tourist*, pp. 27–42 (at p. 33).
57. This is in keeping with what Kunzle sees as "a general pacification of the Che image, in which the gun has been replaced by other (or no) symbols and the association is with doves or other symbols of peace". Although Kunzle is principally concerned with Guevara's legacy in terms of visual culture, his comments are relevant to the context at hand also. See Kunzle, "Chesucristo", p. 101.
58. Saldaña-Portillo, "'On the Road' with Che and Jack", p. 103.
59. Stephen Levin, *The Contemporary Anglophone Travel Novel: The Aesthetics of Self-Fashioning in the Era of Globalisation* (London: Routledge, 2008).
60. Levin, *The Contemporary Anglophone Travel Novel*, p. 32. Levin's typology includes the obsessional, hysteric, and melancholic adventurer. In his terms the melancholic "operates according to a logic of rejection" (p. 36): s/he "either forecloses on the possibility of whole, integrated selfhood altogether, or suffers through the journey as a kind of self-prescribed 'penance'" for what he sees at the centre of all adventure travel, a revolt against the (Lacanian) law. There are two possible outcomes for the melancholic, according to Levin: "either the journey results in a reinvigorated identification with the state that was left behind . . . or, the traveller derives an ethical stance from the fragmentation of selfhood (resigned to alienation) that, frequently, finds an outlet in literary expressivity" (p. 107).
61. Maureen Moynagh's important and illuminating conception of "political tourism", to which I referred earlier (see n22) and with which I have much sympathy, could also be useful in this context, although it would not serve to distinguish Ruggeri in specific terms from Guevara as I aim to do here. See Chapter 5 for further discussion of Moynagh's ideas.
62. Guevara, *The Motorcycle Diaries*, p. 39.
63. Debbie Lisle, *The Global Politics of Contemporary Travel Writing* (Cambridge: Cambridge University Press, 2006), p. 269.
64. Thus, my preference for Derrida's spectrality hinges on his particular conception of mourning. Melancholia, for Freud, is a condition of unresolved mourning, the reaction to the loss of a loved one, or "to the loss of some abstraction which has taken the place of one, such as fatherland, liberty, an ideal, and so on". The idea is predicated on the possibility of "successful" mourning, therefore: "when the work of mourning is completed the ego becomes inhibited and goes free again." In "Mourning and Melancholia" [1917], *The Standard Edition of the Complete Psychological Works of Sigmund Freud*, Vol. XIV, ed. and trans. James Strachey (London: Vintage, 2001 [The Institute of Psycho-Analysis/The Hogarth Press, 1957]), pp. 243–258 (at p. 245). Although he is in agreement with Freud's idea of letting the loved one go, Derrida believes that there is no "successful mourning", that we cannot completely let the other go. Derrida's concept of mourning is predicated on an aporia, therefore, the successful (Freudian) mourning failing and the failed mourning (in Freud's sense) succeeding. For a succinct

and lucid summary of the distinction between Freud and Derrida on these issues, see Mark Dooley and Liam Kavanagh, *The Philosophy of Derrida* (Trowbridge, UK: Acumen, 2007), pp. 75–78.
65. See Dooley and Kavanagh, *The Philosophy of Derrida*, p. 17.
66. Jo Labanyi, "History and Hauntology: Or What Does One Do with the Ghosts of the Past? Reflections on Spanish Film and Fiction of the Post-Franco Period", in Joan Ramón Resina, ed., *Disremembering the Dictatorship: The Politics of Memory in the Spanish Transition to Democracy* (Amsterdam: Rodopi, 2000), pp. 65–82 (at p. 66).
67. Jacques Derrida, *Specters of Marx: The State of the Debt, the Work of Mourning and the New International*, trans. Peggy Kamuf (London: Routledge, 1994), p. 120.
68. Jo Frances Maddern and Peter Adey, "Editorial: Spectro-Geographies", *Cultural Geographies*, 15 (2008), 291–295 (at p. 291).
69. Derrida, *Specters of Marx*, p. 135.
70. The book has been taken to task, for example, by Aijaz Ahmad for "a misrecognition of its moment" (p. 92) and by Tom Lewis in similar terms for its overzealous, premature burial of core Marxist concepts. Lewis writes: "*Specters of Marx*'s 'hauntological politics' must be firmly rejected as incapable of answering the demands of our time" (p. 160). See Ahmad's "Reconciling Derrida: *Specters of Marx* and Deconstructive Politics" (pp. 88–109) and Lewis's "The Politics of 'Hauntology' in Derrida's *Specters of Marx*" (pp. 134–167), both in Michael Sprinker, ed., *Ghostly Demarcations: A Symposium on Jacques Derrida's Specters of Marx* (London: Verso, 1999).
71. Roger Luckhurst, "The Contemporary London Gothic and the Limits of the 'Spectral Turn'", *Textual Practice*, 16, no. 3 (2002), 527–546 (at p. 542).
72. See Rory Carroll, "Spirit of Che Rises Again", *The Guardian*, 4 September 2007, http://www.guardian.co.uk/world/2007/sep/04/rorycarroll.international (accessed 14 July 2008). This is not to suggest, however, that those governments mentioned hold the same leftist credentials. There are important distinctions between these countries, with some (Chile and Brazil, for example) seen to be more moderate than others (such as Venezuela and Bolivia). What these new left-leaning regimes in Latin America do have in common, however, appears to be an aspiration for greater regional integration and a shared focus in government policy on issues of inequality.
73. Simmel, "The Adventurer", p. 190.

NOTES TO CHAPTER 4

1. For example, in her overview of the field in *The Cambridge Companion to Travel Writing*, Susan Basnett makes no mention of Pratt's work. See "Travel writing and gender", in Peter Hulme and Tim Youngs, eds., *The Cambridge Companion to Travel Writing* (Cambridge: Cambridge University Press, 2002), pp. 225–241.
2. Mary Louise Pratt, *Imperial Eyes: Travel Writing and Transculturation* [1992] (London: Routledge, 2008), p. 154.
3. Pratt, *Imperial Eyes*, pp. 154, 165.
4. Giuliana Bruno sums up a principal conflict for nineteenth-century women writers in this respect: "The struggle with self-representation lies at the core of many travel reports . . . women have had not only [to] justify the fact that they left 'the home' but also that they write in constant relation with the fact that they are women." In *Atlas of Emotion: Journeys in Art, Architecture and Film* (London: Verso, 2002), p. 116.

5. See Sara Mills, *Discourses of Difference: An Analysis of Women's Travel Writing and Colonialism* (London: Routledge, 1991) and Indira Ghose, *Women Travellers in Colonial India: The Power of the Female Gaze* (Oxford: Oxford University Press, 1998).
6. Mills, *Discourses of Difference*, p. 3.
7. Sara Mills, *Gender and Colonial Space* (Manchester, UK: Manchester University Press, 2005), p. 168.
8. As Duncan Green explains, this refers to the market restructuring undergone in Mexico and elsewhere in the continent during that decade following the adoption of neoliberal economic policies. See Duncan Green, *The Silent Revolution: The Rise and Crisis of Market Economics in Latin America* (London: Monthly Review Press/Latin American Bureau, 2003).
9. Kristi Siegel, ed., *Gender, Genre and Identity in Women's Travel Writing* (New York: Peter Lang, 2004), p. 5.
10. Bartra writes: "We are looking at a malaise of the cultural heart of Mexican society that also has produced a *fin de siècle* political syndrome, that is to say, symptoms of the critical extinction of the authoritarian political system. If we look at the ideological and political dimensions of the problem, we notice that those dark humors looming on the cultural horizon have made themselves evident in a crisis of nationalism, a demand for democracy, and a search for new forms of identity, as well as in many other ways", in "Tropical Kitsch in Blood and Ink", in Roger Bartra, *Blood, Ink and Culture: Miseries and Splendors of the Post-Mexican Condition*, trans. Mark Alan Healey (Durham, NC: Duke University Press, 2002), pp. 15–43 (at p. 15).
11. In the scholarship to date, Hsu-Ming Teo's article on "Femininity, Modernity and Colonial Discourse" is one of the few studies to provide an analysis of the work of (British) women travellers which straddles the nineteenth and twentieth centuries (1880–1930). Hsu-Ming notes that certain differences in their twentieth-century travel writing can be accounted for in terms of the professionalisation of both travel and its narrativisation. In Helen Gilbert and Anna Johnston, eds., *In Transit: Travel, Text, Empire* (New York: Peter Lang, 2002), pp. 173–190.
12. As Levy and Bruhn point out, the PRI outlasted the Communist Party of Soviet Russia as the longest-ruling party in the world. Mexico is also the only major country in Latin America to have avoided a military coup and a serious communist revolution in the post–World War II period: a position which is thrown into sharp relief in comparison with the rise and fall of authoritarian regimes in its neighbouring countries. In *Mexico: The Struggle for Democratic Development* (Berkeley: University of California Press, 2006), p. 6.
13. One of the most representative of those conflicts occurred on 1 January 1994 when Mexico entered into NAFTA (North American Free Trade Agreement) with North America and Canada. On the same day there began an armed Zapatista uprising in the southern state of Chiapas.
14. Levy and Bruhn, *Mexico: The Struggle for Democratic Development*, p. 107.
15. The neoliberal package includes cuts in government spending, privatisation, deregulation, and the opening up of the economy to international trade and investment, which in Mexico's case was consolidated through its entry into NAFTA. Although standard economic indicators were positive in respect of its first results in the case of Mexico, the benefits of growth were nonetheless distributed very unevenly (Levy and Bruhn, *Mexico: The Struggle for Democratic Development*, p. 12). Less favourable outcomes included a rise in inflation and unemployment, plummeting wages, and an exacerbation of divisions between rich and poor in the country.

16. Jorge Castañeda analyses events during the Salinas and Zedillo administrations in his *Sorpresas te da la vida: México, fin de siglo* (Mexico City: Santillana, 1995). He debates the question of whether Mexico was undergoing a meaningful transition of any kind at this particular stage of its history or whether circumstances indicated rather "ni crisis ni transición, sino un estado de cosas permanente" [neither crisis, nor transition, but a permanent state of affairs] (p. 216).

17. To talk of a corpus of "domestic" travel writing in Mexico is not to imply that it has attained the same level of organisation and renown as travel/writing movements in other countries such as, for example, France, where, as Charles Forsdick points out, the *"Pour une literature voyageuse* movement, a loose grouping of authors which emerged in the 1970s and 1980s ... was consolidated in 1990 with the creation of the Ètonnants Voyageurs festival in Saint-Malo." In "Hidden Journeys: Gender, Genre and Twentieth-Century Literature in French", in Jane Conroy, ed., *Cross-Cultural Travel: Papers from the Royal Irish Academy Symposium on Literature and Travel* (New York: Peter Lang, 2003), pp. 315–323 (at p. 315). Nevertheless, there has been a significant increase in the production of and interest in Mexican travel writing. For more details see Thea Pitman, "Mexican Travel Writing: The Legacy of Foreign Travel Writers in Mexico, or Why Mexicans Say They Don't Write Travel Books", *Comparative Critical Studies*, 4, no. 3 (2007), 209–223.

18. I am indebted to Pitman's work for much of the following contextual detail concerning travel writing in Mexico. For a clarification of the term *crónica de viaje*, see Pitman, "The Construction of National Identity in the Mexican Travel-Chronicle, 1843–1893", *Journeys: The International Journal of Travel and Travel Writing*, 2, no. 1 (2000), 1–23.

19. Famously, Calderón de la Barca's account of her two years' residence in the country was subsequently used as a guide by the United States in their 1847 military campaign against Mexico. For more on this see Michael Costeloe, "Prescott's *History of the Conquest* and Calderón de la Barca's *Life in Mexico*", *The Americas*, 47, no. 3, (1991) 337–348, and my article, "Fetishising Frances Calderón de la Barca", *Women: A Cultural Review*, 17, no. 2 (2006), 171–187.

20. Thea Pitman, "*Cuadernos de viaje*: Contemporary Mexican Travel Chronicles" (unpublished doctoral thesis, University College London, 1999), p. 48. See also her book *Mexican Travel Writing* (Bern: Peter Lang, 2008).

21. Indeed, this can be seen as part of the long-term investment of the postrevolutionary state in Mexico in the creation of national culture. Despite a high level of interventionism, however, this has not necessarily lead to a top-down imposition of culture on society from above, as Anne Rubenstein describes: Mexico has been successful in "allowing an adequate space for dissent and maintaining enough flexibility to respond to those voices", in *Bad Language, Naked Ladies, and Other Threats to the Nation* (Durham, NC: Duke University Press, 1998), p. 4.

22. For example, in the case of Sonora, see Manuel Murrieta Saldívar, *De viaje en Mex-América; crónicas* (Sonora: Instituto Sonorense de Cultura, 1992) and Erasmo Lozano Rocha, *Crónica de un viaje al río San Miguel* (Sonora: Instituto Sonorense de Cultura, 2000).

23. The *Viajes en México* volumes comprise Jorge Tavera Alfaro, ed., *Viajes en Mexico: crónicas mexicanas*, Vol. I (Mexico: Fondo de Cultura Económica, 1984) and Margo Glantz, ed., *Viajes en Mexico: cronicas extranjeras*, Tomo II (Mexico: Fondo de Cultura Económica, 1982).

24. A branch of the Department of Public Education, CONACULTA is the state institution responsible for "formulating and administering national cultural

policies". See Sergio de la Mora, *Cinemachismo: Masculinities and Sexuality in Mexican Film* (Austin: University of Texas Press, 2006) p. 137.
25. In this respect, it confers sponsorships and grants to writers and artists and has a range of different published series. Notwithstanding the controversy and criticism it has engendered as a result of its efforts, CONACULTA has engineered the creation of cultural institutes and grant-awarding bodies in most state capitals of the country, as Pitman notes ("Cuadernos de viaje", p. 95).
26. The one exception is Héctor Perea's *Mexico, crónica en espiral* (Mexico: CONACULTA, 1999). For more on this volume see Thea Pitman, "An Impossible Task? Héctor Perea's *Mexico, crónica en espiral* and the Problems of Writing a Travel-Chronicle of Contemporary Mexico City", *Studies in Travel Writing*, 7, no. 1 (2003), 47–62.
27. Ana Rosa Domenella, "La provincia como bien perdido: crónicas de finales del siglo XX", in *Espacio, viajes y viajeros*, ed. by Luz Elena Zamudio (Mexico City: Aldus, Universidad Autonoma Metropolitana–Iztapalapa, 2004), pp. 294–329. There is one other short article in existence which deals briefly with Puga's volume: see Hillary Mosher's "Literatura de viajes: Textos de identidad, apropiación, y enajenación", *El Cid*, 2003, n.p. http://www.citadel.edu/mlng/elcid/ (accessed 12 April 2007).
28. These writers include, in addition to Bergua, Molina, and Puga: Francisco Hinojosa, Hugo Diego Blanco, Fernando Solana Olivares, Luis Zapata, Orlando Ortiz, Hector Perea, and Alvaro Ruiz Abreu.
29. Cited in Pitman, "Cuadernos de viaje", p. 96.
30. Contributors were given three months to complete their work.
31. Levy and Bruhn, *Mexico: The Struggle for Democratic Development*, p. 26.
32. Elissa J. Rashkin, *Women Filmmakers in Mexico: The Country of Which We Dream* (Austin: University of Texas Press, 2001), p. 3.
33. As Nuala Finnegan points out, it is not that there were no women's voices heard prior to this, just that this is the first time there were significant numbers of them. In "Postcolonial Problems?: Literature, Feminism and Power in Mexico Since 1980", paper delivered at the Gender, Culture and Postcolonial Thought conference, University of Liverpool, November 2004. For more on the misogyny prevalent in Mexicanist literary criticism in respect of women writers, see her article "'Light' Women/'Light' Literature: Women and Popular Fiction in Mexico Since 1980", *Donaire*, 15 (2000), 18–22. Finnegan explores these issues at greater length in her book *Ambivalence, Modernity, Power: Women and Writing in Mexico Since 1980* (Bern: Peter Lang, 2008). "The campaign for political, cultural and economic *modernización*, aggressively implemented from 1982 onwards," she points out, "activates the voices of women in the cultural arena virtually for the first time. These voices are enabled by the modernising project and are thus also deeply implicated in it" (p. 9).
34. Jane Robinson, *Unsuitable for Ladies: An Anthology of Women Travellers* (Oxford: Oxford University Press, 1994), p. xii.
35. Rashkin, *Women Filmmakers in Mexico*, p. 8.
36. See Angel Rama, *The Lettered City*, trans. John Charles Chasteen (Durham, NC: Duke University Press, 1996).
37. Andrea Noble, *Mexican National Cinema* (London: Routledge, 2005), p. 12. In *Ambivalence, Modernity, Power*, Finnegan employs Jacques Derrida's idea of the supplement to conceptualise the location of metropolitan Mexican women writers. The idea of supplementarity, an ambivalent insinuation of sorts into established terms of reference, "antagonis[ing] the implicit

142 Notes

      power to generalise, to produce the sociological solidity" (Bhabha, quoted in Finnegan, p. 21), could also be of use in relation to the women "travel writers" under consideration here.

38. In an article which focuses exclusively on the work of women travel writers in French, however, Forsdick also argues against a separatist view of their work, not least because of the resulting conflation "of a variety of journeys . . . into a falsely unified repository of female experience" (Forsdick, "Hidden Journeys", p. 322).

39. Patrick Holland and Graham Huggan, *Tourists with Typewriters: Critical Reflections on Contemporary Travel Writing* (Ann Arbor: University of Michigan Press, 2000), p. 113.

40. Finnegan, *Ambivalence, Modernity, Power*, p. 14. One exception to this tendency is when gender "intrude[s]" on other significant issues under consideration in Latin American cultural studies, such as the question of subalternity. Nevertheless, even in this case gender tends to signify a particular complexion of poverty, leaving the "privileged female intellectual from Latin America unaccounted for" (p. 15).

41. Pitman, "Cuadernos de viaje", p. 96, n28.

42. Finnegan has written precisely on this subject in the context of Mexico and in respect of one of the writers concerned here, observing crucially that "there is much evidence still to attest to the very marginalised position of women writers in the Mexican literary scene" (See Finnegan, "Light Women", p. 18). On one level, an exclusive association of women's travel writing with autobiography, as Pitman's critique implies, reinforces time-honoured binary distinctions between public and private discourses. On another level, it disallows any process of fictionalisation at work in the travel writing itself. As Susan Bassnett describes, "many of the works by women travellers are self-conscious fictions, and the persona which emerges from the pages is as much a character as a woman in a novel" (Bassnett, "Travel Writing and Gender", p. 234).

43. As Tim Youngs points out, "travel writing is held to be less valuable or accomplished a form than poetry, the drama, the novel, or the short story. The low opinion of it probably arises from its perceived documentary function and from its kinship with other lowly regarded forms: autobiography, journalism, and the travel guide." For more on this, see his article on "The Importance of Travel Writing", *The European English Messenger*, 13, no. 2 (2004), 55–62.

44. Mills, *Discourses of Difference*, p. 5.

45. Pitman, *Mexican Travel Writing*, p. 179.

46. Pitman, *Mexican Travel Writing*, p. 27.

47. Pitman, *Mexican Travel Writing*, p. 93. In addition to the "fragmented subcategories of postnational identity", there is also in evidence in such work "a self-conscious and ironic treatment of the question of identity per se . . . [which] can also be exploited as a means of undermining the authority of the traditional narrative voice in travel writing and of exploring in a more subtle manner the relationships between self and other that travel writing typically describes."

48. Domenella, "La provincia como bien perdido", p. 304.

49. Born in 1960, Bergua is the author of several novels, including *El Umbral* (1993) and *Isla de Bobos* (2007), and a number of works of short fiction. She has a regular column in the Mexican daily *La Jornada*.

50. Ana García Bergua, *Postales del Puerto* (Mexico City: CONACULTA, 1997), p. 9.

51. As Bassnett explains, women travellers are frequently seen as "doubly different" in their departure from normative standards of social behaviour for

women and in their difference from orthodox, male travellers. This notion that women travellers are somehow exceptional, as Bassnett says, "has been one of the classic ways of marginalising women's achievements". "Travel Writing and Gender", p. 228.

52. David Taylor, "Bruce Chatwin: Connoisseur of Exile, Exile as Connoisseur", in Steve Clark, ed., *Travel Writing and Empire: Postcolonial Theory in Transit* (London: Zed Books, 1999), pp. 195–211 (at p. 204).
53. Shirley Foster and Sara Mills, eds., *An Anthology of Women's Travel Writing* (Manchester, UK: Manchester University Press, 2002), p. 10.
54. In this respect, among others, travel writing is a genre of contradictions which "sets itself in opposition to the very economic forces that make it possible". Holland and Huggan, *Tourists with Typewriters*, pp. 52–53.
55. In an article on women travellers in Greece, Efterpi Mitsi considers the use of titles such as *Sketches, Glimpses* and *Impressions* a useful strategy for nineteenth-century women travel writers: their suggestion of a tone of informality, Mitsi suggests, "in the case of women writers may serve as protection against comparison with the great (male) writers such as Byron or Chateaubriand". Mitsi goes on to point out, however, that "many [Victorian women] travellers emphasised the scholarly preparation for their journey, aspiring beyond the status of tourist". Efterpi Mitsi, "Women Travellers and Modern Tourism", *The European English Messenger*, 12, no. 1 (2003), 25–29 (at pp. 26–27)
56. See Pitman, "Mexican Travel Writing".
57. Silvia Molina is a prize-winning author of a number of novels published since 1977. These include *La mañana debe seguir gris* (1977, which won the Premio Xavier Villaurrutia that year), *Asención Tun* (1983), *La familia vino del norte* (1987), *Imagen de Héctor* (1990). Her novel *El amor que me juraste* (1998) is kind of fictional travel narrative: for more on that see Finnegan, *Ambivalence, Modernity, Power*, pp. 54–73. Until her death in 2004 María Luisa Puga was one of Mexico's most renowned and respected contemporary women writers. Her debut was *Las posibilidades del odio* (1978), a travel novel about Africa. Other novels include *Pánico o peligro* (1983) and *Inventar ciudades* (1998).
58. Molina, for example, did not use the associated travel grant for a journey to Campeche at all, according to the parameters of the commission. I am grateful to Pitman for this information.
59. The vocabulary of psychology, pathology, and "disease" that I am employing is of course potentially highly problematic, especially in the context of a discussion of women who have conventionally been characterised by psychoanalytic theorists such as Freud as "hysterics". Nevertheless, it is the figurative property of this vocabulary which has currency in my argument here, especially as I take my cue in what follows from its use in supporting theoretical and critical material.
60. Molina has written a separate volume on Campechan culture: *Campeche, Punta del ala del país: Poesía, narrativa y teatro* (Mexico: CONACULTA, 1991).
61. In fact Molina, like other travellers considered in this volume, studied anthropology (Molina, *Campeche, imagen de una eternidad*, p. 56).
62. For more on this, see Deborah Reed-Danahay, ed., *Auto/Ethnography; Rewriting the Self and the Social* (Oxford: Berg, 1997), p. 4. Reed-Danahay's description of the autoethnographer points to an increasing difficulty in maintaining binary categories in the field of anthropology, a topic which is also at the heart of James Clifford's work. See his essay "Spatial Practices: Fieldwork, Travel and the Disciplining of Anthropology", in *Routes: Travel*

and Translation in the Late Twentieth Century (Cambridge: Harvard University Press, 1997), pp. 52–91.
63. *Chilango/a* is a colloquial—and often pejoratively used—term for an inhabitant of Mexico City.
64. *Disfraz* translates both as disguise and fancy dress costume.
65. See, for example, Molina's interview with Gabriella de Beer, *Escritoras mexicanas contemporáneas: cinco voces* (Mexico: Fondo de Cultura Económica, 1999), p. 97.
66. Juan Vives Rocabert, "El extranjero y sus hijos", in Fanny Blanck-Cereijid and Pablo Yankelevich, eds., *El otro, el extranjero* (Mexico City: Zorza, n.d.) pp. 49–66 (at p. 62).
67. The D.F. is a widely-used epithet to refer to Mexico City.
68. Clifford foregrounds these difficulties in the context of the ethnographic field trip: "Alternate forms of travel/fieldwork, whether indigenous or diasporic, grapple with many problems similar to those of conventional research: problems of strangeness, privilege, miscomprehension, stereotyping, and political negotiation of the encounter" in *Routes*, p. 78.
69. See Molina, *Campeche, imagen de una eternidad*, p. 44. Héctor Pérez Martínez was a journalist, editor, writer, and statesman who served as governor and as Secretario de la Gobernación under Miguel Alemán. Martínez wrote a book on the archaeology and history of the Yucatán, and, as a politician, founded welfare and educational programmes during his tenure as governor.
70. Rosi Braidotti usefully sums up their idea in her description of the global capitalist economy: "Advanced capitalism looks like a system that promotes feminism without women, racism without races, natural laws without nature, reproduction without sex, sexuality without genders, multiculturalism without ending racism, economic growth without development and cash flow without money . . . welcome to capitalism as schizophrenia!" Rosi Braidotti, *Transpositions: On Nomadic Ethics* (Cambridge: Polity Press, 2006), pp. 58–59.
71. Lisa Adkins, *Revisions: Gender and Sexuality in Late Modernity* (Buckingham, UK: Open University Press, 2002), p. 62.
72. Fredric Jameson. "Postmodernism and Consumer Society", in Hal Foster, ed., *The Anti-Aesthetic: Essays on Postmodern Culture* (Port Townsend, Washington: Bay Press, 1983), pp. 111–125 (at p. 119).
73. Gilles Deleuze and Felix Guattari, *Anti-Oedipus: Capitalism and Schizophrenia* (Minneapolis: University of Minnesota Press, 1983), p. 246.
74. Jonah Peretti, "Capitalism and Schizophrenia: Contemporary Visual Culture and the Acceleration of Identity Formation/Dissolution", www.datawranglers.com/negations/issues/96w/96w_peretti (accessed 17 April 2007).
75. Bartra, *Blood, Ink and Culture*, p. 14.
76. Some of Puga's work in the volume had been published previously in *El Economista* and *Mexico Desconocido*, a specialist travel magazine also published by CONACULTA. It is precisely in this respect that Puga "contravenes" the parameters of the commission and genre, according to Pitman.
77. Whereas English has the verb "to countrify", it is not an entirely appropriate translation in this instance: my translation of the verb "to ruralise" attempts to convey the "foreignness" of the term even in Spanish.
78. In depicting the experience of internal or domestic migration in these terms, Puga implicitly conveys a sense of the magnitude of Mexico's centralisation. Indeed, the resistance to translation appears to be intended, for Puga writes that "los fuereños no son militantes de nada, andan en busca de su vida y ésta no es traducible a otros idiomas" [strangers are not militants of anything, they are in search of life and that isn't translatable into any language] (23).

79. Michael Herzfeld, "The Taming of the Revolution: Intense Paradoxes of the Self", in Deborah Reed-Danahay, ed., *Auto/Ethnography; Rewriting the Self and the Social*, pp. 169–194 (at pp. 173–174).
80. In this respect there appears to be some convergence with Jacques Derrida's conception of the foreigner, for whom language is a crucial issue: "[The foreigner] has to ask for hospitality in a language which by definition is not his own, the one imposed on him by the master of the house, the host, the king, the lord, the authorities, the nation, the State, the father, etc. This personage imposes on him translation into their own language, and that's the first act of violence." In Jacques Derrida and Anne Dufourmantelle, *Of Hospitality: Anne Dufourmantelle invites Jacques Derrida to Respond*, trans. Rachel Bowlby (Stanford, CA: Stanford University Press, 2000), p. 15.
81. In Mexico and elsewhere in Latin America, the "usted" [you] form of address is much more ubiquitous than the "tú" [you informal] form, although in some instances it does have a similar usage as it has in Spain, that is, for addressing unknown or elder persons or in order to emphasise distance and politeness.
82. Jamaica Kincaid, *A Small Place* (London: Virago, 1988). Holland and Huggan describe Kincaid's book as "tantamount to a moral crusade against white racism . . . vehemently antiwhite, vehemently antitourist" in *Tourists with Typewriters*, pp. 51–52.
83. Nevertheless, following Pitman's thesis in "Mexican Travel Writing", Puga's *crónicas* are implicitly set up in counterpoint to their colonial generic heritage.
84. As Sara Ahmed describes, the stranger is usually conceived as "the outsider in the nation space whose behaviour seems unpredictable and beyond control". Sara Ahmed, *Strange Encounters: Embodied Others in Post-Coloniality* (London: Routledge, 2000), p. 36.
85. There appear to be two distinct categories of "otherness" for Puga beyond that figure of the *fuereño*—foreigners and tourists. It is for the tourist, however, that the author reserves her deepest contempt, in which respect there are some similarities with Kincaid. The tourist is "metiche, irrespetuoso, prepotente y sucio" [nosy, disrespectful, arrogant, and dirty] (27), "un perfecto imbécil o un perfecto soñador" [a perfect imbecile or dreamer] (24). This is part of a more general critique of tourism throughout Puga's book. Whilst recognising its potential economic benefits, the author is concerned with the environmental disadvantages and cultural shortcomings of the industry and argues instead for what she calls, echoing her famous compatriot and literary precursor Rosario Castellanos, "un turismo de otro modo" (5). See also n100.
86. Emily Hind, *Entrevistas con quince escritoras mexicanas* (Madrid: Iberoamericana, 2003), p. 175.
87. Madan Sarup, "Home and Identity", in George Robertson et al., eds., *Travellers' Tales: Narratives of Home and Displacement* (London: Routledge, 1994), pp. 93–104 (at p. 101–102).
88. As such, Zygmunt Bauman suggests that strangers are endemic in the city spaces of our "liquid times": "cities are spaces where strangers stay and move in close proximity to one another . . . that presence . . . is a never-drying source of anxiety and of an aggression that is usually dormant, yet erupts time and again" in *Liquid Times: Living in an Age of Uncertainty* (Cambridge: Polity Press, 2007), p. 85.
89. Nevertheless, in his thesis on "the foreigner question", Derrida provides a contemporary context for the illustration of his ideas—namely, Algeria (*Of Hospitality*, pp. 141–147).
90. This is not to say that Braidotti's theory has not been useful for conceptualising matters of gender and travel. For a Braidottian reading of women's road

narratives, for example, see Deborah Paes de Barros, *Fast Cars and Bad Girls: Nomadic Subjects and Women's Road Stories* (New York: Peter Lang, 2004).
91. Rosi Braidotti, *Nomadic Subjects* (New York: Columbia University Press, 1994), pp. 23, 31.
92. Braidotti, *Nomadic Subjects*, p. 36.
93. Indeed, in Deleuze and Guattari's formulation "the rhizome has no beginning or end: it is always in the middle, between things, interbeing, *intermezzo*", *A Thousand Plateaus: Capitalism and Schizophrenia* (Minneapolis: University of Minnesota Press, 1987), p. 25.
94. The kind of politics of location that is embedded in Puga's poetics of strangerhood also incidentally underpins the work of Braidotti, who writes of her commitment to "the task of providing politically informed maps of the present, convinced of the usefulness of a situated approach as a critical tool to achieve an enlarged sense of objectivity and a more empowering grasp of the social", terms which are no less applicable to Puga in this case. See Braidotti, *Transpositions*, p. 7.
95. Those elections were deemed to be the most honest in Mexico's history to that date.
96. Susan Kaufman Purcell and Luis Rubio, eds., *Mexico under Zedillo* (Boulder, CO: Lynne Reiner Publishers, 1998), p. 5.
97. For example, Zedillo created a Judicial Council to monitor the conduct of judges and set their budgets, "the first time the judicial branch had formal control of its own budget" (Levy and Bruhn, *Mexico: The Struggle for Democratic Development*, p. 105).
98. Purcell and Rubio, *Mexico under Zedillo*, pp. 7, 31.
99. Castañeda, *Sorpresas te da la vida*, p. 216.
100. Caren Kaplan, *Questions of Travel: Postmodern Discourses of Displacement* (Durham, NC: Duke University Press, 1996), p. 87
101. Ahmed, *Strange Encounters*, p. 5.
102. Kaplan, *Questions of Travel*, pp. 66, 89.
103. The second part of the book would appear to comprise some kind of manifesto of Puga's thesis for this alternative form of tourism based on cultural exchange rather than commerce. This part of the travel book comprises a lengthy portrait of an artisans' workshop called "El Molino" in the nearby village of Erongarícuaro. The workshop runs courses for children of all backgrounds who come from all over Mexico to study there, and for whom the most favourable outcome of their stay, according to Puga, is "ese inesperado descubrimiento del otro, de lo otro, de lo diferente" [that unexpected discovery of the other, of otherness, and difference] (75). The *taller* [workshop] thus offers both adults and children "un buen intercambio humano" [a good human exchange] (75) where they can learn that "se puede ser de otra manera" [one can be another way] (76).
104. Bartra, "The Mexican Office", *Blood, Ink and Culture*, pp. 3–14 (at p. 14).
105. Bartra, "The Mexican Office", p. 14.
106. Ahmed, *Strange Encounters*, p. 88.

NOTES TO CHAPTER 5

1. William Anthony Nericcio, "'Remembering': What is Truth at the Border?", in Harry Polkinhorn, Gabriel Trujillo Muñoz, and Rogelio Reyes, eds., *Border Lives: Personal Essay on the US-Mexico Border/Vidas fronterizas: La crónica en la frontera México-Estados Unidos* (Mexicali: Binational Press, 1995), pp. 97–114 (at p. 108).

2. Alicia Schmidt Camacho, "Migrant Melancholia: Emergent Discourses of Mexican Migrant Traffic in Transnational Space", *South Atlantic Quarterly*, 105, no. 4 (2006), 831–861 (at p. 833).
3. José Manuel Valenzuela Arce, "Centralidad de las fronteras: procesos socioculturales en la frontera Mexico-EEUU", in Hermann Herlinghaus and Mabel Moraña, eds., *Fronteras de la modernidad en América Latina* (Pittsburgh: University of Pittsburgh Press, 2003), pp. 159–182 (at p. 162).
4. Jorge Durand and Douglas S. Massey, eds., *Crossing the Border: Research from the Mexican Migration Project* (New York: Russell Sage Foundation, 2004), p. 1.
5. In the area of cinema, for example, this body of work includes films such as Patricia Riggen's *La misma luna [Under the Same Moon]* (2007) and Gregory Nava's *Bordertown* (2006).
6. This tendency might well also be seen as a particular strain of a broader post-9/11 shift towards a so-called New Realism. David Boyle, in *Authenticity: Brands, Fakes, Spin and the Lust for Real Life* (London: Flamingo, 2003), sees the emergence of New Realism as a reaction to the hyperreal, as a search for something "authentic".
7. See Debra Castillo and María Socorro Tabuenca Córdoba, *Border Women: Writing from La frontera* (Minneapolis: University of Minnesota Press, 2002), p. 4. Other recent "bi-focal" studies include Robert McKee Irwin, *Bandits, Captives, Heroines and Saints: Cultural Icons of Mexico's Northwest Borderlands* (Minneapolis: University of Minnesota Press, 2007) and Claudia Sadowski-Smith, *Border Fictions: Globalisation, Empire, and Writing at the Boundaries of the United States* (Charlottesville: University of Virginia Press, 2008).
8. Martínez's *Crossing Over*, for example, also exists in Spanish translation: *Cruzando la frontera: La crónica implacable de una familia mexicana que emigra a Estados Unidos* (Mexico: Planeta, 2003).
9. See, for example, Luis Humberto Crosthwaite, *Instrucciones para cruzar la frontera* (Mexico City: Joaquín Mortiz, 2002) and Rosario Sanmiguel, *Bajo el puente: Relatos desde la frontera. Under the Bridge: Stories from the Border*, trans. John Pluecker (Houston: Arte Público Press, 2008).
10. See Peter Bishop, "To Witness and Remember: Mapping Reconciliation Travel" (pp. 180–198); Maureen Moynagh, "The Political Tourist's Archive: Susan Meiselas's Images of Nicaragua" (pp. 199–212); and Bill Ashcroft, "Afterword: Travel and Power" (pp. 229–241), all in Julia Kuehn and Paul Smethurst, eds., *Travel Writing, Form and Empire: The Poetics and Politics of Mobility* (London: Routledge, 2009).
11. Bishop, "To Witness and Remember", p. 194.
12. Rubén Martínez, *The Other Side: Notes from the New L.A., Mexico City and Beyond* (New York: Vintage, 1993 [Verso, 1992]), p. 168. His work also includes *The New Americans* (New York: The New Press, 2004).
13. Martínez, *The Other Side*, pp. 3, 5.
14. Martínez, *Crossing Over: A Mexican Family on the Migrant Trail* (New York: Picador, 2001), pp. 18, 2. All further references to this work will be made in parentheses after quotations in the text.
15. Luis Alberto Urrea's first book was *Across the Wire: Life and Hard Times on the Border* (New York: Anchor, 1993). His other work includes collections of poetry, such as *Ghost Sickness* (El Paso: Cinco Puntos Press, 1997); a memoir, *Nobody's Son: Notes from an American Life* (Tucson: University of Arizona Press, 1998); and, more recently, a novel based on the life of Teresa, Santa de Cabora, *The Hummingbird's Daughter* (New York: Little, Brown, 2006). See also the author's website www.luisurrea.com (accessed 27 February 2009).

16. Urrea, *By the Lake of Sleeping Children* (New York: Anchor, 1996), p. 4.
17. Luis Alberto Urrea, *The Devil's Highway: A True Story* (New York: Little, Brown, 2004), p. 31. All further references to this work will be made in parentheses after quotations in the text. The same incident frames John Annerino's account of border crossing in the company of undocumented Mexican migrants, *Dead in Their Tracks: Crossing America's Desert Borderlands* (New York: Four Walls Eight Windows, 1999). Annerino describes in his preface how he gifted a copy of his travel book to Mexican President Vicente Fox because "the border is a war zone and a killing ground that continues to be ignored," p. xi.
18. For obvious reasons, the telling of the migrant's story to or by an ethnographer has historically been something of an expediency in this context (as in others). The tradition in this particular region includes titles such Ruth Behar's *Translated Women: Crossing the Border with Esperanza's Story* (Boston: Beacon, 1993) and Ramón "Tianguis" Pérez's *Diary of an Undocumented Immigrant*, trans. Dick J. Reavis (Houston: Arte Público Press, 1991). Of course, migrants' border narratives take a plethora of other forms, including the popular *retablo*, photography and music, which have all been well documented elsewhere. See, for example, Jorge Durand and Douglas S. Massey, *Miracles on the Border: Retablos of Mexican Migrants to the United States* (Tucson: University of Arizona Press, 1995); Rudy Adler, Victoria Criado, and Brett Huneycutt, *Border Film Project: Photos by Migrants and Minutemen on the US-Mexico Border* (New York: Abrams, 2007); and www.theborderfilmproject.com (last accessed 27 February 2009).
19. José David Saldívar, *Border Matters: Remapping American Cultural Studies* (Berkeley: University of California Press, 1997), p. 139.
20. Saldívar, *Border Matters*, p. 135.
21. As Urrea writes sardonically in *By the Lake of Sleeping Children*: "I often find myself leading mini-safaris to the southland's favourite representation of hell. You know the drill by now: we go to some shacks, maybe stop at an orphanage or two, gobble fish tacos . . . Everyone loves the dump—cameras fly out of purses, and wanderers walk into the trash, furtively glancing at me over their shoulders so they can be sure they're not *really* in danger" (p. 37).
22. Saldívar, *Border Matters*, p. 140.
23. José Pablo Villalobos, "Up Against the Border: A Literary Response", in Ana María Matanzas, ed., *Border Transits: Literature and Culture Across the Line* (Amsterdam: Rodopi, 2007), pp. 35–52 (p. 43). Recent travel alerts issued by the U.S. State Department have been effective in warning tourists to stay away from Tijuana, however, and the city saw a corresponding dearth of visitors in 2009 during what would otherwise have been a conventionally buoyant spring break period, due to an escalation in drugs-related violence along the border. This has led to fears in Mexico about a potential collapse in its tourist industry: as Nuala Finnegan put it, "Mexico's killing grounds are killing tourism" (personal communication, 31 March 2009).
24. María Antonia Oliver-Rotger, "Ethnographies of Transnational Migration in Rubén Martínez's *Crossing Over*", in Matanzas, ed., *Border Transits*, pp. 181–203 (at p. 183).
25. For a good overview of these debates, see Georg M. Gugelberger, ed., *The Real Thing: Testimonial Discourse and Latin America* (Durham, NC: Duke University Press, 1996).
26. James Clifford and George Marcus, eds., *Writing Culture: The Poetics and Politics of Ethnography* (Berkeley: University of California Press, 1986), p. 9.
27. Clifford and Marcus, eds., *Writing Culture*, p. 9.

28. Ashcroft, "Travel and Power", p. 230.
29. Ashcroft, "Travel and Power", pp. 237–238.
30. Ashcroft, "Travel and Power", p. 240.
31. Moynagh, "The Political Tourist's Archive", p. 200.
32. Moynagh, "The Political Tourist's Archive", p. 211.
33. During the nineteenth century, in the face of burgeoning US expansionism, *mestizo* Mexicans were encouraged by their government to settle there, along with Chinese, Mennonite, and Kickapoo Indian migrants, who were given portions of land to set up home in the area.
34. Andrea Noble, *Mexican National Cinema* (London: Routledge, 2005), p. 151.
35. Since the 1980s, refugees from Central America (known by the Border Patrol as "Other than Mexicans") have notably swelled the ranks of undocumented border crossers.
36. Also in the mid-1990s, San Diego residents parked cars along the border at night and switched on their headlights to "light up the border" in "a symbolic display of solidarity with the deterrence approach of the U.S. government". Patricia L. Price, *Dry Place: Landscapes of Belonging and Exclusion* (Minneapolis: University of Minnesota Press, 2004), p. 115.
37. "Between 1965 and 1985 85% of undocumented entries [to the United States] were offset by departures, yielding a relatively modest new increment to the US population", Durand and Massey, *Crossing the Border*, p. 6.
38. Durand and Massey, eds., *Crossing the Border*, pp. 11, 12. Cerrutti and Massey found evidence that fraudulent legalisation programmes established under the auspices of IRCA also pulled into migration many Mexicans who would not otherwise have left for the United States. Marcela Cerrutti and Douglas S. Massey, "Trends in Mexican Migration to the US, 1965–1995", in Durand and Massey, eds., *Crossing the Border*, pp. 17–43. Moreover, the increasing feminisation of migration is another of the unintended consequences of policies of border enforcement. For more on this, see Katharine M. Donato and Evelyn Patterson, "Women and Men on the Move: Undocumented Border Crossing", in Durand and Massey, eds., *Crossing the Border*, pp. 111–129.
39. Saldívar, *Border Matters*, p. 96.
40. Price, *Dry Place*, p. 115. Quotation from Debbie Nathan, *Women and Other Aliens: Essays from the US-Mexico Border* (El Paso: Cinco Puntos Press, 1991), p. 12. Since the beginning of 2009, following a record year of over 6,000 drug-related murders there, Washington has dispatched a high number of federal agents and equipment to the southwest border region while President Felipe Calderón has sent more than 10,000 Mexican troops to the border.
41. Durand and Massey, eds., *Crossing the Border*, p. 12.
42. Ricardo C. Ainslie, "Cultural Mourning, Immigration, and Engagement: Vignettes from the Mexican Experience", in Marcelo M. Suárez-Orozco, ed., *Crossings: Mexican Immigration in Interdisciplinary Perspectives* (Cambridge, MA: Harvard University Press, 1998), pp. 285–305 (at p. 288).
43. According to Ainslie, La Pulga creates "a temporary visual/sensory illusion that one is back home in Mexico", "Cultural Mourning", p. 291.
44. See Peggy Levitt's response to Ainslie in the same volume, p. 303.
45. Schmidt Camacho, "Migrant Melancholia", pp. 838, 839.
46. Wendy Wheeler, "Melancholic Modernity and Contemporary Grief: The Novels of Graham Swift", in Roger Luckhurst and Peter Marks, eds., *Literature and the Contemporary: Fictions and Theories of the Present* (Harlow: Pearson Education, 1999), pp. 63–79 (at p. 65).

47. Wheeler, "Melancholic Modernity", p. 65. She contrasts this to "the self-destructive melancholias of modernity", the product of its "harsh individualism".
48. For more on this, see Chapter 3.
49. For small boats and swimmers the river is not much of a deterrent in any case. See Brent Ashabranner and Paul Conklin, *The Vanishing Border: A Photographic Journey along our Frontier with Mexico* (New York: Dodd, Mead & Company, 1987).
50. See Saldívar, *Border Matters*, pp. 13–14.
51. Claire Fox, *The Fence and the River: Culture and Politics at the US-Mexico Border* (Minneapolis: University of Minnesota Press, 1999), p. 3.
52. What was known in pre-Columbian times as Gran Chichimeca is now a region sometimes broadly referred to as MexAmérica, which for Chicanos encompasses the mythical Aztlán. In turn, Américo Paredes used the term "Greater Mexico" to refer to "all the areas inhabited by people of a Mexican culture—not only within the present limits of the Republic of Mexico but in the United States as well—in a cultural rather than a political sense." Américo Paredes, *A Texas-Mexico Cancionero: Folksongs of the Lower Border* [1975] (Austin: University of Texas Press, 1995), p. xiv.
53. Those Mexicans who stayed in the North after 1848 (who were at first conceived as "la familia ausente" [the absent family], or "el otro Mexico" [the other Mexico]) were increasingly deemed, in pejorative terms, to have undergone a process of "apochamiento" [transformation into a *pocho*]. From this juncture onwards the Mexican migrant became a traitor in the south, deemed to have lost or abandoned their national identity. See Valenzuela, "Centralidad de las fronteras".
54. Gloria Anzaldúa, *Borderlands/La frontera: The New Mestiza* (San Francisco: Ann Lute Books, 1987), p. 24.
55. Castillo and Tabuenca Córdoba, *Border Women*, p. 3.
56. Javier Durán, "De la guerra y otros demonios: heterotopías y (des)territorialización en la narrativa fronteriza mexicana y chicana", *Arizona Journal of Hispanic Cultural Studies*, 4 (2000), 105–129 (at p. 106).
57. Castillo and Tabuenca Córdoba, *Border Women*, p. 3.
58. Guillermo Gómez Peña, *The New World Border: Prophecies, Poems and Loqueras for the End of the Century* (San Francisco: City Lights Books, 1996), p. 33.
59. See, for example, Nestor García Canclini, *Hybrid Cultures: Strategies for Entering and Leaving Modernity*, trans. Christopher L. Chiappari and Silvia L. López (Minneapolis: University of Minnesota Press, 1995) and Sergio Gómez Montero, *The Border: The Future of Postmodernity*, trans. Harry Polkinhorn (San Diego: San Diego State University Press, 1994).
60. Homi Bhabha, *The Location of Culture* (London: Routledge, 1994), p. 7.
61. Eduardo Barrera, "Aliens in Heterotopia: An Intertextual Reading of the Border Patrol Museum", in Pablo Vila, ed., *Ethnography at the Border* (Minneapolis: University of Minnesota Press, 2003), pp. 166–181 (at p. 166).
62. George Yúdice, *The Expediency of Culture: Uses of Culture in the Global Era* (Durham, NC: Duke University Press, 2004), pp. 252–253.
63. Cited by Pablo Vila in "The Limits of American Border Theory", in *Ethnography at the Border*, pp. 306–341 (at p. 311).
64. Castillo and Tabuenca Córdoba, *Border Women*, p. 27.
65. Vila, *Ethnography at the Border*, p. 307.
66. Arturo J. Aldama, "Millennial Anxieties: Borders, Violence and the Struggle for Chicana/o Subjectivity", *Arizona Journal of Hispanic Cultural Studies*, 2 (1998), 41–62 (at p. 46).

67. Vila, *Ethnography at the Border*, p. 315.
68. John Beverley, "The Real Thing", in Gugelberger, ed., *The Real Thing*, pp. 266–286 (at p. 266).
69. Dylan Evans, *An Introductory Dictionary of Lacanian Psychoanalysis* (London: Routledge, 1996), p. 159.
70. Evans, *An Introductory Dictionary of Lacanian Psychoanalysis*, p. 160.
71. Sean Homer, *Jacques Lacan* (London: Routledge, 2005), p. 94.
72. Slavoj Žižek, *Welcome to the Desert of the Real* (London: Verso, 2002), p. 19.
73. See his essay "The Real and Its Vicissitudes", in *Looking Awry: An Introduction to Jacques Lacan Through Popular Culture* (Cambridge, MA: MIT Press, 1992), pp. 21–47 (at p. 23).
74. Tony Myers, *Slavoj Žižek* (London: Routledge, 2003), p. 26. Žižek also locates the radiation from Chernobyl in the dimension of the Real: "No matter what we say about [the radiation], it continues to expand, to reduce us to the role of impotent witnesses. The rays are thoroughly *unrepresentable*, no image is adequate to them . . . we do not see or feel radioactive rays . . . it would be quite possible to persist in our commonsense attitude and maintain that all the panic provoked by Chernobyl resulted from the confusion and exaggeration of a few scientists." In "The Real and Its Vicissitudes", p. 36.
75. Martínez, *Crossing Over*, p. 325.
76. Other books worthy of mention in this respect include Annerino, *Dead in Their Tracks*; Charles Bowden, *Down by the River: Drugs, Money, Murder and the Family* (London: Simon & Schuster, 2002); and Ted Conover, *Coyotes: A Journey across the Borders with America's Illegal Migrants* (New York: Vintage, 1987).
77. Patrick Holland and Graham Huggan, *Tourists with Typewriters: Critical Reflections on Contemporary Travel Writing* (Ann Arbor: University of Michigan Press, 2000), p. 9.
78. The travel narrative, writes Steve Clark, "is addressed to the home culture . . . that to which is refers cannot be verified, hence the ready and habitual equation of traveller and liar." "Introduction", in Steve Clark, ed., *Travel Writing and Empire: Postcolonial Theory in Transit* (London: Zed Books, 1999), pp. 1–28 (at p. 1).
79. Debbie Lisle, *The Global Politics of Contemporary Travel Writing* (Cambridge: Cambridge University Press), p. 29.
80. For a critique of that position, however, see my article "Road to Nowhere? *Los autonautas de la cosmopista* by Julio Cortázar and Carol Dunlop", in Kuehn and Smethurst, eds., *Travel Writing, Form and Empire*, pp. 213–227.
81. Oliver-Rotger, "Ethnographies of Transnational Migration", p. 185.
82. Dennis Porter, *Haunted Journeys: Desire and Transgression in European Travel Writing* (Princeton, NJ: Princeton University Press, 1991), p. 5.
83. Postmemory, Hirsch continues, characterises "the experience of those who grow up dominated by narratives that preceded their birth, whose own belated stories are evacuated by the stories of the previous generation shaped by traumatic events that can neither be understood nor recreated". Although Hirsch develops this idea in specific relation to the experience of the children of Holocaust survivors, she admits to its potential resonance in the context of other second-generation memories of cultural or collective traumatic experiences or events. See Marianne Hirsch, *Family Frames: Photography, Narrative, and Postmemory* (Cambridge, MA: Harvard University Press, 1997), p. 21.
84. Indeed, the more time he spends in Cherán the greater his ambivalence about crossing the border with the volatile brother-in-law of the deceased men,

Wense. On one level, he confesses that he thinks to cross is "the writerly thing to do" (99), but on another feels a burden of responsibility, despite his own inadequacies: "to Wense I'm the older brother ... the one who should know about the border and its risk and how to cross it without losing your life, because, after all, the fortifications on the line are my country's ideas, not his" (99). Indeed, Martínez does not cross the border with Wense or his wife Rosa in the end, as planned, preferring instead to fly back to spend Christmas with his own family in Los Angeles.

85. Slavoj Žižek, *Welcome to the Desert*, p. 11.
86. For more on this see Holland and Huggan, *Tourists with Typewriters*, pp. 27–65.
87. Among whom feature "the *sans papier* in France; the inhabitants of the *favelas* in Brazil, people in African-American ghettos in the USA ... those who are perceived as recipients of humanitarian aid". Žižek, *Welcome to the Desert*, p. 92. See also Giorgio Agamben, *Homo Sacer: Sovereign Power and Bare Life*, trans. Daniel Heller-Roazen (Stanford, CA: Stanford University Press, 1998).
88. To cite just one example from *Crossing Over*, Martínez's early encounter with a Cherán schoolteacher, José Luis Macías: "Now that school will be letting out for the summer, he's going to see about getting a passport and a visa to go be with [his wife and children in Wisconsin]. And if he doesn't get his visa, well, he's just going to have to go illegally. And he thinks that the people of the United States should understand this, that there should be some kind of diplomatic negotiation. Maybe a *bracero* programme, like in the old days. You know, people moving back and forth according to their needs—and of course the needs of the bosses in the United States. Simple and just" (48).
89. Shlomith Rimmon-Kenan, *Narrative Fiction: Contemporary Poetics* (London: Routledge, 1983), p. 113. The juxtaposition of several voices in one text in this manner has the property of being "a miniature reflection of the nature of all texts and language" (indeed, for Jacques Derrida it foregrounds language's inherent linguistic iterability). One of the pitfalls of the citational character of free indirect discourse, however, is that "deprives this phenomenon as well as the whole of literature of its privileged differential status" (pp. 115, 116).
90. Emile Benveniste, *Problems in General Linguistics*, trans. Mary Elizabeth Meek (Coral Gables: University of Miami Press, 1971), p. 201. The second-person narrative voice, however, also implies the (authorial narrative) "I". As Benveniste elaborates, "'You' is necessarily designated by 'I' and cannot be thought of outside a situation set up by starting with 'I.'" So while Urrea of necessity eschews the position of the first-person narrator in this travelogue, because the account is of another's journey, it is implicit in his other narrative choices.
91. Ivan Callus, "Comparatism and (Auto)thanatography: Death and Mourning in Blanchot, Derrida, and Tim Parks", *Comparative Critical Studies*, 1, no. 3 (2004), 337–358 (at pp. 340, 343).
92. Lisle, *The Global Politics of Contemporary Travel Writing*, p. 30.
93. Judith Butler, *Precarious Life: the Powers of Mourning and Violence* (London: Verso, 2004), p. 20.
94. This idea is consonant with her proposal in *Giving an Account of Oneself* in which she argues that the narrative "I" is predicated on a fictive process and constructed upon an essential opacity, which can in turn occasion an ethics "based on our shared, invariable, and partial blindness about ourselves." Butler, *Giving an Account of Oneself* (New York: Fordham University Press, 2005), p. 41. In that book she contends that the "I" is of necessity a social theorist or what she calls a "speculative philosopher": "The 'I' can neither

tell the story of its own emergence nor the conditions of its own possibility without bearing witness to a state of affairs to which one could not have been present, which are prior to one's own emergence as a subject who can know, and so constitute a set of origins that one can narrate only at the expense of authoritative knowledge. Narration is surely possible under such circumstances, but it is, as Thomas Keenan has pointed out, surely fabulous" (p. 37).
95. Butler, *Precarious Life*, p. 30.
96. Angela McRobbie, "Vulnerability, Violence and (Cosmopolitan) Ethics", *British Journal of Sociology*, 57, no. 1 (2006), 69–86 (at p. 84). For Marjorie Jolles, the book presents "[Butler's] most direct, demanding and relevant voice." Marjorie Jolles, "Butler, J. (2004), Precarious Life: The Powers of Mourning and Violence", *Journal of Communication Inquiry*, 31 (2007), 370–376 (at p. 375).
97. Malini Johar Schueller, "Decolonising Global Theories Today", *Interventions*, 11, no. 2 (2009), 235–254, p. 249. Schueller argues that global theories such as Butler's (and Agamben's notion of "bare life") "in which a West-centered humanism parades as universalism" can operate as "colonising forces which it is our ethical task to resist, to decolonise" (p. 236).
98. Butler, *Precarious Life*, p. 8. In a similar vein, in her more recent collection of essays, Butler is preoccupied by the use of pronouns in respect of the idea of responsibility: "Is it only as an 'I', that is, as an individual, that I am responsible? Could it be that when I assume responsibility what becomes clear is that who 'I' am is bound up with others in necessary ways . . . In effect, could it be that through the process of assuming responsibility the 'I' shows itself to be, at least partially, a 'we'?" In *Frames of War: When Is Life Grievable?* (London: Verso, 2009), p. 35.
99. Insofar as photography has a democratising and aestheticizing quality, the inclusion of thirteen photographs by documentary photographer Joseph Rodriguez in *Crossing Over* also seems apposite in this respect, attesting both to the broader collaborative nature of the travelogue's production and to a further decentering of the travelling (narrative) "I". The very wording of the book's dedication ("for Joseph Rodriguez, whose eyes helped mine to see") underscores those collective efforts but also shores up that time-honoured association between the photographic gaze and empirical truth, what Sontag calls the "heroism of vision" conventionally attributed to the photographer. See Susan Sontag, *On Photography* (Harmondsworth, UK: Penguin, 1979), p. 69.
100. Jan Borm, "Defining Travel: On the Travel Book, Travel Writing and Terminology", in Glenn Hooper and Tim Youngs, eds., *Perspectives on Travel Writing* (Aldershot, UK: Ashgate, 2004), pp. 13–26 (at p. 17).
101. Butler, *Precarious Life*, p. 34.
102. Butler, *Precarious Life*, pp. 30, 46.
103. Maureen Moynagh, *Political Tourism and Its Texts* (Toronto: University of Toronto Press, 2008), p. 3.
104. See James Clifford, *Routes: Travel and Translation in the Late Twentieth Century* (Cambridge, MA: Harvard University Press, 1997), p. 39.

NOTES TO THE AFTERWORD

1. Janet Woolf, "On the Road Again: Metaphors of Travel in Cultural Criticism", *Cultural Studies*, 7, no. 2 (1993), 224–239 (at p. 235).

154 *Notes*

2. Quoted in Patrick Holland and Graham Huggan, *Tourists with Typewriters: Critical Reflections on Contemporary Travel Writing* (Ann Arbor: University of Michigan Press, 2000), p. 200.
3. Holland and Huggan, *Tourists with Typewriters*, pp. 202–203.
4. Thea Pitman, *Mexican Travel Writing* (Bern: Peter Lang, 2008), p. 178.
5. In an essay based on that inaugural lecture, Youngs provides further details in that respect. See Tim Youngs, "The Importance of Travel Writing", *The European English Messenger*, 13, no. 2 (2004), 55–62. It is worth adding that in terms of publishing alone, the recently increased number of annual issues of the journal *Studies in Travel Writing* and the establishment of a series of critical studies of travel writing at Routledge provide further grounds on which to invalidate those apocalyptic assumptions. In fact, as Youngs writes elsewhere, "travel writing studies in now in fashion", although it has yet to become "institutionalised in the way that postcolonial studies has." See Tim Youngs, "Where Are We Going? Cross-Border Approaches to Travel Writing", in Glen Hooper and Tim Youngs, eds., *Perspectives on Travel Writing* (Aldershot, UK: Ashgate, 2004), pp. 167–180 (at p. 171).
6. See Richard Coker, "Swine Flu: Fragile Systems Will Make Surveillance and Mitigation a Challenge", *British Medical Journal*, 9 May 2009, 1087–1088.
7. Figures from the WHO. See http://www.who.int/csr/don/2009_07_06/en/index.html (accessed 13 July 2009).
8. That the death toll has been highest in Mexico has led to widespread internal criticism of that country's government in dealing with health issues. Indeed, Calderón's lack of presence during the crisis also received censure. See "Gobierno mexicano atrapado en 'danza de cifras' sobre gripe", http://www.lajornadanet.com/diario/archivo/2009/abril/30/5.html (accessed 7 May 2009).
9. Coker, "Swine Flu: Fragile Systems", p. 1087.
10. Andrea Noble, *Mexican National Cinema* (London: Routledge, 2005), p. 172.
11. Michael Barrett, "Pandemic's Progress: We Saw It Coming", *New Statesman*, 4 May 2009, pp. 14–15.
12. Stephen Gibbs, "Mexican economy squeezed by swine flu", http://news.bbc.co.uk/go/pr/fr/-/1/hi/world/americas/8026113.stm (accessed 7 May 2009).
13. Malini Johar Schueller, 'Decolonising Global Theories Today', *Interventions*, 11, no. 2 (2009), 235–254 (at p. 237).
14. Holland and Huggan, *Tourists with Typewriters*, p. 198.
15. Paul Smethurst, "Introduction", in Julia Kuehn and Paul Smethurst, eds., *Travel Writing, Form, and Empire: The Poetics and Politics of Mobility* (London: Routledge, 2009), pp. 1–18 (at p. 11).
16. Stuart Hall, "The Local and the Global: Globalisation and Ethnicity", in Anne McClintock, Aamir Mufti, and Ella Shoat, eds., *Dangerous Liaisons: Gender, Nation, and Postcolonial Perspectives* (Minneapolis: University of Minnesota Press, 1997), pp. 173–187 (at p. 183).
17. Howard Markel and Alexandra Stern, "Blaming the Flu on Mexicans Is Immoral. And Foolish", *The New Republic: A Journal of Politics and the Arts*, 30 April 2009, http://blogs.tnr.com/tnr/blogs/the_treatment/archive/2009/04/30/scapegoating-mexicans.aspx (accessed 12 May 2009).
18. Barrett, "Pandemic's Progress", p. 14.
19. Some conditions do pertain, however, to particular ethnic, religious, or geographically located groups, e.g. Ashkenazy Jews are more prone to certain genetic disorders and thalassaemia occurs with particular prevalence in inhabitants of Mediterranean and Middle Eastern countries. My thanks to Mark McPhail for this information.

20. The porcine connotation lead Vassiliou to declare a rapid renaming of the virus to the "novel flu virus" to avoid any misleading link with pigs or the pork industry.
21. Duncan Turnbull, "Swine Flu Needs to Be Rebranded", *Guardian*, 7 May 2009, http://www.guardian.co.uk/commentisfree/2009/may/07/swin-flu-rebranding (accessed 8 May 2009).
22. Quoted in Markel and Stern, "Blaming the Flu on Mexicans", n.p.
23. Woolf, "On the Road Again", p. 235.
24. Debbie Lisle, *The Global Politics of Contemporary Travel Writing* (Cambridge: Cambridge University Press, 2006), p. 262.
25. Lisle, *The Global Politics of Contemporary Travel Writing*, p. 268.
26. See 'Bolivia calls time on bizarre world of prison frequented by tourists', *Guardian*, 8 July 2009, http://www.guardian.co.uk/world/2009/jul/08/bolivia-bans-tourists-entering-jail#history-byline (accessed 9 July 2009).

Bibliography

Adkins, Lisa. *Revisions: Gender and Sexuality in Late Modernity*. Buckingham and Philadelphia: Open University Press, 2002.
Adler, Rudy, Victoria Criado, and Brett Huneycutt. *Border Film Project: Photos by Migrants and Minutemen on the US-Mexico Border*. New York: Abrams, 2007.
Agamben, Giorgio. *Homo Sacer: Sovereign Power and Bare Life*. Translated by Daniel Heller-Roazen. Stanford, CA: Stanford University Press, 1998.
Ahmed, Sara. *Strange Encounters: Embodied Others in Post-Coloniality*. London and New York: Routledge, 2000.
Ainslie, Ricardo C. "Cultural Mourning, Immigration, and Engagement: Vignettes from the Mexican Experience". In *Crossings: Mexican Immigration in Interdisciplinary Perspectives*, edited by Marcelo M. Suárez-Orozco. Cambridge, MA: Harvard University Press, 1998, pp. 285–305.
Aldama, Arturo J. "Millennial Anxieties: Borders, Violence and the Struggle for Chicana/o Subjectivity". *Arizona Journal of Hispanic Cultural Studies*, 2 (1998), 41–62.
Andermann, Jens. *Mapas de poder: Una arqueología literaria del espacio argentino*. Rosario, Argentina: Beatriz Viterbo, 2000.
Anderson, Jon Lee. *Che Guevara: A Revolutionary Life*. New York: Grove Press, 1997.
Annerino, John. *Dead in Their Tracks: Crossing America's Desert Borderlands*. New York: Four Walls Eight Windows, 1999.
Anzaldúa, Gloria. *Borderlands/La frontera: The New Mestiza*. San Francisco: Ann Lute Books, 1987.
Appadurai, Arjun. "Disjuncture and Difference in the Global Cultural Economy". In *Global Culture: Nationalism, Globalisation and Modernity* [A Theory, Culture and Society Special Issue], edited by Mike Featherstone. London and New Delhi: Sage Publications, 1990, pp. 295–310.
———. *Modernity at Large: Cultural Dimensions of Globalisation*. Minneapolis: University of Minnesota Press, 1996.
Ashabranner, Brent, and Paul Conklin. *The Vanishing Border: A Photographic Journey along our Frontier with Mexico*. New York: Dodd, Mead & Company, 1987.
Ashcroft, Bill. "Afterword: Travel and Power." In *Travel Writing, Form, and Empire: The Poetics and Politics of Mobility*, edited by Julia Kuehn and Paul Smethurst. London: Routledge, 2009, pp. 229–241.
Barrett, Michael. "Pandemic's Progress: We Saw It Coming". *New Statesman*, 4 May 2009, pp. 14–15.
Bartra, Roger. *Blood, Ink and Culture: Miseries and Splendors of the Post-Mexican Condition*. Translated by Mark Alan Healey. Durham, NC, and London: Duke University Press, 2002.

Bassnett, Susan. "Travel writing and gender". In *The Cambridge Companion to Travel Writing*, edited by Peter Hulme and Tim Youngs. Cambridge: Cambridge University Press, 2002, pp. 225–241.

Bauman, Zygmunt. *Liquid Times: Living in an Age of Uncertainty*. Cambridge: Polity Press, 2007.

———. *Wasted Lives: Modernity and its Outcasts*. Cambridge: Polity Press, 2004.

Beck, Ulrich. *Risk Society: Towards a New Modernity*. Translated by Mark Ritter. London: Sage, 1992.

Behar, Ruth. *Translated Women: Crossing the Border with Esperanza's Story*. Boston: Beacon, 1993.

Behdad, Ali. *Belated Travellers: Orientalism in the Age of Colonial Dissolution*. Durham, NC, and Cork: Duke and Cork University Presses, 1994.

———. "The Politics of Adventure: Theories of Travel, Discourses of Power". In *Travel Writing, Form and Empire: The Poetics and Politics of Mobility*, edited by Julia Kuehn and Paul Smethurst. London and New York: Routledge, 2009, pp. 80–94.

Benveniste, Emile. *Problems in General Linguistics*. Translated by Mary Elizabeth Meek. Coral Gables: University of Miami Press, 1971.

Bhabha, Homi. *The Location of Culture*. London and New York: Routledge, 1994.

Blanton, Casey. *Travel Writing: The Self and the World*. New York: Twayne, 1997.

Borm, Jan. "Defining Travel: On the Travel Book, Travel Writing and Terminology". In *Perspectives on Travel Writing*, edited by Glenn Hooper and Tim Youngs. Aldershot, UK: Ashgate, 2004, pp. 13–26.

Bowden, Charles. *Down by the River: Drugs, Money, Murder and the Family*. London and New York: Simon & Shuster, 2002.

Boyle, Catherine. "Violence in Memory: Translation, Dramatization and Performance of the Past in Chile". In *Cultural Politics in Latin America*, edited by Anny Brooksbank Jones and Ronaldo Munck. Basingstoke, UK: Macmillan, 2000, pp. 93–112.

Boyle, David. *Authenticity: Brands, Fakes, Spin and the Lust for Real Life*. London: Flamingo, 2003.

Braidotti, Rosi. *Nomadic Subjects*. New York: Columbia University Press, 1994.

———. *Transpositions: On Nomadic Ethics*. Cambridge: Polity Press, 2006.

Brennan, Timothy. *At Home in the World: Cosmopolitanism Now*. Cambridge, MA: Harvard University Press, 1997.

Brooksbank Jones, Anny, and Ronaldo Munck, eds. *Cultural Politics in Latin America*. Basingstoke, UK: Macmillan, 2000.

Brown, Matthew. *Adventuring Through the Spanish Colonies: Símon Bolívar, Foreign Mercenaries and the Birth of New Nations*. Liverpool: Liverpool University Press, 2006.

———. "Richard Vowell's Not-so-Imperial Eyes: Travel Writing and Adventure in Nineteenth-Century Hispanic America". *Journal of Latin American Studies*, 38 (2006), 95–122.

Brunner, José Joaquín. "Notes on Modernity and Postmodernity in Latin American Culture". In *The Postmodernism Debate in Latin America*, edited by John Beverley, José Oviedo, and Michael Aronna. Durham, NC: Duke University Press, 1995, pp. 34–54.

Bruno, Giuliana. *Atlas of Emotion: Journeys in Art, Architecture and Film*. London: Verso, 2002.

Buck, Daniel. "Sequels to a Patagonian Journal". *Americas*, 52, no. 5 (2000), 6–13.

Butler, Judith. *Frames of War: When Is Life Grievable?* London: Verso, 2009.

———. *Giving an Account of Oneself*. New York: Fordham University Press, 2005.

———. *Precarious Life: the Powers of Mourning and Violence*. London and New York: Verso, 2004.

Butler, Shannon Marie. *Travel Narratives in Dialogue: Contesting Representations of Nineteenth-Century Peru*. New York: Peter Lang, 2008.
Cabañas, Miguel A. *The Cultural "Other" in Nineteenth-Century Travel Narratives: How the United States and Latin America Described Each Other*. Lewiston, NY, and Lampeter UK: Edwin Mellen, 2008.
Cahill, Tim, *Road Fever: A High-Speed Travelogue*. London: Fourth Estate, 1992.
Callus, Ivan. "Comparatism and (Auto)thanatography: Death and Mourning in Blanchot, Derrida, and Tim Parks". *Comparative Critical Studies*, 1, no. 3 (2004), 337–358.
Castañeda, Jorge. *Compañero: The Life and Death of Che Guevara*. Translated by Marina Castañeda. New York: Alfred A. Knopf, 1997.
——. *Sorpresas te da la vida: México, fin de siglo*. Mexico City: Santillana, 1995.
Castillo, Debra, and María Socorro Tabuenca Córdoba. *Border Women: Writing from La frontera*. Minneapolis: University of Minnesota Press, 2002.
Cerda, Susana. "Placing Oneself in Conflict Zones: Gabriel García Márquez, Jorge Ibargüegoitia and Juan Villoro". Unpublished doctoral thesis, University of Warwick, UK, 2008.
Chambers, Iain. *Migrancy, Culture and Identity*. London and New York: Routledge, 1994.
Chatwin, Bruce. *In Patagonia*. [1977] London: Vintage, 1998.
Clark, Steve, ed. *Travel Writing and Empire: Postcolonial Theory in Transit*. London: Zed Books, 1999.
Clifford, James. *Routes: Travel and Translation in the Late Twentieth Century*. Cambridge and London: Harvard University Press, 1997.
Clifford, James, and George Marcus, eds. *Writing Culture: The Poetics and Politics of Ethnography*. Berkeley and London: University of California Press, 1986.
Coker, Richard. "Swine Flu: Fragile Systems Will Make Surveillance and Mitigation a Challenge". *British Medical Journal*, 9 May 2009, pp. 1087–1088.
Conover, Ted. *Coyotes: A Journey across the Borders with America's Illegal Migrants*. New York: Vintage, 1987.
Costeloe, Michael. "Prescott's *History of the Conquest* and Calderón de la Barca's *Life in Mexico*". *The Americas*, 47, no. 3, (1991), 337–348.
Cronin, Michael. *Across the Lines: Travel, Language, Translation*. Cork: Cork University Press, 2000.
——. *Translation and Globalisation*. London and New York: Routledge, 2003.
Crosthwaite, Luis Humberto. *Instrucciones para cruzar la frontera*. Mexico City: Joaquín Mortiz, 2002.
Darwin, Charles. *The Voyage of the Beagle: Journal of Researches into the Natural History and Geology of the Countries Visited During the Voyage of HMS Beagle Round the World, Under the Command of Captain Fitz Roy, R.N.* Chatham: Wordsworth Classics, 1997.
Davies, Catherine, ed. *The Companion to Hispanic Studies*. London: Arnold, 2002.
de Beer, Gabriella. *Escritoras mexicanas contemporáneas: cinco voces*. Mexico: Fondo de Cultura Económica, 1999.
Deleuze, Gilles, and Felix Guattari. *Anti-Oedipus: Capitalism and Schizophrenia*. Minneapolis: University of Minnesota Press, 1983.
——. *Kafka: Toward a Minor Literature*. [1975] Translated by Dana Polan. Minneapolis: University of Minnesota Press, 1986.
——. *A Thousand Plateaus: Capitalism and Schizophrenia*. Minneapolis: University of Minnesota Press, 1987.
Derrida, Jacques and Anne Dufourmantelle. *Of Hospitality: Anne Dufourmantelle Invites Jacques Derrida to Respond*. Translated by Rachel Bowlby. Stanford: Stanford University Press, 2000.

Derrida, Jacques. *Specters of Marx: The State of the Debt, the Work of Mourning and the New International.* Translated by Peggy Kamuf. London: Routledge, 1994.
Domenella, Ana Rosa. "La provincia como bien perdido: crónicas de finales del siglo XX". In *Espacio, viajes y viajeros*, edited by Luz Elena Zamudio. Mexico City: Aldus, Universidad Autónoma Metropolitana–Iztapalapa, 2004, pp. 294–329.
Dooley, Mark, and Liam Kavanagh. *The Philosophy of Derrida.* Trowbridge: Acumen, 2007.
Durán, Javier. "De la guerra y otros demonios: heterotopías y (des)territorialización en la narrativa fronteriza mexicana y chicana". *Arizona Journal of Hispanic Cultural Studies*, 4 (2000), 105–129.
Durand, Jorge and Douglas S. Massey eds. *Crossing the Border: Research from the Mexican Migration Project.* New York: Russell Sage Foundation, 2004.
———. *Miracles on the Border: Retablos of Mexican Migrants to the United States.* Tucson and London: University of Arizona Press, 1995.
Evans, Dylan. *An Introductory Dictionary of Lacanian Psychoanalysis.* London and New York: Routledge, 1996.
Fey, Ingrid E., and Karen Racine, eds., *Strange Pilgrimages: Exile, Travel and National Identity in Latin America, 1800s–1990s.* Wilmington, DE: Scholarly Resources, 2000.
Finnegan, Nuala. *Ambivalence, Modernity, Power: Women and Writing in Mexico Since 1980.* Bern: Peter Lang, 2008.
———. "'Light' Women/ 'Light' Literature: Women and Popular Fiction in Mexico Since 1980". *Donaire*, 15 (2000), 18–22.
Fombona, Jacinto. *La Europea necesaria: Textos de viaje de la época modernista.* Rosario, Argentina: Beatriz Viterbo, 2005.
Forsdick, Charles. "Hidden Journeys: Gender, Genre and Twentieth-Century Literature in French". In *Cross-Cultural Travel: Papers from the Royal Irish Academy Symposium on Literature and Travel*, edited by Jane Conroy. New York: Peter Lang, 2003, pp. 315–323.
———. *Travel in Twentieth-Century French and Francophone Cultures: The Persistence of Diversity.* Oxford: Oxford University Press, 2005.
Foster, Shirley, and Sara Mills, eds. *An Anthology of Women's Travel Writing.* Manchester, UK: Manchester University Press, 2002.
Foucault, Michel. "Of Other Spaces". Translated by Jay Miskowiec. *Diacritics*, 16, no. 1 (1986), 22–27.
Fox, Claire. *The Fence and the River: Culture and Politics at the US-Mexico Border.* Minneapolis: University of Minnesota Press, 1999.
Freud, Sigmund. "Mourning and Melancholia" [1917], *The Standard Edition of the Complete Psychological Works of Sigmund Freud*, Vol. XIV. Translated and edited by James Strachey. London: Vintage, 2001 [The Institute of Psycho-Analysis/The Hogarth Press, 1957], pp. 243–258.
Fussell, Paul. *Abroad: British Literary Travelling Between the Wars.* Oxford and New York: Oxford University Press, 1980.
Gallagher, Mark. *Action Figures: Men, Action Films and Contemporary Adventure Narratives.* New York and Basingstoke, UK: Palgrave Macmillan, 2006.
García Bergua, Ana. *Postales del Puerto.* Mexico City: CONACULTA, 1997.
García Canclini, Nestor. *Hybrid Cultures: Strategies for Entering and Leaving Modernity.* Translated by Christopher L. Chiappari and Silvia L. López. Minneapolis: University of Minnesota Press, 1995.
Ghose, Indira. *Women Travellers in Colonial India: The Power of the Female Gaze.* Oxford: Oxford University Press, 1998.
Giardinelli, Mempo. *Final de novela en Patagonia.* Barcelona: Ediciones B, 2000.

———. "Todos somos patagónicos". http://www.todoteca.com.ar/modules.php?name=News&file=print&sid=48 (accessed 25 July 2007).
Gibbs, Stephen. "Mexican Economy Squeezed by Swine Flu". http://news.bbc.co.uk/go/pr/fr/-/1/hi/world/americas/8026113.stm (accessed 7 May 2009).
Gilbert, Helen, and Anna Johnston, eds. *In Transit: Travel, Text, Empire*. New York: Peter Lang, 2002.
Giménez Hutton, Adrian. *La Patagonia de Chatwin*. Buenos Aires: Sudamericana, 1999.
Glantz, Margo, ed. *Viajes en Mexico: crónicas extranjeras*, Tomo II. Mexico: Fondo de Cultura Económica, 1982.
Gómez Montero, Sergio. *The Border: The Future of Postmodernity*. Translated by Harry Polkinhorn. San Diego: San Diego State University Press, 1994.
Gómez Peña, Guillermo. *The New World Border: Prophecies, Poems and Loqueras for the End of the Century*. San Francisco: City Lights Books, 1996.
González Echeverría, Roberto. *Myth and Archive: A Theory of Latin American Narrative*. Cambridge: Cambridge University Press, 1990.
Graham-Yooll, Andrew. "Light at the End of the Tunnel: The New Writers of Latin America". *The Antioch Review*, 52, no. 4 (1994), 566–579.
Green, Duncan. *The Silent Revolution: The Rise and Crisis of Market Economics in Latin America*. London and New York: Monthly Review Press/Latin American Bureau, 2003.
Green, Martin. *Dreams of Adventure, Deeds of Empire*. London: Routledge and Kegan Paul, 1980.
Greenblatt, Stephen. *Marvelous Possessions: The Wonder of the New World*. Chicago: University of Chicago Press, 1991.
Guevara, Ernesto Che. *The Motorcycle Diaries: A Journey around South America*. Translated by Ann Wright. London: Fourth Estate, 1996.
Gugelberger, Georg M., ed. *The Real Thing: Testimonial Discourse and Latin America*. Durham, NC, and London: Duke University Press, 1996.
Guillermoprieto, Alma. *Looking for History: Dispatches from Latin America*. New York: Vintage, 2001.
Hall, Stuart. "The Local and the Global: Globalisation and Ethnicity". In *Dangerous Liaisons: Gender, Nation, and Postcolonial Perspectives*, edited by Anne McClintock, Aamir Mufti, and Ella Shoat. Minneapolis: University of Minnesota Press, 1997, pp. 173–187.
Harley, J. B. "Deconstructing the Map". In *Human Geography: An Essential Anthology*, edited by John Agnew, David N. Livingstone, and Alisdair Rogers. Oxford: Blackwell, 1996, pp. 422–443.
Hassett, John. "Luis Sepúlveda: *Nombre de torero, Patagonia Express, Historia de una gaviota y del gato que le enseño a volar*". *Chasqui*, 26, no. 2 (1997), 149–151.
Herlihy, David V. *Bicycle: The History*. New Haven, CT, and London: Yale University Press, 2004.
Hetherington, Kevin. *The Badlands of Modernity: Heterotopia and Social Ordering*. London and New York: Routledge, 1997.
Hind, Emily. *Entrevistas con quince escritoras mexicanas*. Madrid/Frankfurt: Iberoamericana/Vervuert, 2003.
Hirsch, Marianne. *Family Frames: Photography, Narrative, and Postmemory*. Cambridge, MA: Harvard University Press, 1997.
Holland, Patrick, and Graham Huggan. *Tourists with Typewriters: Critical Reflections on Contemporary Travel Writing*. Ann Arbor: University of Michigan Press, 2000.
Homer, Sean. *Jacques Lacan*. London and New York: Routledge, 2005.
Huggan, Graham. *The Postcolonial Exotic*. London and New York: Routledge, 2001.

Hulme, Peter. *Colonial Encounters: Europe and the Native Caribbean, 1492–1797.* London and New York: Methuen, 1986.
Hulme, Peter, and Tim Youngs, eds. *The Cambridge Companion to Travel Writing.* Cambridge: Cambridge University Press, 2002.
Iparraguirre, Sylvia. "Patagonia: historia y ficción, Documento histórico y novela: una experiencia de escritura". *Páginas de Guardia,* 1 (2006), 101–116.
Jaffe, Aaron. *Modernism and the Culture of Celebrity.* Cambridge: Cambridge University Press, 2005.
Jagoe, Eva-Lynn. "Buenos Aires and the Aesthetics of Defamiliarization". *Journal of Latin American Cultural Studies,* 17, no. 3 (2008), 299–315.
———. *The End of the World as They Knew It: Writing Experiences of the Argentine South.* Lewisburg, PA: Bucknell University Press, 2008.
Jameson, Fredric. "Postmodernism and Consumer Society". In *The Anti-Aesthetic: Essays on Postmodern Culture,* edited by Hal Foster. Washington: Bay Press, 1983, pp. 111–125.
Jolles, Marjorie. "Butler, J. (2004) Precarious Life: The Powers of Mourning and Violence". *Journal of Communication Inquiry,* 31 (2007), 370–376.
Kaplan, Caren. *Questions of Travel: Postmodern Discourses of Displacement.* Durham, NC: Duke University Press, 1996.
Kaufman Purcell, Susan, and Luis Rubio, eds. *Mexico under Zedillo.* Boulder, CO: Lynne Reiner Publishers, 1998.
Kincaid, Jamaica. *A Small Place.* London: Virago, 1988.
Kowalewski, Michael, ed. *Temperamental Journeys: Essays on the Modern Literature of Travel.* Athens and London: University of Georgia Press, 1992.
Kuehn, Julia, and Paul Smethurst, eds. *Travel Writing, Form and Empire: The Poetics and Politics of Mobility.* London and New York: Routledge, 2009.
Kunzle, David. "Chesucristo: Fusions, Myths, and Realities". *Latin American Perspectives,* 35 (2008), 97–115.
Labanyi, Jo. "History and Hauntology: Or What does one do with the Ghosts of the Past? Reflections on Spanish Film and Fiction of the Post-Franco Period". In *Disremembering the Dictatorship: The Politics of Memory in the Spanish Transition to Democracy,* edited by Joan Ramón Resina. Amsterdam: Rodopi, 2000, pp. 65–82.
Lazzara, Michael J. *Chile in Transition: The Poetics and Politics of Memory.* Gainesville: University Press of Florida, 2006.
Leed, Eric. *The Mind of the Traveller: From Gilgamesh to Global Tourism.* New York: Basic Books, 1992.
Levin, Stephen M. *The Contemporary Anglophone Travel Novel: The Aesthetics of Self-Fashioning in the Era of Globalisation.* London and New York: Routledge, 2008.
Lévi-Strauss, Claude, *Tristes Tropiques.* Translated by John and Doreen Weightman. London: Penguin, 1992.
Levy, Daniel, and Kathleen Bruhn. *Mexico: The Struggle for Democratic Development.* Berkeley and London: University of California Press, 2006.
Lindsay, Claire. "Fetishising Frances Calderón de la Barca". *Women: A Cultural Review,* 17, no. 2 (2006), 171–187.
———. "Road to Nowhere? *Los autonautas de la cosmopista* by Julio Cortázar and Carol Dunlop." In *Travel Writing, Form, and Empire: The Poetics and Politics of Mobility,* edited by Julia Kuehn and Paul Smethurst. London and New York: Routledge, 2009, pp. 213–227.
Lisle, Debbie. *The Global Politics of Contemporary Travel Writing.* Cambridge: Cambridge University Press, 2006.
Livon-Grosman, Ernesto. "Lo abierto y lo cerrado: el espacio patagónico en la literatura de viaje", *Ciberletras,* 5 (2001), http://www.lehman.cuny.edu/ciberletras/v05.html (accessed 21 July 2004).

——. *Geografías imaginarias: el relato de viaje y la construcción del espacio patagónico*. Rosario, Argentina: Beatriz Viterbo, 2003.
Logan, Joy. "'Discovering the Real': Travels in Patagonia". *Romance Studies*, 21 (1992), 63–70.
Lozano Rocha, Erasmo. *Crónica de un viaje al río San Miguel*. Sonora, Mexico: Instituto Sonorense de Cultura, 2000.
Luckhurst, Roger. "The Contemporary London Gothic and the Limits of the 'Spectral Turn'". *Textual Practice*, 16, no. 3 (2002), 527–546.
MacCannell, Dean. *The Tourist: A New Theory of the Leisure Class* [1976]. Berkeley and London: University of California Press, 1999.
Maddern, Jo Frances, and Peter Adey. "Editorial: Spectro-Geographies". *Cultural Geographies*, 15 (2008), 291–295.
Magee, Paul. *From Here to Tierra del Fuego*. Urbana and Chicago: University of Illinois Press, 2000.
Markel, Howard, and Alexandra Stern. "Blaming the Flu on Mexicans is Immoral. And Foolish". *The New Republic: A Journal of Politics and the Arts*, 30 April 2009, http://blogs.tnr.com/tnr/blogs/the_treatment/archive/2009/04/30/scapegoating-mexicans.aspx (accessed 12 May 2009).
Marshall, P. David. "New Media–New Self: The Changing Power of Celebrity". In *The Celebrity Culture Reader*. London and New York: Routledge, 2006, pp. 634–644.
Martí, José. "Nuestra América". In *Ensayos y crónicas*, edited by José Olivio Jiménez. Madrid: Muchnik, 1995, pp. 117–126.
Martínez, Rubén. *Crossing Over: A Mexican Family on the Migrant Trail*. New York: Picador, 2001.
——. *Cruzando la frontera: La crónica implacable de una familia mexicana que emigra a Estados Unidos*. Mexico: Planeta, 2003.
——. *The New Americans*. New York and London: The New Press, 2004.
——. *The Other Side: Notes from the New L.A., Mexico City and Beyond*. New York: Vintage, 1993 [Verso, 1992].
Masiello, Francine. *The Art of Transition: Latin American Culture and Neoliberal Crisis*. Durham, NC: Duke University Press, 2001.
Matanzas, Ana María, ed. *Border Transits: Literature and Culture across the Line*. Amsterdam and New York: Rodopi, 2007.
McGuire, James. *Peronism without Perón: Unions, Parties and Democracy in Argentina*. Stanford, CA: Stanford University Press, 1997.
McKee Irwin, Robert. *Bandits, Captives, Heroines and Saints: Cultural Icons of Mexico's Northwest Borderlands*. Minneapolis: University of Minnesota Press, 2007.
McRobbie, Angela. "Vulnerability, Violence and (Cosmopolitan) Ethics". *British Journal of Sociology*, 57, no. 1 (2006), 69–86.
Mills, Sara. *Discourses of Difference: An Analysis of Women's Travel Writing and Colonialism*. London and New York: Routledge, 1991.
——. *Gender and Colonial Space*. Manchester, UK: Manchester University Press, 2005.
Mitsi, Efterpi. "Women Travellers and Modern Tourism". *The European English Messenger*, 12, no. 1 (2003), 25–29.
Molina, Silvia. *Campeche, imagen de una eternidad*. Mexico: CONACULTA, 1996.
Moraña, Mabel, Enrique Dussel, and Carlos A. Jáuregui, eds. *Coloniality at Large: Latin America and the Postcolonial Debate*. Durham, NC: Duke University Press, 2008.
Moreno, Francisco P. *Viaje a la Patagonia Austral 1876–1877*. Estudio preliminar de Raúl Rey Balmaceda. Buenos Aires: Sol/Hachette, 1969 [1879].
Mosher, Hillary. "Literatura de viajes: Textos de identidad, apropiación, y enajenación". *El Cid*, 2003, n.p. http://www.citadel.edu/mlng/elcid/ (accessed 12 April 2007).

Moss, Chris. *Patagonia: A Cultural History*. Oxford: Signal, 2008.
Moynagh, Maureen. *Political Tourism and Its Texts*. Toronto: University of Toronto Press, 2008.
———. "The Political Tourist's Archive: Susan Meiselas's Images of Nicaragua." In *Travel Writing, Form and Empire*, edited by Julia Kuehn and Paul Smethurst. London: Routledge, 2009, pp. 199–212.
Murray, Nicholas. *Bruce Chatwin*. Bridgend, UK: Seren Books, 1993.
Murrieta Saldívar, Manuel. *De viaje en Mex-America: Crónicas*. Sonora, Mexico: Instituto Sonorense de Cultura, 1992.
Myers, Tony. *Slavoj Žižek*. London and New York: Routledge, 2003.
Nathan, Debbie. *Women and Other Aliens: Essays from the US-Mexico Border*. El Paso: Cinco Puntos Press, 1991.
Nericcio, William Anthony. "'Remembering': What Is Truth at the Border?" In *Border Lives: Personal Essay on the US-Mexico Border/Vidas fronterizas: La crónica en la frontera México-Estados Unidos*, edited by Harry Polkinhorn, Gabriel Trujillo Muñoz, and Rogelio Reyes. Mexicali and Calexico, Mexico: Binational Press, 1995, pp. 97–114.
Noble, Andrea. *Mexican National Cinema*. London and New York: Routledge, 2005.
Nouzeilles, Gabriela. "Patagonia as Borderland: Nature, Culture and the Idea of the State". *Journal of Latin American Cultural Studies*, 8, no. 1 (1999), 35–48.
———. "Touching the Real: Alternative Travel and Landscapes of Fear". In *Writing Travel: The Poetics and Politics of the Modern Journey*, edited by John Zilcosky. Toronto: University of Toronto Press, 2008, pp. 195–210
Nouzeilles, Gabriela, and Graciela Montaldo, eds. *The Argentina Reader: History, Culture, Politics*. Durham, NC: Duke University Press, 2002.
Oliver-Rotger, María Antonia, "Ethnographies of Transnational Migration in Rubén Martínez's *Crossing Over*". In *Border Transits: Literature and Culture Across the Line*, edited by Ana María Matanzas. Amsterdam and New York: Rodopi, 2007, pp. 181–203.
Paredes, Américo. *A Texas-Mexico Cancionero: Folksongs of the Lower Border* [1975]. Austin: University of Texas Press, 1995.
Peñaloza, Fernanda. "Appropriating the 'Unattainable': The British Travel Experience in Patagonia". In *Informal Empire in Latin America: Culture, Commerce, and Capital*, edited by Matthew Brown. Oxford: Blackwell/Society of Latin American Studies, 2008, pp. 149–172.
———. "Ethnographic Curiosity and the Aesthetics of Othering: Nineteenth-Century British Representations of Argentine Patagonia". Unpublished doctoral thesis, University of Exeter, 2004.
Peretti, Jonah. "Capitalism and Schizophrenia: Contemporary Visual Culture and the Acceleration of Identity Formation/Dissolution". www.datawranglers.com/negations/issues/96w/96w_peretti (accessed 17 April 2007).
Pérez Mejía, Angela. *A Geography of Hard Times: Narratives about Travel to South America, 1780–1849*. Translated by Dick Cluster. New York: State University of New York Press, 2004.
Pérez, Ramón "Tianguis". *Diary of an Undocumented Immigrant*. Translated by Dick J. Reavis. Houston: Arte Público Press, 1991.
Perreault, Thomas and Patricia Martin. "Geographies of Neoliberalism in Latin America". *Environment and Planning A*, 37, no. 2 (2005), 191–201.
Perry, Richard O. "Argentina and Chile: The Struggle for Patagonia 1843–1881". *The Americas*, 36, no. 3 (1980), 347–363.
Pfister, Manfred. "Bruce Chatwin and the Postmodernization of the Travelogue". *Literature Interpretation History*, 7, nos. 2–3 (1996), 253–267.

Phillips, Richard. *Mapping Men and Empire: A Geography of Adventure*. London and New York: Routledge, 1997.
Piglia, Ricardo. "Ernesto Guevara: The Last Reader". *Journal of Latin American Cultural Studies*, 17, no. 3 (2008), 261–277.
Pitman, Thea. "The Construction of National Identity in the Mexican Travel-Chronicle, 1843–1893". *Journeys: The International Journal of Travel and Travel Writing*, 2, no. 1 (2000), 1–23.
———. "*Cuadernos de viaje*: Contemporary Mexican Travel Chronicles". Unpublished doctoral thesis, University College London, 1999.
———. "An Impossible Task? Héctor Perea's *Mexico, crónica en espiral* and the Problems of Writing a Travel-Chronicle of Contemporary Mexico City". *Studies in Travel Writing*, 7, no. 1 (2003), 47–62.
———. "Mexican Travel Writing: The Legacy of Foreign Travel Writers in Mexico, or Why Mexicans Say They Don't Write Travel Books". *Comparative Critical Studies*, 4, no. 2 (2007), 209–223.
———. *Mexican Travel Writing*. Bern: Peter Lang, 2008.
Polezzi, Loredana. *Translating Travel: Italian Travel Writing in English Translation*. Aldershot, UK: Ashgate, 2001.
Porter, Dennis. *Haunted Journeys: Desire and Transgression in European Travel Writing*. Princeton, NJ, and Oxford: Princeton University Press, 1991.
Pratt, Mary Louise. *Imperial Eyes: Travel Writing and Transculturation* [1992]. London and New York: Routledge, 2008.
Price, Patricia L. *Dry Place: Landscapes of Belonging and Exclusion*. Minneapolis: University of Minnesota Press, 2004.
Puga, María Luisa. *Crónicas de una oriunda del kilómetro X en Michoacán*. Mexico City: CONACULTA, 1995.
Quemain, Miguel Angel. "'No soy un escritor chileno': Entrevista con Luis Sepúlveda". *Quimera*, 121 (1993), 20–24.
Rama, Angel. *The Lettered City*. Translated by John Charles Chasteen. Durham, NC: Duke University Press, 1996.
Rashkin, Elissa J. *Women Filmmakers in Mexico: The Country of Which We Dream*. Austin: University of Texas Press, 2001.
Reed-Danahay, Deborah, ed. *Auto/Ethnography; Rewriting the Self and the Social*. Oxford and New York: Berg, 1997.
Richard, Nelly. *Residuos y metáforas: Ensayos de crítica cultural sobre el Chile de la transición*. Santiago: Cuarto Propio, 1998.
Rimmon-Kenan, Shlomith. *Narrative Fiction: Contemporary Poetics*. London and New York: Routledge, 1983.
Robertson, Roland. "Glocalisation: Time-Space and Homogeneity-Heterogeneity". In *Global Modernities*, edited by Mike Featherstone, Scott Lash, and Roland Robertson. London: Sage, 1995, pp. 25–44.
Robinson, Jane. *Unsuitable for Ladies: An Anthology of Women Travellers*. Oxford: Oxford University Press, 1994.
Rojek, Chris. *Celebrity*. London: Reaktion, 2001.
Romero, Luis Alberto. *A History of Argentina in the Twentieth Century*. Translated by James P. Brennan. University Park: Pennsylvania State University Press, 2002.
Ruggeri, Andrés. *América en bicicleta*. Buenos Aires: Ediciones del Sol, 2001.
Sadowski-Smith, Claudia. *Border Fictions: Globalisation, Empire, and Writing at the Boundaries of the United States*. Charlottesville and London: University of Virginia Press, 2008.
Said, Edward. "Travelling Theory". In *The World, the Text and the Critic*. Cambridge, MA: University of Harvard Press, 1983, pp. 157–181.

Saldaña-Portillo, María Josefina. "'On the Road' with Che and Jack: Melancholia and the Legacy of Colonial Racial Geographies in the Americas". *New Formations*, 47 (2002), 87–108.
Saldívar, José David. *Border Matters: Remapping American Cultural Studies*. Berkeley and London: University of California Press, 1997.
Sánchez-Blanco, Cristina. "Mempo Giardinelli y la percepción de la región patagónica a través de la experiencia de un viaje: De la construcción literaria del espacio natural y universal de la 'modernidad' a la literatura de viajes contemporánea social y local". Unpublished doctoral dissertation, University of Cinncinati, 2005.
Sanmiguel, Rosario. *Bajo el puente: Relatos desde la frontera. Under the Bridge: Stories from the Border*. Translated by John Pluecker. Houston: Arte Público Press, 2008.
Sarup, Madan. "Home and Identity". In *Travellers' Tales: Narratives of Home and Displacement*, edited by George Robertson et al. London and New York: Routledge, 1994, pp. 93–104.
Schmidt Camacho, Alicia. "Migrant Melancholia: Emergent Discourses of Mexican Migrant Traffic in Transnational Space". *South Atlantic Quarterly*, 105, no. 4 (2006), 831–861.
Schueller, Malini Johar. "Decolonising Global Theories Today". *Interventions*, 11, no. 2 (2009), 235–254.
Scott, David. *Semiologies of Travel: From Gautier to Baudrillard*. Cambridge: Cambridge University Press, 2004.
Sepúlveda, Luis. *Full Circle: A South American Journey*. Translated by Chris Andrews. Melbourne: Lonely Planet, 1996.
———. *Patagonia Express*. Barcelona: Tusquets, 1995.
Shakespeare, Nicholas. *Bruce Chatwin*. London: Vintage, 2000.
Shullenberger, Geoffrey. "That Obscure Object of Desire: Machu Picchu as Myth and Commodity". *Journal of Latin American Cultural Studies*, 17, no. 3 (2008), 317–333.
Siegel, Kristi, ed. *Gender, Genre and Identity in Women's Travel Writing*. New York: Peter Lang, 2004.
Simmel, Georg. "The Adventurer". In *On Individuality and Social Forms*. Chicago: University of Chicago Press, 1971, pp. 187–198.
Smith, Sidonie. *Moving Lives: Twentieth-Century Women's Travel Writing*. Minneapolis: University of Minnesota Press, 2001.
Sontag, Susan. *On Photography*. Harmondsworth, UK: Penguin, 1979.
Sprinker, Michael, ed. *Ghostly Demarcations: A Symposium on Jacques Derrida's Specters of Marx*. London and New York: Verso, 1999.
Szurmuk, Mónica. *Women in Argentina: Early Travel Narratives*. Gainesville: University of Florida Press, 2000.
Tavera Alfaro, Jorge, ed. *Viajes en Mexico: crónicas mexicanas*, Vol. I. Mexico: Fondo de Cultura Económica, 1984.
Taylor, David. "Bruce Chatwin: Connoisseur of Exile, Exile as Connoisseur". In *Travel Writing and Empire: Postcolonial Theory in Transit*, edited by Steve Clark. London: Zed Books, 1999, pp. 195–211.
Taylor, Marcus. *From Pinochet to the "Third Way": Neoliberalism and Social Transformation in Chile*. London: Pluto Press, 2006.
Thacker, Andrew. "Journey with Maps: Travel Theory, Geography and the Syntax of Space". In *Cultural Encounters: European Travel Writing in the 1930s*, edited by Charles Burdett and Derek Duncan. Oxford: Berghahn, 2002, pp. 11–28.
Theroux, Paul. *Fresh-Air Fiend: Travel Writings 1985–2000*. Boston and New York: Houghton Mifflin Harcourt, 2000.

———. *The Old Patagonia Express: By Train through the Americas*. New York: Washington Square Press, 1980.
Thompson, Krista A. *An Eye for the Tropics: Tourism, Photography and Framing the Caribbean*. Durham, NC: Duke University Press, 2007.
Todorov, Tzvetan. "The Journey and Its Narratives". In *The Morals of History*, translated by Alyson Waters. Minneapolis: University of Minnesota Press, 1995, pp. 60–70.
Tschiffely, Aimé. *Southern Cross to Pole Star*. London: Heinemann, 1933.
———. *This Way Southward: An Account of a Journey through Patagonia to Tierra del Fuego*. London: The Book Club, 1941.
Turnbull, Duncan. "Swine Flu Needs to Be Rebranded", *Guardian*, 7 May 2009. http://www.guardian.co.uk/commentisfree/2009/may/07/swin-flu-rebranding (accessed 8 May 2009).
Urrea, Luis Alberto. *Across the Wire: Life and Hard Times on the Border*. New York: Anchor, 1993.
———. *By the Lake of Sleeping Children*. New York: Anchor, 1996.
———. *The Devil's Highway: A True Story*. New York: Little, Brown, 2004
———. *Ghost Sickness*. El Paso: Cinco Puntos Press, 1997.
———. *The Hummingbird's Daughter*. New York: Little, Brown, 2006.
———. *Nobody's Son: Notes from an American Life*. Tucson: University of Arizona Press, 1998.
Valenzuela Arce, José Manuel. "Centralidad de las fronteras: procesos socioculturales en la frontera Mexico-EEUU". In *Fronteras de la modernidad en América Latina*, edited by Hermann Herlinghaus and Mabel Moraña. Pittsburgh: University of Pittsburgh Press, 2003, pp. 159–182.
Vieyra, Hernán Santiváñez. "La Patagonia a traves de sus viajeros", *Revista de Occidente*, 218–219 (1999), 141–153.
Vila, Pablo, ed. *Ethnography at the Border*. Minneapolis: University of Minnesota Press, 2003.
Vivanco, Luis A., and Roberto J. Gordon. *Tarzan Was an Eco-Tourist and Other Tales in the Anthropology of Adventure*. Oxford and New York: Berghahn, 2006.
Vives Rocabert, Juan. "El extranjero y sus hijos". In *El otro, el extranjero*, edited by Fanny Blanck-Cereijid and Pablo Yankelevich. Mexico City: Zorza, n.d., pp.49–66.
von Humboldt, Alexander. *Personal Narrative of a Journey of the Equinoctial Regions of the New Continent*. Abridged and translated with an introduction by Jason Wilson and a historical introduction by Malcolm Nicolson. London: Penguin 1995.
Weyland, Kurt. "Neoliberalism and Democracy in Latin America: A Mixed Record". *Latin American Politics and Society*, 46, no. 1 (2004), 135–157.
Wheeler, Wendy. "Melancholic Modernity and Contemporary Grief: The Novels of Graham Swift". In *Literature and the Contemporary: Fictions and Theories of the Present*, edited by Roger Luckhurst and Peter Marks. Harlow, UK: Pearson Education, 1999, pp. 63–79.
Williams, Gareth. *The Other Side of the Popular: Neoliberalism and Subalternity in Latin America*. Durham, NC: Duke University Press, 2002.
Wilson, Jason. "Travel Literature". In *Encyclopedia of Latin American Literature*, edited by Verity Smith. Chicago and London: Fitzroy Dearborn, 1997, p. 803.
Woolf, Janet. "On the Road Again: Metaphors of Travel in Cultural Criticism". *Cultural Studies*, 7, no. 2 (1993), 224–239.
Youngs, Tim. "The Importance of Travel Writing". *The European English Messenger*, 13, no. 2 (2004), 55–62.
———. "Punctuating Travel: Paul Theroux and Bruce Chatwin". *Literature and History*, 6, no. 2 (1997), 73–88.

———. "Where Are We Going? Cross-Border Approaches to Travel Writing". In *Perspectives on Travel Writing*, edited by Glen Hooper and Tim Youngs. Aldershot, UK: Ashgate, 2004, pp. 167–180.
Yúdice, George. *The Expediency of Culture: Uses of Culture in the Global Era.* Durham, NC: Duke University Press, 2003.
Ziff, Tricia. *Che Guevara: Revolutionary and Icon.* London: V&A Publications, 2006.
Žižek, Slavoj. *Looking Awry: An Introduction to Jacques Lacan through Popular Culture.* Cambridge, MA: MIT Press, 1992.
———. *Welcome to the Desert of the Real.* London: Verso, 2002.
Zweig, Paul. *The Adventurer.* London: Dent, 1974.

Index

A

Across the Wire (Urrea), 95, 96
adventure, 2, 3, 11, 12, 16, 18, 22, 23, 31, 39, 40, 45, 47–48, 50, 52, 62, 106, 107, 115, 119, 121n12, 127n28, 129n58, 131n89, 136n46, 136n53, 137n56, 137n60; Georg Simmel on, 63, 65; imprimatur of, 58–61; spectral, 65
Agier, Michel, 87
Ahmed, Sara, 15, 90, 145n84
AIDS, 104
Ainslie, Ricardo, 101, 102
Allende, Isabel, 29
Allende, Salvador, 23, 25, 27, 63
Amazon, 12, 28, 49, 59, 64, 129n58
América en bicicleta [*America by Bike*] (Ruggeri), 52–53, 58, 59–63, 65
Andermann, Jens, 19, 38
Andes, 11, 49, 59, 132n98, 134n5
anti-imperialism, 36, 50, 53. *See also* colonialism, imperialism
anthropology, 15, 47, 92, 97, 143n62
Anzaldúa, Gloria, 95, 102, 103
Appadurai, Arjun, 1, 15, 43
Argentina, 14, 18, 19, 20, 34, 42, 43, 46, 49, 54, 124n58; under Menem, 23, 65
Arlt, Roberto, 19
Art of Transition, The (Masiello), 14
Ashcroft, Bill, 94, 98, 99,
autobiography, 30, 47, 73, 106, 142nn42–43; "reflexive autobiography", 28
autoethography, 78–84, 96–98
Aylwin, Patricio, 23

B

Bachelet, Michelle, 24, 65
Barrett, Michael, 116, 119
Bartra, Roger, 15, 68, 84, 90, 139n10
Bauman, Zygmunt, 43, 87
Beck, Ulrich, 24, 128n46
Behdad, Ali, 35, 48,
belatedness, 15, 35, 38, 55, 125n7, 151n83
Benítez, Fernando, 75
Benveniste, Emile, 111
Bingham, Hiram, 50
Bishop, Peter, 94
Bhabha, Homi, 103
Blanton, Casey, 26, 27
Bolivia, 54, 55, 63, 65, 120, 138n72
Borm, Jan, 11, 113, 123n46
Borderlands/La frontera (Anzaldúa), 102
Border Patrol, 94, 100, 107, 108, 111
border theories, critique of, 102–4
Boyle, Catherine, 33
bracero programme, 99, 152n88
Braidotti, Rosi, 15, 88, 144n70, 145n90, 146n94
Brân, Zoë, 29
Brazil 9, 52, 57, 62, 64, 138n72, 152n87
Brennan, Timothy, 31, 32, 130n69
Brown, Matthew, 48, 58
Brunner, José Joaquín, 24
Bryson, Bill, 3
Buenos Aires Tour (Macchi), 6
Burton, Richard, 4
Butler, Judith, 15, 17, 93, 152n94, 153n98; on vulnerability, 112–114
Butler, Shannon Marie, 9, 10

C

Cahill, Tim, 39
Calderón de la Barca, Frances, 69, 75

Callus, Ivan, 112
Campeche, imagen de una eternidad [Campeche, Image of an Eternity] (Molina), 78–80, 82, 83
Caribbean, 12, 55
cartography, 18, 19, 20, 132n102
Castillo, Debra and María Socorro Tabuenca Córdoba, 93, 103
Castañeda, Jorge, 49, 50, 89, 140n16
Castro, Fidel, 55, 61, 62
Cavallo, Domingo, 23
celebrity, 48, 53, 54, 57–58, 61
Chambers, Iain, 38
Chatwin, Bruce, 16, 21, 27, 29, 32, 33, 109, 124n49, 127n31, 129n53; conception of Patagonia, 45; *In Patagonia*, 16, 22–23, 25–26, 34, 36, 37, 76, 129n57, 131n84; *The Songlines*, 30
Chávez, Hugo, 65
Chile, 14, 18, 25, 27, 33, 49, 50, 63, 65, 66, 124n52, 127n37, 128n43, 138n72; redemocratisation in, 20, 23–24
Clark, Steve, 5, 151n78
Clifford, James, 3, 6, 98, 114, 121n6, 143n62, 144n68
CNN, 94, 104
Colombia, 49
colonialism, 67, 105; anti-colonialism, 36, 50, 53; neo-colonialism, 15, 125n63; postcolonialism, 67; Spanish, 50. *See also* imperialism
Columbus, Christopher, 58
CONACULTA (Mexican Council for Arts and Culture), 16, 70–72, 75, 78, 84, 140n24, 141n25
Convertibility Law, 23
Correa, Rafael, 65
Cortázar, Julio, and Carol Dunlop, 37, 39, 105
cosmopolitanism, 109
crónica de viaje, 11, 69
Crónicas de una oriunda del kilómetro X en Michoacán [Chronicles of a native of Kilometre X in Michoacán] (Puga), 16, 84, 85, 87, 88
Cronin, Michael, 31, 33
Crossing Over: A Mexican Family on the Migrant Trail (Martínez), 17, 92–93, 94, 97, 104, 106–108, 113, 114, 147n8, 152n88, 153n99
Crosthwaite, Luis Humberto, 93

Cuba, 12, 16, 48, 52, 54, 55, 59, 60, 62, 63, 65, 99; U.S. embargo of, 48, 55, 134n6

D

Dalrymple, William, 29
Darwin, Charles, 18, 37, 40, 132n99, 134n13; "Darwin's delay", 134n13
Death and the Maiden (Dorfman), 33
Deleuze, Gilles and Felix Guattari, 15, 44, 82, 83–84, 89, 124n60, 146n93
Derrida, Jacques, 15, 16, 49, 64, 65, 137n64, 141n37, 145n80, 145n89, 152n89; hauntology, 64. *See also* spectrality
Devil's Highway, The (Urrea), 17, 92, 93, 95–96, 107, 108–111, 113–114
Diarios de motocicleta: Notas de viaje [The Motorcycle Diaries] (Guevara), 16, 49–50, 51, 52, 136n48
Díaz del Castillo, Bernal, 75
Discourses of Difference (Mills), 67
discovery, 4, 18, 34, 50, 121n12
displacement, 26, 27, 38, 75, 79, 80, 84, 87–90, 101, 121n6, 127n31; "harmonious deterritorialisation", 27, 32, 45
Domenella, Ana Rosa, 70, 75
domestic travel, 6–7; Paul Theroux on 6
Dorfman, Ariel, 33
Durán, Javier, 102
Durand, Jorge and Douglas Massey, 100

E

environmentalism, 22, 28, 129n88, 145n85
erotics of travel, 36
ethnography, 12, 17, 47, 78, 79, 95, 98; "ethico-fictive", 93, 105, 114. *See also* autoethnography
Evans, Dylan, 104
exile, 3, 4, 22, 28, 45; of Mempo Giardinelli, 34, 37; of Luis Sepúlveda, 25, 26, 27, 45; as theme in travel writing, 26, 27
exoticism, 2, 15, 16, 21, 22, 31, 32, 33, 82, 124n60; "politico-exotic", 31. *See also* Brennan, Timothy

Expediency of Culture, The (Yúdice), 103
exploration, 47, 52, 106; military, 4; New World, 3, 4; scientific, 18
EZLN (Ejército Zapatista de Liberación Nacional [Zapatista Army of National Liberation]), 88–89

F
fact and fiction, boundary between, 92, 105, 111
Featherstone, Mike, 24
feminism, 67
Final de novela en Patagonia [*Novel's End in Patagonia*] (Giardinelli), 16, 20, 34–43, 46
Finnegan, Nuala, 73, 141n33, 141n37, 142n42, 148n23
Fitzroy, Robert, 18
Forsdick, Charles, 5, 7, 72–3, 140n17, 142n38
Foster, Shirley, 17, 77
Foucault, Michel, 16, 20, 78, 133n108, 133n111; on heterotopia, 44
Fox, Claire, 102
Frei, Eduardo, 24
Freud, Sigmund, 63, 68, 101–102, 137n64, 143n59; uncanny (umheimlich), 68. *See also* melancholy
Fussell, Paul, 7, 10, 123n42

G
Galeano, Eduardo, 29
Gallagher, Mark, 58, 60
García Bergua, Ana, 2, 67, 68, 71, 73, 79, 80, 84, 109, 142n49; *Postales del puerto* [*Postcards from the Port*], 16, 75–78, 80
García Bernal, Gael, 49
García Canclini, Nestor, 103
García Márquez, Gabriel, 10, 29, 31, 55
Gadsden purchase, 102
gender, 3, 14, 15, 17, 66–67, 68–78, 82–83, 91, 142n40, 145n90
Gender and Colonial Space (Mills), 67
Ghose, Indira, 67
Giardinelli, Mempo, 2, 20–21, 23, 33, 45, 120, 130n81, 132n101; *Final de novela en Patagonia* [*Novel's End in Patagonia*], 16, 20, 34–43, 46

Giddens, Anthony, 24
globalisation, 9, 12, 15, 16, 21, 22, 24, 28, 41, 46, 63, 65, 77, 87, 98, 117, 118
Gómez Montero, Sergio, 103
Gómez Peña, Guillermo, 90, 91, 94, 103
González Echeverría, Roberto, 4, 121n12
Graham, María, 66
Granado, Alberto, 53–54
Green, Martin, 58
Guadalupe Hidalgo, Treaty of, 103
Guevara de la Serna, Ernesto Che, 48, 49–57, 60, 61, 62, 63, 65, 134n9, 134n12, 135n34, 136n48, 137n57; *Diarios de motocicleta: Notas de viaje* [*The Motorcycle Diaries*], 16, 49, 51, 52, 136n48
Guillermoprieto, Alma, 50

H
Hall, Stuart, 118
Herzfeld, Michael, 85
heterotopia, 16, 20, 44–46, 133nn108–109, 133nn111 & 115; Deleuze and Guattari and, 44
Hetherington, Kevin, 44, 133n109
Hicks, Emily, 103
Hirsch, Marianne, 106
home, 2, 4, 5, 6–7, 26, 27, 32, 37, 68, 79, 88, 90, 94, 101, 114, 115, 116, 138n4, 151n78
Hudson, W.H., 18, 19
Huggan, Graham, 31; Patrick Holland and, 11, 18, 33, 34, 55, 56, 73, 77, 115, 118, 124n49, 125n7, 129n53
Hulme, Peter, 5, 58
Humboldt, Baron Alexander von, 4, 66
hybridity, 102, 103, 105

I
Ibargüengoitia, Jorge, 3
IMF (International Monetary Fund), 13, 124n51
Imperial Eyes (Pratt), 8, 9, 66
imperialism, 18, 61, 67, 118; neoimperialism, 63. *See also* antiimperialism
Independence, Wars of, 58
In Patagonia, 16, 22–23, 25, 26, 34, 36, 37, 76, 129n57, 131n84

Iparraguirre, Silvia, 21, 22, 126n21
IRCA (Immigration Reform and Control Act), 100
irony, 40, 56, 70, 82, 108

J
Jagoe, Eva-Lynn, 19, 20
journalism, 71, 142n43

K
Kaplan, Caren, 89, 90
Kowalewski, Michael, 5, 6

L
Lacan, Jacques, 93, 102, 104
Lagos, Ricardo, 24
landscape, 22, 26, 39, 42, 43, 53, 84, 86, 108; emptiness of in Patagonia, 16, 21, 26; mountain, 20, 41
language, 5, 6, 8, 29, 33, 93, 108, 119–120, 125n3, 144n78, 145n80, 152n89
Lazzara, Michael, 24
Lechner, Norbert, 24
Leed, Eric, 34, 60
Levin, Stephen L., 11, 48, 63, 137n60
Lévi-Strauss, Claude, 47–48, 62, 115; "entropology", 115; *Tristes Tropiques*, 47
Levy, Daniel and Kathleen Bruhn, 68–9, 72
Life in Mexico (Calderón de la Barca), 69
Lisle, Debbie, 39, 46, 64, 105, 107, 112, 120
Livon-Grosman, Ernesto, 19, 21, 125n3
Location of Culture, The (Bhabha), 103
Lonely Planet, 29, 30, 31; *Journeys* series, 25, 29
Los autonautas de la cosmopista [*The Autonauts of the Cosmopiste*] (Cortázar and Dunlop), 37, 105
Luchetti, Karina, 62
Luckhurst, Roger, 65

M
Macchi, Jorge, 6
Machu Picchu, 50, 120
Magee, Paul, 22
Magellan, Ferdinand, 18, 58
Mansilla, Lucio, 19
maps, 132n102

Markel, Howard and Alexandra Stern, 119
Martí, José, 52
Martínez, Rubén, 94–99, 112–114, 120, 152n84; *Crossing Over: A Mexican Family on the Migrant Trail*, 17, 92–93, 94, 97, 104, 106–108, 147n8, 152n88, 153n99; *The Other Side: Notes from the New L.A., Mexico City, and Beyond*, 94
Masiello, Francine, 14, 124n58, 127n37
McCannell, Dean, 2
melancholy, 15, 50, 63, 68, 83, 101, 114, 137n64, 150n47
Menem, Carlos, 23, 41, 42, 43
Mexican Travel Writing (Pitman), 74
Mexico, 6, 8, 9, 23, 34, 42, 50, 52, 67, 68–70, 72, 73, 77, 78, 82, 84, 88–89, 90, 93, 99, 101, 115, 116–117, 118, 119, 138n12, n15, 140n16, n21, 148n23; border with United States, 11, 17, 92, 94, 102, 106: developments in fortification of border with United States, 100; border as dimension of the "Real", 104; Revolution, 90
Mexico Around Me (Miller), 75
migrants, 26, 80–81, 92; undocumented, 17, 94, 95, 100–101, 105, 106, 110, 112, 114
migration, 3, 38, 94, 95, 113, 114n78; Mexico-U.S., 99–102, 149n38
Mills, Sara, 17, 67, 74, 77, 82,
modernity, 9, 16, 21, 14, 28, 39, 40, 40, 44, 65, 84, 90, 91; adventurer and, 137n56; heterotopia and, 133n109; political tourism and, 135n22
modes of transport, 48: automobile, 39–40; bicycle, 47, 56–57, 60; foot, 96, 100; horse, 40
Molina, Silvia, 2, 16, 67, 78–84, 90, 143nn57–58, 143nn60–61; *Campeche, imagen de una eternidad* [*Campeche, Image of an Eternity*], 78–80, 82, 83
Morales, Evo, 65
Moraña, Mabel, 2, 15, 125n63
Moreno, Francisco Perito, 19, 20, 22, 38, 39, 126n26
Moss, Chris, 19, 20, 126n19, 127n33

Motorcycle Diaries, The (Guevara). See *Diarios de motocicleta*
mourning, 15, 17, 93, 101, 112–114, 137n64
Moynagh, Maureen, 3, 51, 94, 98, 99, 114, 134n9, 134n12, 135n22, 137n61
Murray, Nicholas, 30
myths, 2, 4, 11, 18, 19, 20, 21, 22, 36, 118, 120

N

NAFTA (North American Free Trade Agreement), 88
nationalism, 7, 50, 139n10
neoliberalism, 7–8, 12–14, 33, 55, 69, 92, 119, 124n51, 124n52; in Argentina, 23, 65; in Chile, 23–24, 128n43; in Mexico, 67–69; "Washington Consensus", 13
Newby, Eric, 29
New World Border, The (Gómez Peña), 94, 103
Noble, Andrea, 72, 116
nomadism, 15, 16, 22, 23, 25, 26, 45, 109, 121n6; "nomadic consciousness", 88, 90. See also Braidotti, Rosi
nostalgia, 35, 36, 43, 45
Nouzeilles, Gabriela, 19, 20, 21, 22, 40, 44–45, 126n26, 127n28

O

Odyssey (Homer), 11
O'Hanlon, Redmond, 11, 131n93
Old Patagonia Express, The (Theroux), 29
Oliver-Rotger, María Antonia, 97, 106
Operation Desert Storm, 100
Operation Hold the Line, 100
Operation Rio Grande, 100
Operation Safeguard, 100
Operation Wetback, 100
otherness, 16, 36, 74, 80, 90, 98, 103, 104, 106, 113, 114, 118, 145n85, 146n103, 149n35, 150n53, 153n98
Other Side: Notes from the New L.A., Mexico City, and Beyond, The (Martínez), 94
Other Side of the Popular, The (Williams), 14

P

PAN (Partido Acción Nacional), 69
parody, 39, 105, 125n7
Patagonia, 11, 16, 18–19, 20, 21–22, 25, 26, 27, 28, 32, 34, 35, 36, 38, 39, 40, 41–43, 44, 45, 46, 59, 118
Patagonia Express [*Full Circle: A South American Journey*] (Sepúlveda), 16, 20, 25–33
Payno, Manuel, 75
Payró, Roberto, 18, 19
Peñaloza, Fernanda, 18, 125n5
Perea, Hector, 6
Peretti, Jonah, 84
Pérez Martínez, Héctor, 82
Pérez Mejía, Angela, 5
Perreault, Thomas and Patricia Martin, 12, 13, 121n51
Pfister, Manfred, 22
Phillips, Richard, 58, 61
Pigafetta, Antonio, 18
Piglia, Ricardo, 9, 50, 136n38
Pinochet, Augusto, 23, 24, 26, 27, 63, 124n52, 127n37
Pitman, Thea, 5, 8, 9, 69–70, 73–74, 78, 115, 142n47
photography, 134n9, 153n99
Polezzi, Loredana, 5, 37
Polo, Marco, 58
Porter, Dennis, 2, 4, 10, 106, 123n42
postcolonial theory, 15, 87, 97, 125n63
postmemory, 80, 106
postmodern aesthetic, 22, 73–74, 110, 120,
postmodernity, 16, 17, 21, 43, 44, 45, 46, 65, 83, 90, 101, 103, 104, 108
Postales del puerto (García Bergua), 16, 75–78, 80
Pratt, Mary Louise, 3–4, 7, 8–9, 17, 52, 66–67, 102; "capitalist vanguard", 66; "contact zone", 8, 102. See also *Imperial Eyes*
Precarious Life: The Powers of Mourning and Violence (Butler), 112–114
PRD (Partido de la Revolución Democrática), 69
PRI (Partido Revolucionario Institucional), 69
Puga, María Luisa, 2, 67, 68, 71, 72, 73, 77, 78, 84–90, 143n57, 144n76, 144n78, 145n85,

146n94, 146n103; *Crónicas de una oriunda del kilómetro X en Michoacán* [*Chronicles of a Native of Kilometre X in Michoacán*], 16, 84, 85, 87, 88

R
Raban, Jonathan, 11
race, 50, 82, 89, 103, 144n70
Rama, Angel, 72
Rashkin, Elissa, 72
Reed-Danahay, Deborah E., 79
reflexive modernization, 24. *See also* globalisation
refugees, 87
Richard, Nelly, 33
risk society, 24. *See also* globalisation
Road Fever (Cahill), 39
Robinson, Jane, 72
Robinson Crusoe (Defoe), 11
Rojek, Chris, 57
Romero, Luis Alberto, 23, 42
Rosaldo, Renato, 103
Ruggeri, Andrés, 16, 2, 47–49, 120; *América en bicicleta* [*America by Bike*], 52–53, 58, 59–63, 65
Rulfo, Juan, 42

S
Saldaña-Portillo, María Josefina, 50
Saldívar, José David, 96, 97, 100; "*transfrontera* contact zone", 102
Salinas de Gotari, Carlos, 69, 70
Salles, Walter, 49
Sánchez-Blanco, Cristina, 34, 41, 132n101
Santiváñez Vieyra, Hernán, 21, 40, 126n26
Sanmiguel, Rosario, 93
schizophrenia, 17, 78; capitalism as 82, 83–84, 144n70
Schmidt Camacho, Alicia, 101, 102
Schueller, Malini Johar, 112
Scott, David, 5
Secure Fence Act, 100
Sepúlveda, Luis, 2, 20–21, 34, 36, 43, 45, 128n47, 129nn58–60; *Patagonia Express* [*Full Circle: A South American Journey*], 16, 20, 25–33
Shakespeare, Nicholas, 22
Shullenberger, Geoffrey, 50
Simmel, Georg, 16, 49, 137n56; on adventure, 62–63, 65
Sinclair, Iain, 6
Small Place, A (Kincaid), 86
Smethurst, Paul, 118
Songlines, The (Chatwin), 22, 30
Spain, 25, 26, 27, 87, 128n47, 145n81
Specters of Marx (Derrida), 64–65, 138n70
spectrality, 49, 63–65, 92, 105, 114, 137n64
Spicer-Escalante, Juan Pablo, 38
Spivak, Gayatri Chakravorty, 97
strangers, 84, 85–88; fetishization of, 90
subalternity, 14, 142n40
sublime, 40–43
swine flu, 116, 119, 120; progress of, 116, 117–118; economic effects of, 117

T
testimonio, 97, 98
thanatography, 93, 105, 112
Taylor, David, 22, 26, 127n31
Theroux, Paul, 3, 6, 16, 18, 26, 27, 29
Todorov, Tzvetan, 6
tourism, 1–2, 22, 42, 71, 77, 80, 117, 120, 135n22, 137n61, 145n85, 146n103, 148n23; literary, 16, 34, 45, 46; political, 51, 55, 98–99, 114
tourist gaze, 86
tourists, 1, 2, 4, 36, 52, 86, 96, 115, 120, 145n85, 148n23; traveller-tourist dichotomy, 40, 50
translation, 28–33
Translation and Globalisation (Cronin), 31
travel writing, definitions and terms, 7, 8, 10–11, 123n41; affiliations between travel and writing, 38; end of, 115; in Latin America, 8–10; non-existence of in Mexico, 115; postcolonial travel writing, 118
travellee, 9, 26, 79, 81
Tristán, Flora, 66
Tristes Tropiques (Lévi-Strauss), 47
Tschiffely, Aimé, 40

U
uncanny (unheimlich), 68

United States of America, 9, 13, 69, 93, 94, 95, 96, 99, 100, 108, 116, 117, 118
Urrea, Luis Alberto, 2, 94–99, 101, 104, 105, 120, 147n15, 148n21, 152n90; *Across the Wire*, 95, 96; *The Devil's Highway*, 17, 92, 93, 95–96, 107, 108–111, 113–114
U.S.-Mexican War, 102
utopia, 20, 46, 90, 103, 133n108, n111. *See also* heterotopia

W
Waugh, Evelyn, 115
Weyland, Kurt, 13, 23, 124n52
Wheeler, Wendy, 101
Whitehead, Neil, 4
WHO (World Health Organisation), 116
Williams, Gareth, 7, 14–15
Wilson, Jason, 4, 7, 9–10, 11
Winnicott, Donald, 101
women travellers, 66–68, 76, 77, 138n4, 142n42, n51, 143n55; and home, 90; publication/reception of in Mexico 67, 72, 73–75, 141n33, 142n42
Woolf, Janet, 115, 119–120

World Bank, 13

V
Valenzuela Arce, José Manuel, 92, 102
Vargas Llosa, Mario, 69
Venas abiertas de América Latina [Open Veins of Latin America] (Galeano), 29
Venezuela, 49, 65, 138n72
Viaje a la Patagonia austral [Journey to Austral Patagonia] (Moreno), 22, 38
Viajes en México [Journeys in Mexico] series, 70
Vila, Pablo, 103, 104
Vivanco, Luis A. and Robert J. Gordon, 48
Vives Rocabert, Juan, 81

Y
Youngs, Tim, 5, 27, 115, 142n43, 154n5; and Glen Hooper, 123n46
YouTube, 120
Yúdice, George, 103

Z
Zedillo, Ernesto, 69, 82, 88–89
Žižek, Slavoj, 104, 108

For Product Safety Concerns and Information please contact our EU
representative GPSR@taylorandfrancis.com
Taylor & Francis Verlag GmbH, Kaufingerstraße 24, 80331 München, Germany

www.ingramcontent.com/pod-product-compliance
Lightning Source LLC
Chambersburg PA
CBHW070614300426
44113CB00010B/1531